Women Agency, Culture, and Crime in Education:
A Critical Study of Acquaintance Rape in Zimbabwe's Higher Education

Phinias Tafirei

Langaa Research & Publishing CIG
Mankon, Bamenda

Publisher:
Langaa RPCIG
Langaa Research & Publishing Common Initiative Group
P.O. Box 902 Mankon
Bamenda
North West Region
Cameroon
Langaagrp@gmail.com
www.langaa-rpcig.net

Distributed in and outside N. America by African Books Collective
orders@africanbookscollective.com
www.africanbookscollective.com

ISBN-10: 9956-553-32-8

ISBN-13: 978-9956-553-32-7

© Phinias Tafirei 2024

Dedication

This book is dedicated to my late mother, Gamuchirai Chipo Mhunhundowarwa, and father, Phinias Tafirei (Senior) who passed on before its completion and publication, and my Great Ancestor Mudyiravanji Gomarara (Magurupira) Bere, who inspired me to excel and advance academically and socially.

Acknowledgements

This book is my reworked Doctor of Philosophy thesis from the University of South Africa. I would like to express my heartfelt gratitude to the following people who generously assisted in the completion of my thesis, and some also in the reworking of the thesis to its current book form:

- My supervisor, Professor Regis Chireshe for his patient guidance, support, expert criticism, advice, informative and educative comments and encouragement in the development of my PhD thesis which read: *Factors affecting higher education students' perceptions of acquaintance rape in Masvingo Province, Zimbabwe.*
- My family for its unwavering support in a multitude of ways.
- he Ministry of Higher and Tertiary Education, Science, Innovation and Technology Development in, Zimbabwe, for granting me permission to undertake my study in institutions for higher education in Masvingo.
- The participating colleges and the Masvingo Polytechnic for taking time in answering my questionnaires.
- Participants for their willingness to share their views unreservedly on such a sensitive topic.
- My mother, for her advice and encouragement to always advance academically. I could not have done it if it was not for her words of wisdom.
- Martin, Tatenda, Fanikiso, Professor Tawanda Majoko, Professor Issac Mhute and Professor Jeriphanos Makaye for being my best friends and companions during my academic journey.
- Professor Extraordinarius Dr. Munyaradzi Mawere for his meticulous editing of my PhD thesis before it was reworked into a book and after, and for assisting in publishing this book.
- The ALMIGHTY GOD for his grace and mercy and for giving me the strength and wisdom to complete this study.
- My wife, Vimbai for her unwavering moral and material support.
- UNISA Financial Aid Bureau for the postgraduate bursary which lessened my financial burden.

Table of Contents

Chapter 1

The Problem and Its Context

1.1 Introduction

It is one Thursday afternoon at Vumbu Polytechnic (not real name) where I have been a lecturer for the past ten years. It is a sport day, and other students and staff members are busy with different activities around the college. As I am passing by one classroom, I hear John (not his real name) talking to a friend, Tamuka as they are going about their chores: "Yaah, that Stella (not her real name), my classmate is so sweet. Yesterday, we were doing some biology homework in my room, and as I was explaining the concepts, ummm I started fondling her breasts, and the two of us ended up having sex. She only resisted a little bit, but I managed to 'get in'. Besides being a classmate, she is not my girlfriend as you know and I never proposed love from her, but she did not scream. I really enjoyed myself and I wish if I can get another chance". "Oh, John that was rape!" retorted Tamuka. "No, it wasn't rape Tamuka. She did not report it. Neither did she scream," answered back John. I remained by the classroom window as the two continued with their conversation, and when they saw me, they quickly changed the subject of their talk. But from what I had heard, this was undoubtedly a case of acquaintance rape – rape committed in the name of acquaintance.

As can be seen from the anecdote above, acquaintance rape is a complex problem with no easy solution. As has been noted, the crime is intimately associated with culture, peer pressure, alcohol and policy, legislation or law. Its widespread prevalence reflects inappropriate norms about sexual behaviour that are deeply ingrained among all sectors of the society including institutions of higher education. This book investigates factors affecting higher education students' perceptions of acquaintance rape in Masvingo Province (heretofore referred to as Masvingo) of Zimbabwe as a precursor for proposing a model to eradicate or at least reduce it in institutions of higher education. To this end, this chapter presents the problem and its context. This includes the background to the study, statement of the problem, research questions, research objectives, significance of the book, assumptions, limitations, and delimitations of the study, definition of terms and organisation of the book. The next sub-heading presents the background to the book.

1.2 Background to the Book

Acquaintance rape is coercive sexual activity directed at someone whom the perpetrator knows *closely* (Gravelin, 2017:4; Biernat & Bucher, 2019:2). It is also referred to as date rape (Santrock, 2005:257). This type of rape can take place between people who know each other such as lovers, friends, ex-lovers or between a sister-in law and a brother-in-law or college mates (Santrock, 2005:257). For Duffy and Artwater (2012:312), acquaintance rape is forced sexual activity without a partner's consent. Thacker (2017:89) contends that acquaintance rape is a major problem that takes place as people socialise and interact with each other especially in institutions where they stay together. These include higher education institutions. Boswell and Spade (2010:136) propound that sexual assault between acquaintances consists of non-consensual sexual activities that can include sex and fondling. Non-consensual implies that there is some use of force, intimidation or manipulation, or that one of the parties is unable to give consent. Clarkson, Keating and Cunningham (2007:279) argue that certain crimes are defined in such a manner that they can only be committed without the victim's consent. Acquaintance rape is one of the examples of such crimes. This suggests that acquaintance rape as a form of crime may not be easily reported to the police because of cultural reasons, gender stereotypes, peer pressure, policy, legislation or law, familial bonds, and other factors that are beyond the scope of this book. The tendency not to report acquaintance rape cases, as is seen with Stella's story above, mainly due to abovementioned factors motivated the researcher to write this book. Miller and Cheveallier (2018:1) observe that perpetrators may interpret signs of friendliness in a victim as an interest in sexual activity, and thus be inclined to force sexual activity despite the victim's protest. Further, that individuals are attracted to the opposite sex or have sexual interest in someone emanates from cultural practices (Gravelin, Biernat & Bucher, 2019: 15). This is because cultural markers often determine the level of intimacies that are formed in social relationships.

From the foregoing, it can be noted that the prevalence of acquaintance rape varies according to regions and context. According to data obtained by the European Union prevalence survey, the 2014 Fundamental Rights Agency (FRA) survey on sexual violence against ladies, a broad category in which acquaintance rape falls, one in ten women in the European Union (11%) is a victim of acquaintance rape. The experience of acquaintance rape stretches from the age of 15 up to 49 (Right to Be Free from Rape, 2018:3). Dixie (2017:35) notes that one in every five women and one in every sixteen males are sexually assaulted by their acquaintances while attending college. As for the World Health Organisation's (WHO, 2017:2) survey, lifetime acquaintance rape cases reported by women victims aged 15 to 49 years ranged from 6% in Japan.

Withowska and Menckel (2005) carried out a study on perceptions of acquaintance rape in Swedish high school students with a random sample of 1, 038 high school girls born in 1993. In another Swedish study by Hostile Hallways (2001:53), 78% of both boys and girls in high schools stated that acquaintance rape was prevalent in their schools. The study shows that female high school students in Sweden are exposed to a variety of inappropriate and/or unacceptable behaviour of a sexual nature or one based on sex that may infringe their right to a supportive, respectful and safe learning environment or/and their dignity. From the above studies, it was found that the female gender is more vulnerable to acquaintance rape than the male gender, this is because, culturally, males are expected to be aggressive towards love. In Israel (see Lightfoot & Evans, 2000:1; Ziera, Astor & Benbenshty, 2012:152) and in sub-Saharan Africa, for instance, in Nigeria (Odu & Olusegun, 2012:10; Ajuwon, Olaleye, Faromoju, Ladipo & Akin Jimoh, 2001:146; Okeke, 2011:39; Oshiname, Ogunwale, Ajuwon, 2013:137) and in Zimbabwe (Mapolisa & Stevens, 2004:18; Mutekwe, Modiba & Maposa,2012:115; Mapfumo, Shumba & Chireshe,2007:15), it was found out that acquaintance rape is perpetrated mostly by men whilst most victims of acquaintance rape are women. Mapfumo, Shumba, and Stevens' (2007) studies were, for instance, conducted on male students. The same applies to Mutekwe, Modiba and Maposa's 2012 studies. As a point of departure, the present book sought to explore the extent to which acquaintance rape affects both male and female students' perceptions of rape in institutions of higher learning in Masvingo of Zimbabwe.

The book also sought to examine the claim that acquaintance rape is more prevalent in cultures that have a general acceptance of violence such as societies that accept beating as a form of discipline as is the case with Zimbabwean societies (Matlin, 2008:428). Armstrong (1989:69) asserts that some societies permit beating as discipline, so it might be possible too that someone might feel that he/she is able to take advantage of someone he/she knows and make sexual advancements.. Rape culture, among other factors, is also behind the causes of acquaintance rape. Miattal, Signh and Verma (2017:2) view rape culture as a set of values and beliefs that provide an environment conducive for rape to occur or to be committed. As for Burt (1980: 218), rape culture is a pervasive ideology that effectively supports or excuses sexual assault such as *chiramu* (fowl play with the younger sister/brother of your wife/husband); a broad term in which acquaintance rape falls. According to Johnson and Johnson (2017:2), the term also applies to generic culture surrounding and promoting rape, not the specific settings which are said to be important in defining relationships between men and women.

Boswell and Spade (2010:134) opine that some fraternities, abusive attitudes towards women, some cultural parameters, traditional gender prejudices, and stereotypes trigger acquaintance rape. Similarly, LaPlante, McComick and Brannigan (2010:338) propound that in many cultures men are viewed as initiators of sex and women as either passive partners or active resisters of sex.

In most European countries, factors that cause acquaintance rape include frequent alcoholic drinking to such a point that one is unable to resist sexual advances, or use of recreational drugs which might impair judgment or make it difficult to resist sexual advances (Dixie, 2017:8). Matlin (2008:433) observed that excessive consumption of alcohol and drug abuse distort reality and impair judgment, hence can be among factors which influence acquaintance rape. Familiarity and some beliefs about sexual roles such as thinking that someone who provides financial support has the right to expect sexual favours as well as prior history of rape or sexual victimisation are among other causes of acquaintance rape (see also, Kottak, 2000:63; Santrock, 2005:257; Matlin, 2008:432; Boswell & Spade, 2010:136). Looking at the political economy of sex, Santrock (2005:258) observes that most people choose to engage in sexual intercourse or other sexual activities at their free will, but some people force others to engage in it.

Studies by Dixie (2017:35); Santrock (2005:256); Kottak (2000:63); and Koss, Dinero & Siebel (1988:133) reveal that acquaintance rape is an increasing problem in high schools and college campuses in the United States of America. This resonates with Zeira, Astor and Benbenishty's (2001:150) earlier observation that acquaintance rape is common in the United States of America and other English-speaking cultures. Santrock (2005:257) also observed that nearly 200

000 rapes are reported to the police each year in the United States of America. Dziech's (2003:146) study also established that between 20% and 40% of undergraduate women students have been raped on college campuses in the United States of America by someone they knew. In all these incidents, no-one was reported. These under-reported and unreported cases lead to post-traumatic psychological disorders on the victims of acquaintance rape (Deane, 2018:86).

There are various factors which contribute to the perpetration of acquaintance rape. Lisak, Gardinier, Nicksa and Cote 's (2010:318) study in the United States of America found that 3% (63) of 2500 male participants on college campuses reported that they engaged in acts that constitute acquaintance rape or attempted rape. Many of the male participants also admitted having committed multiple rapes on acquaintances. Though without explaining the reason(s), the same study established that male college mates who participated in aggressive athletic activities at campuses were found to be more accepting of rape myths and violence and were involved in more sexual coercion than their peers. In this study, athletes were more often labelled as perpetrators of sexual assault on college campuses than any other group. Factors which contribute to acquaintance rape stretch from economic, social and political ones. As for Howard and Wang (2005:372), rape myth acceptance such as : girls who claim that they were raped are just looking for attention, rape only happens to girls, if a guy pays for the date, he deserves sex, girls who wear short skirts or tight tops are looking for sex, when a girl says "no" she really means "yes", only strangers and dirty old men in most cases are perceived as possible candidates for committing rape, girls who are raped are asking for it and that rape is just about sex are some of the factors which cause acquaintance rape among others.

As has been highlighted earlier, many studies on acquaintance rape were carried out in the United States Of America (see for example, Dixie,2017:42; De Leon, 2013:10 ; Do & Mark, 2020:1; Dekeseredy *et al.*, 2007:295; Dupalo, 2012:1; Johnson & Johnson, 2017:9; Finn,1997:vi; Rhodes,2019:v) in the United Kingdom (Sleath & Bull,2017:1) ; in New Zealand (Bohner *et al*, 2010:287) in Germany (Boswell & Spade, 2010:143) and in Australia (Xenos& Smith,2001:1103). In Asian countries, studies on acquaintance rape were done particularly in India (Ben-David & Schneider, 2005:385; Mittal, *et al*, 2017:1), in Israel (Lightfoot& Evans, 2000:1; Zeira *et al*, 2012:152) and in sub-Saharan Africa, Nigeria in particular (Odu& Olusegun,2012:10, Ajuwon *et al*, 2001:146; Okeke, 2011:39;

Oshniname *et al.*, 2013:137), in Zimbabwe (Mapolisa & Stevens, 2004:18; Mutekwe *et al*, 2012:115; Mapfumo *et al*, 2007:1). However, Carlson *et al*, (2015:82) note that there are different perceptions of acquaintance rape among students in institutions of higher education. As such, the present book sought to fill the cultural, gender, peer pressure, policy, legislation or law gaps between Europe, Asia, Australia, America, and sub-Saharan Africa, with particular reference to Masvingo.

Deming (2017:8) asserts that men's sexuality is seen as more natural, acceptable and uncontrollable than women's sexuality hence many men and women excuse acquaintance rape by affirming that men cannot control their natural urges. This view by Deming is debatable but more other scholars have supported the view. Dixie (2017:41), for instance, observed that across cultures, males were widely believed to be dominant, independent, aggressive, achievement oriented, and enduring while females were widely believed to be nurturing, affiliative, less esteemed and more helpful in times of distress. Biologically inherited differences such as intelligence and temperament in human beings affect their actions, thinking and behaviour and are the reason why during the interaction and socialisation process some elements of society might end up being either victims or perpetrators of acquaintance rape (Hunter & Colander, 2010:79).

For Freud, instincts (unlearned psychological drives) are the primary sources of psychic energy hence they are the main causes of acquaintance rape. Instincts have their origins in the biological needs and metabolic processes of organisms hence they are said to be responsible for all behaviours. Within Freud's psychic energy, the sexual instinct is a major life instinct and differs from other instincts such as those related to hunger and elimination in that gratification of the sexual instinct is necessary for the survival of these species whereas gratification of other instincts is necessary for the survival of the individual. However, for Friedrich Engels in his *The origin of the family...*, the modern individual family is founded on the open or concealed domestic slavery of the wife which suggests that women are often disadvantaged in issues of love relationships with men. Salkind (2004:115) reiterates that these life instincts are maintained and continue to develop through *libido*. Clemons (2002:249) observes that through socialisation, other people alter thoughts, feelings and behaviour of others and sometimes they alter their own behaviour in order to adhere to social norms. Acquaintance rape perpetrators create settings for social influence and in the process, victims will also alter their thoughts, feelings, and behaviour, and as a result there will be confusion as to whether acquaintance rape exists, or it is just a mere social construct. In such a situation, acquaintance rape may occur while both victims and perpetrators are quite unaware of its existence.

The existence of acquaintance rape cases stretches from Europe, the United States of America, Australia, Asia and Africa. A survey conducted by World Health Organisation (2017:2) in Japan, for example, revealed that reported acquaintance rape cases are low (constituting only 6% of the country's population). The World Health Organisation's (2017:2) book concurs with Kishwar's (1999:128) earlier book in India and Paludi's (2004:157) book in China which also highlighted a high prevalence of acquaintance rape. Very few studies on acquaintance rape have been carried out in sub-Saharan. Based on the complexities associated with acquaintance rape at least perceptionally, the researcher was motivated to embark on exploring the factors affecting students in higher education's perceptions of acquaintance rape in Masvingo of Zimbabwe. Absence of acquaintance rape not only protects human rights but also helps to avoid psychological disorders in victims. If acquaintance rape is reduced, students' mental and physical health would improve during their stay in college campuses (Deane, 2018:86).

In general, males are more likely than females to agree with myths and beliefs supportive of perceptions of acquaintance rape towards women, to blame and show less empathy for the victim and regard behaviours associated with victims as less serious. Howard and Wang (2005:372) observe that males can also be raped by their acquaintances despite their sexual orientation, appearance, physical size or strength. Bohner *et al.* (2006:293) propounds that perceived rape myth acceptance of others affect men's rape proclivity; that is, if men were told that others in their peer group had a high level of acceptance of rape myth, their own rape proclivity increased. Thus, this book sought to establish the factors affecting higher education students' perceptions of acquaintance rape in Masvingo as a context for improving the welfare of students in institutions of higher education.

The situations pertaining to acquaintance rape perceptions in Europe, the Unites States of America, Australia, and Asia is not exceptional to the sub-Saharan Africa. Like in other continents, acquaintance rape is also a challenge in all levels of education across all academic fields in Africa. In Kenya, for example, Okeke's (2011:5) findings indicated that girls experienced frequent acquaintance rape in and out of school despite the Sexual Offences Act enacted by the Kenyan Parliament in 2006. This is reverberated by Abuya, Onsomu, Moore and Sangwe's (2014:115) study which established that acquaintance rape is common among girls attending high schools in urban slums in Nairobi Kenya. The studybook found that 31% of young Kenyan women aged 15-24 reported acquaintance rape with a majority experiencing sexual debut due to coercion.

At least at continental level, a high proportion of female students in colleges and universities across the African continent have experienced acquaintance rape from male faculty staff and students (Okeke, 2011). According to Okeke's (2011:6) studies, there are different trends and forms of acquaintance rape being experienced by women students in several institutions of higher learning in Nigeria. Worse still, victims of acquaintance rape experience degrading verbal remarks, unwanted touching and other types of gender- based violence (Adeokun, 2004:5; Abati, 2006:2). Banya (2003:6) also found that 37.7% of women students in a university in Tanzania have been raped by male faculty members. Similarly, Haruhanga (2006:63) reported that 42% of women students in Makerere University in Uganda have been raped by male faculty members and peers.

Elaborating on socialisation of women in some African cultures, Okeke's (2011:12) study notes that the way women are socialised, for example, among the Igbos of Anambra states encourages acquaintance rape. Most women students come to universities lacking a solid foundation in science technology education right from secondary schools and so they tend to seek academic help from male faculty staff members and peers. In the process, they tend to be exposed to acquaintance rape. Okeke (2011:12) notes that college and university life is associated with adolescence, a stage also associated with sexual activeness and experimentation. Ashford and LeCroy (2010:463) observe that heterosexuality among adolescents might sound like a gender stereotype; that during this stage of development, males aggressively search for sexual experience with females and, in the process, can commit acquaintance rape unaware of the crime. More females than males report being involved in acquaintance rape; they interpret it as a way of being in love and as a result they fall victim to the malpractice (Weiten & LIoyd, 2002:428). This interpretation makes acquaintance rape even more problematic as it teases out the concepts of love and agency in terms of what these entail and where they start and end (see Archer, 2004). Santrock (2005:259) notes that acquaintance rape can be triggered by the perception that oral sex is something you can do with someone you are not intimate with; intercourse being reserved for the special person.

As has already been alluded to, the prevalence and age of acquaintance rape victims varies internationally. Rossetti (2001:16) indicated that in Botswana 68% of all the recorded 2260 acquaintance rape cases are experienced by girls in secondary schools and tertiary institutions, 14% are experienced by girls in primary schools. Similarly, related findings were established by Leach and Machakanya (2000:150) who found that 27% of 6500 girls in junior secondary schools in Ghana have experienced forced sex and over 50% have also been sexually harassed. Human Rights Watch report (2001:4) also states that thousands of girls in schools across South Africa encountered acquaintance rape.

According to the study carried by the African Union Commission (2004:64), besides culture, gender, peer pressure, policy, legislation or law, social orientation, political and economic conflict in many African countries have also exposed the worst form of objectification of women and abuse of their rights as citizens. African women's subordinate social status and gender discrimination expose them to experience acquaintance rape differently from men and women in other countries of the world (African Union Commission, 2004:5). For Boswell and Spade (2010:134), attitudes towards sexuality and rape are based on individual and psychological interpretations of both victims and perpetrators. Adler, Mueller and Laufer (2007:254) argue that the explanations of acquaintance rape fall into two categories, that is psychological and socio-cultural, but its causes remain speculative. In their cultural practices, most students and ordinary people seem not to know or recognise acquaintance rape as the latter do not exist, at least from a cultural point of view. This book sought to establish if Zimbabwean culture was one of the factors affecting higher education students' perceptions of acquaintance rape in Masvingo.

Although acquaintance rape may not be regarded as serious as rape by a stranger, it, nevertheless, has the same repercussions as any type of rape. Mwamwenda (2010:179) notes that according to the African cosmos and realities as well as the Karanga ethnic culture, a dominant in Masvingo, it is normally acceptable and justified for a sister's husband to force his wife's young sister to have sex with him or a husband to force his wife to have sex against her will. The reason why this type of rape is complicated is that it often occurs without any form of physical violence applied but usually during playing, thereby leaving the victim without any distinguishable evidence to support his/her claim. On the other hand, Mbigi and Maree (2006:2) observe that African customs and practices as well as the fear of being accused of having "led the man on" and being labelled a loose woman make it difficult for both victim and perpetrator to come out in the open.

Consistent with international studies, acquaintance rape is also rampant in co-educational schools in Masvingo (Mutekwe *et al.*, 2012:115). Of the girls interviewed, 75% cited common examples of sexual abuse as teasing, humiliation, verbal bullying or assault and unnecessary ridicule by boys. These are the common tactics which are applied in perpetrating acquaintance rape. Besides boys, young teachers also ask for sexual favours from school girls (Mapfumo *et al.*, 2007:515).

Thacker (2017:95) concurs with Shumba and Matina (2002:42) that victims and perpetrators normally perceive acquaintance rape differently and are likely to suffer differently. This might be due to either individual differences or background and experiences of both victims and perpetrators. Based on the stated assumption that acquaintance rape is prevalent in most higher education institutions in Masvingo, the researcher investigated whether culture, peer pressure, policy, legislation or law and the gender of students in institutions of higher education in Masvingo affect their perceptions of acquaintance rape or not.

To the knowledge of the researcher, there is dearth of studies in Masvingo on acquaintance rape. The few available related studies include Kambarami's (2006) patriarchy and female subordination in Zimbabwe; Chireshe and Chireshe's (2009) sexual harassment of female students in three selected High Schools in Masvingo Urban, Zimbabwe; Shumba, Gwirai, Shumba, Maphosa, Chireshe, Gudyanga and Makura's (2008) pupils' perceptions of sexual abuse by teachers in Zimbabwean Schools. The researcher greatly appreciates book results gathered by Kambarami's (2006), Chireshe and Chireshe (2009) and Shumba, *et al.* (2008) using qualitative approach and found that females are highly susceptible to both sexual abuse rape (a broad term in which acquaintance falls) and acquaintance rape as they interact and socialise with significant others. However, the studies did not look at students' perceptions of acquaintance rape, especially in settings such as higher institutions in Zimbabwe. Thus, the present book sought to explore factors affecting students in higher education's perceptions of acquaintance rape in Masvingo using quantitative approach. This book focused on students' perceptions and not any other groups of people like college administrators, non-academic staff or ordinary people's perceptions of acquaintance rape because most students in institutions of higher education are in the adolescent stage. Adolescents are generally experimental in nature, and they do that in the context of cultural beliefs, gender stereotypes, prejudices and peer pressure. Doshi (2014:8) observes that students in institutions of higher education are also more likely to experience sexual abuses and misconducts since they are sexually active.

European, American, Australian, Asian and other sub-Saharan studies cited in the background to the book were conducted in different contexts to triangulate data from different cultural regions, gender perspectives, policy implementation and interaction practices and experiences among peers in the present book. Studies internationally, regionally and in sub-Saharan Africa revealed that there are no clear policies governing acquaintance rape. The next subheading presents the statement of the problem.

1.3 Statement of the Problem

The ideal situation in institutions of higher education is where there is a clear policy which protects the welfare and wellbeing of students against acquaintance rape (Human Rights Watch, 2017:2) among other abuses. The background to the book has underscored that there is a high incidence of acquaintance rape around the world (Dixie, 2017:41; Harsey & Freyd 2020:4; Santrock, 2005:256; Hodges, 2000:436; Kishwar, 1999:128; Paludi, 2003:457; Matlin, 2008:428; Human Rights Watch report, 2001:4). It has also underlined that acquaintance rape is rampant in high schools, colleges and universities across nations (Chireshe & Chireshe, 2009; Shumba *et al.*, 2008; Shumba & Matina, 2002; Dixie, 2017; Johnson & Johnson, 2017; National Victims Centre, 1999; Santrock, 2005; Kottack, 2000; Koss *et al.*, 1988; Lyness, 2009; Dziech, 2003; Withowska & Menckel, 2005; Abuya *et al.*, 2014; Rosetti, 2001; Leach *et al.*, 2000; Human Rights Watch Report, 2001; Okeke, 2011; Banya, 2003; Mapfumo, *et al.*, 2007).

Furthermore, the background to the book highlighted that no studies have been carried out in Zimbabwe and in particular in Masvingo that focus on factors affecting higher education students' perceptions of acquaintance rape. Yet, absence of acquaintance rape does not only protects human rights but also helps to avoid psychological disorders in victims. In fact, if acquaintance rape is reduced, students' mental and physical health would improve during their stay in college campuses (Deane, 2018:86). It is in this light that the present book sought to establish the factors that affect students' perceptions of acquaintance rape. Students are adolescents who are energetic hence they are very much interested in sexual issues as well as exploring new things (Santrock, 2005:257). Unfortunately, there are no clear policies at least in Zimbabwe that promote positive perceptions to acquaintance rape. Lack of such policies which foster positive perceptions of acquaintance rape would continue to expose students in higher education institutions to victimisation. Thus, this book sought to establish the factors affecting higher education students' perceptions of acquaintance rape in Masvingo.

The next sub-heading presents the main research question.

1.4 Main Research Question

This book sought to answer the following main research question: What are the factors affecting higher education students' perceptions of acquaintance rape in Masvingo of Zimbabwe?

1.4.1 Sub-research questions

In order to answer that main research questions, the following sub-research questions guided the book:

1.4.1.1 To what extent does culture affect students in higher education's perceptions of acquaintance rape in Masvingo?

1.4.1.2 To what extent does gender affect students in higher education's perceptions of acquaintance rape in Masvingo?

1.4.1.3 How does peer pressure affect students in higher education's perceptions of acquaintance rape in Masvingo?

1.4.1.4 How does policy, legislation or law affect students in higher education's perceptions of acquaintance rape in Masvingo?

1.5 Research Objectives

The main objective of this book was to establish factors affecting higher education students' perceptions of acquaintance rape in Masvingo of Zimbabwe. In order to achieve this main objective, ancillary objectives such as those below were sought:

1.5.1. To establish the extent to which culture affects students in higher education's perceptions of acquaintance rape in Masvingo.
1.5.2. To examine the influence of gender on students in higher education's perceptions of acquaintance rape in Masvingo.
1.5.3. To determine the influence of peer pressure on students in higher education's perceptions of acquaintance rape in Masvingo.
1.5.4. To establish the role of policy, legislation or law on students in higher education's perceptions of acquaintance rape in Masvingo.

1.6 Research Methodology

The research design adopted for this study was descriptive survey. The study deployed techniques for selecting the research sample, sampling procedure, and instrumentation (questionnaires and document analysis). This was to make sure that the quality of data harvested from the field is reasonably high.

1.7 Rationale Of The Study

Contribution to body of knowledge
It is anticipated that this book will develop a functional model that will help students in higher education to positively identify effects and instances of acquaintance rape. The knowledge that the book hopes to generate will promote a safe environment for students in higher education. This is against the background that acquaintance rape is still a grey area in Zimbabwe. The novelty of this book lies in its ability to provide an alternative way of looking at acquaintance rape.

Contribution to Communities
Acquaintance rape perpetrators come from the communities. When they are addicted to acquaintance rape, the effects are felt more by the communities they come from. This book will assist the communities to identify cases of acquaintance rape and know what

to do realising that a member within their community is affected by this form of rape. They will also know to what extent the government and other stakeholders protect their interests.

Contribution to policy making

The victims and the perpetrators will know the pitfalls of the regulations in place. Any pitfalls in the legislation affects individuals, the communities and the government. Consequently, the communities and government will not achieve the best without support of all the stakeholders. The policy makers will also be kept abreast with current trends so that appropriate mechanisms can be instituted with the view of benefitting the students in higher education and elsewhere. This will help policy makers to institute appropriate policies to arrest the problem.

The next subheading presents theoretical framework.

1.8 Theoretical Framework

This book on factors affecting higher education students' perceptions of acquaintance rape in Masvingo Province is informed by Bandura's Social Learning Theory book. Social Learning Theory postulates that human social behaviour of any type, that is good or bad, is learned primarily by observing, copying as well as imitating actions of significant others (De Leon,2013:ix) in society. The theory explains that the process of learning takes place within a social context. As such, this book examined the influence of culture, gender, peer pressure and policy, legislation or law on the perceptions of students in higher education's perceptions of acquaintance rape. The process of social learning theory in traditional psychology and social cognitive learning in modern psychology (Santrock, 2005:56) consists of instrumental learning that occurs either actively or directly through reward and punishment. The stated factors above and others affect human beings' behaviour, actions and social interactions as well as perceptions (Zindi & Makotore, 2015:47).

It should be reiterated that the present book, unlike that of Van der Bruggen and Grubb (2014:523) which used the Just World Theory, was guided by the Social Learning Theory to establish participants' perceptions towards acquaintance rape. The Just World Theory postulates that people perceive the world to be fair hence they deserve what they get (Lambert & Raichel, 2000:855). The body of literature is consistent with the theory of social learning that underpins the book which stipulates that individuals are products of the society tend to share certain behaviours and attitudes towards certain phenomena. The tendency of sharing certain behaviours and perceptions is not exceptional to acquaintance rape myth acceptance.

Social Learning Theory explains how both victims and perpetrators' perceptions are influenced by the environment in which they live. Viewed in this way, men learn to perceive risks differently from women (Dejoy, 1992:237; Boholm, 1998:135). Ellis (1989:45) propounds that individuals learn life skills through the process of socialisation appropriate for their genders and cultures regarding their expected behaviours in society and, as such, gendered violence is normative. The difference in the way they view risks may bring about different perceptions towards different social constructs. Finucare, Slovic, Mertz and Satter (2000:170) also observe that there is a significant gender difference in relation to trust between men and women. This process of socialisation through cultural norms often has contradictory views towards women (Robinson-Beverly & Schwartz, 2004). According to Johnson and Johnson (2017:2), social learning teaches human beings that aggressive behaviour during sex is natural and normal. In many African cultures, for example, it is natural that men make sexual advances toward women who may appear as if they are not interested in sex even though they will be. The individual in the society can learn favourable definitions that could increase the probability to act in a particular way. On the other hand, the individual can learn unfavourable definitions that may possibly reduce the probability to engage in particular behaviour (De Leon, 2013:5). In this way, acquaintance rape is viewed as an extreme form of sanctioned male-female sexual interactions.

Social Learning Theory has a distinctive attribute; that is, the advanced capability for observational learning that enables individuals to display their knowledge and skills rapidly through information conveyed to them by modelling influences without experiencing the tedious as well as hazardous process of learning by response consequences. In line with social learning theory, Burgess and Akers (1966:128) proposed seven principles that demonstrated the social learning process:

1. Criminal behaviour is learned according to the principles of operant conditioning.

2. Criminal behaviour is also learned in both nonsocial situations that are reinforcing or disc criminative and through social

interactions in which the individual's behaviour or of another person is reinforcing or discriminative for criminal behaviour.

3. The principal part of learning a criminal behaviour occurs in groups which comprise the individual's major source of reinforcements.

4. Learning of criminal behaviour including specific techniques, attitudes, perceptions, and avoidance procedures, is a function of the effective and available reinforcers, and the existing reinforcement contingencies.

5. Specific class of behaviours which are learned and their frequency of occurrence are also a function of the reinforcers which are effective and available and the rules or norms by which these reinforcers are applied.

6. Criminal behaviour is a function of norms which are discriminative for criminal behaviour, the learning of which takes place when such behaviour is more highly reinforced than noncriminal behaviour.

7. The strength of criminal behaviour is a direct function of the amount, frequency, and probability of its reinforcement. Deviant or conforming behaviour depends on past and present rewards and punishments. The assumption of criminal behaviour in this theory is that it is learned by the same process and mechanisms as conforming behaviour.

Burgess and Akers (1966:6) note that social learning is critical in that it enables psychologists to interpret how the process of learning occurs. The significant others with whom an individual chooses to interact either actively or passively play a fundamental role in providing a context in which social learning occurs. Any behaviour whether good or bad is strengthened through positive and negative reinforcement and is also weakened by positive punishment as well as loss of rewards. The continuation of both deviant and conforming behaviour depends on both past and present rewards and punishment. Thus, this book sought to establish higher education students' perceptions of acquaintance rape with special reference to culture, policy, legislation or law.

In this book, Bandura's Social Learning Theory enabled the researcher to establish factors affecting students in Masvingo's institutions of higher education's perceptions of acquaintance rape as well as to understand differences in perceptions of both victims and perpetrators of acquaintance rape. These differences are normally seen as human beings symbolically and verbally interact in their social settings. The central point of social learning theory is that interactive behaviour producing meaning for the current book is significant in that "... human beings do not act individually but interact with each other, thus reacting to each other in a different way" (Kombo & Tromp, 2009:57). This makes interaction between and among individuals very critical as it prompts different perceptions. Perceptions depend on different factors and as such individuals perceive acquaintance rape as they observe, copy, and their peers and significant others; as such students in institutions of higher learning, just like any other ordinary people, perceive acquaintance rape differently.

In this study, the researcher encountered both victims and perpetrators of acquaintance rape in institutions of higher learning in Masvingo. Through daily interactions or socialisation in general, perpetrators observe and imitate peers and significant others' tactics and responses to acquaintance. The gist of traditional education as conveyed through culture is centred on social cognitive learning theory, observational learning and modelling (Bandura, 1978:12). Social learning theory also enabled the researcher to interpret as well as spell out how students in higher education perceive acquaintance rape as a social construct. In social learning theory internationally, regionally and in the sub-Saharan African context, there is a perception that society denounces the term acquaintance rape but normalises the act (Johnson & Johnson, 2017:3).

According to Bandura's social learning theory, human beings give meaning of other people's actions and deeds as well as of themselves as they socialise and interact with each other (Cohen *et al.*, 2011:65). Using the Social Learning Theory as a base, the book argues that human beings depend on their culture, gender, peer pressure and policy, legislation or law to classify experiences, interact and socialise with each other and teach abstractions to others (Oltedal *et al.*, 2004:17). Consequently, in this book the Social Learning Theory gave lenses through which to establish how culture, gender, peer pressure and policy, legislation or law can affect students' perceptions of acquaintance rape in institutions of higher learning in Masvingo.

Informed by the Social Learning Theory, the researcher got a base for studying how cultural adherence, peer pressure, gender and policy, legislation or law affect people's perceptions and understanding of acquaintance rape as a social vice (risk) (Oltedal *et al.*, 2004:1). Social learning theory, therefore, enabled the researcher to assess how human beings learn about themselves and how other people react to their behaviour. Thus, this book sought to investigate the factors affecting students in higher education students' perceptions of acquaintance rape.

It is also important to note that Bandura's Social Learning Theory postulates that human behaviour is a product of the society, hence acquaintance rape as a social vice is such a product. In sexual relationships, there are a lot of interpretations and misinterpretations of actions, behaviours and deeds (Sampson, 2002:12; Thacker, 2017:95; Hills, Pleva, Selb & Cole, 2020:1) which are pertinent to this book. In their day-to-day interactions with each other, students influence each other on social skills hence they end up having misperceptions and ambiguous communication of acquaintance rape (Roe, 2004:7). These social skills improve students' (adolescents) peer relations. Santrock (2005:358) observes that conglomerate strategies which are taught by peers include demonstrations or modelling of appropriate social skills, discussions, reasoning about the use of reinforcement for their enactment in actual social situations

According to Bandura's Social Learning Theory, it is the society, not the individual, which dictates societal norms and moral values (Dube & Tagutanazvo, 2002:27; Koss 2000:1332; Deming, 2017:12). Most university and college students are adolescents, so their perceptions of acquaintance rape are also affected by peer pressure, gender, societal culture and even loose policy, legislations or laws among other variables (Santrock, 2005:351; Dixie, 2017:42; Grub & Harrower, 2008:65; Johnson & Johnson, 2017:1). This view corroborates Oltedal *et al.*'s (2004:17) argument that human beings depend on each other and culture to classify their experiences. This book thus sought to establish the influence of culture, gender, peer pressure and policy, legislation or law on students in higher education's perceptions of acquaintance rape.

Viewed in this way, Social Learning Theory proved to be a vital tool for this study in exploring the above issues. The next subheading presents assumptions of the study.

1.9 Assumptions of the Study

In this study the following assumptions were made:

1.9.1 Acquaintance rape is prevalent in institutions of higher education in Masvingo Province of Zimbabwe as well as the world over.

1.9.2 Most victims of acquaintance rape are not at liberty to disclose their encounters.

1.9.3 Both female and male victims and perpetrators of acquaintance rape have different perceptions of it.

1.10 Limitations of the Study

The main limitation of the study was that the researcher, as a full-time lecturer, was not able to visit the institutions of higher learning as often as he would have wanted to due to time constraints because he had to balance work and research. Limited financial resources also placed restrictions on the areas that were covered since the researcher needed to travel from his work place to other institutions of Higher and Tertiary Education, Science, Innovation and Technology Development. Because of these limitations, the study was carried out in only chosen institutions of higher education in Masvingo. Thus, its findings cannot be generalised to all other higher education institutions in Masvingo with accurate statistical precision but only to the three randomly sampled institutions of higher education.

1.10.1 Overcoming the limitations

The problem of limited time to move to other colleges, sourcing and pilot testing instruments was mitigated through going on a vacation leave so that the researcher could be free from work. Since the researcher is a full-time employee, he applied for leave to collect data. On monetary constraints, the researcher applied for a bursary (scholarship) from the University of South Africa so that he could carry out his studies timeously and effectively. In fact, the bursary helped the researcher with money for tuition fees, data collection, typing, data processing and other services needed in the study. The problem of limiting the study to only 3 institutions of higher education was solved by application of triangulation of data. Lack of access to certain sites and sensitivity of the phenomenon was encountered by triangulation of data from quantitative sources, qualitative sources and document analysis.

The next subheading presents delimitation of the study.

1.11 Delimitation of the Study

This study focused on the factors affecting higher education students' perceptions of acquaintance rape. The researcher confined himself to factors affecting higher education students' perceptions of acquaintance rape from Masvingo only. The target group in this study consisted of principals, vice principals, hostel wardens, assistant hostel wardens, nursing sisters, disciplinary chairpersons and students randomly chosen from the three conveniently chosen institutions of higher education.

The next subheading presents definition of terms.

1.12 Definition of Terms

To understand the key concepts of this book, it is necessary to clarify them to avoid misinterpretations.

1.12.1 Acquaintance rape

Machisa, Jina, Labuschagne, Vetten, Lisa, Loots, Swemmer, Meyersfeld and Jewkes (2017:18) define acquaintance rape as rape committed by someone with whom a victim has a relationship such as boyfriend, husband, ex-boyfriend, or ex-husband. Acquaintance rape is usually influenced by cultural practices, beliefs, attitudes, norms, values, taboos, mores, customs, and folkways of individuals and groups. In the context of this research, acquaintance rape refers to rape committed by a college mate, boyfriend or anyone known by the victim.

1.12.2 College student

Hackett and Claire (2013:101) define a college student as a learner at an institution of higher learning or a person who goes to college and is studying something. In the context of this present study, college student refers to a registered learner at colleges and universities.

1.12.3 Culture

Cobb (2001:33) defines culture as the behavioural patterns, beliefs and all other products of a particular group or people that are passed on from generation to generation. In the context of this book, culture refers to a tie which consists of food, common thoughts, common practices, norms, taboos, mores, values, attitudes, beliefs, dress, language and folkways as guiding individuals' behaviour.

1.12.4 Gender

According to Schneider and Silverman (2008:51), gender refers to socially constructed women and men's roles and responsibilities. In this book, gender refers to how people are perceived and expected to think and act as women and men.

1.12.5 Gender stereotypes

National Adolescent sexual and Reproductive health Strategy (2010:2015) defines gender stereotypes as socially constructed beliefs about men and women. In the context of this book, gender stereotypes refer to labels or tags associated with men and women in their social setup.

1.12.6 Peer pressure

De Leon (2013:15) defines peer pressure as doing something just because others of the same

age, experiences and academic or professional status are doing it. In the context of this book,

peer pressure refers to an act of copying and imitating age mates.

1.12.7 Perceptions

Johnson and Johnson (2017:7) define perception as the way in which people interpret or understand the message our sensory systems have processed. We interpret these messages or the environment using our five senses. So, by knowing perceptions we can better understand how people are organised to deal with their environment and, in turn, why they behave as they do. In the context of this book, perceptions refer to views or opinions held by individuals or the way they sense the world around them.

1.12.8 Rape culture

Peter and Besley (2019:460) define rape culture as a common practice among college students in which rape and sexual assault are normalised due to their high prevalence. This practice among college students is against societal disposition towards sexuality and gender issues. In the context of this book, rape culture refers to a common practice at a college or university in which rape among college mates is accepted and justified by students themselves.

1.12.9 Rape myths

Miattal, Signh and Verma (2017:2) define rape myths as a complex set of cultural beliefs that support male sexual aggression against females by blaming female victims of acquaintance rape and praising male perpetrators. In the context of this book, rape myths refer to all practices which justify that males have rights to have sex with females at their free will and that females are regarded as males' sexual objects.

1.12.10 Sexual abuse

Arora and Narayanan (2005:12) define **sexual abuse** as "any actual or threatened physical intrusion of a sexual nature, by force or under unequal or coercive conditions." In the context of this book, sexual abuse is any sexual activity perpetrated by someone without the victim's consent.

1.12.11 Sexual assault

Sovino and Turvey (2011: 1) define sexual assault as a non-consensual sexual contact. From this perspective, both rape and sexual assault are coercive acts. In the context of this book, sexual assault encompasses rape since rape is a form of non-consensual sexual activity and it entails sexual penetration.

1.12.12 Sexual consent

According to Dixie (2017:36), sexual consent is when a partner or person engages in sexual intercourse at his or her free will. This is to say, the partner has the power of contrary choice affording him/her an opportunity to make choice to engage (or not engage) in sex. In sexual relationships, a partner should say "yes" for him or her to engage in sexual intercourse. In Zimbabwe, a person who is eighteen years and above can agree or refuse to have sex with his or her partner. This is to say that in Zimbabwe, at least legally, sexual consent is defined by what they call the age of majority (eighteen years) which automatically grants one the power of contrary choice.

In the context of this book, sexual consent refers to accepting to have sexual intercourse with a sexual partner.

1.12.13 Sexual harassment

Arora and Narayanan (2005: 12) define **sexual harassment** as any unsolicited sexual advance, comment, expressed or implied, or any other communication of a sexual nature. These criminal acts are generally associated with requests for sexual favours, sexual advances or other sexual conducts. Giving in is either directly or indirectly, but such a condition affects decision making. Such a condition also creates behaviour and an environment which is intimidating or uncomfortable for the victim. The harasser continues with such behaviour despite the victim's objection. Sexual harassment is pervasive and occurs in different social environments across the world. In Islam, Muslim men are enjoined to lower their gaze when walking in public, while in the United Kingdom, sexual harassment is a racialised issue, and the question of who is watching is as important as the complicated definition of sexual harassment. It involves sexual activities such as rape. Where the abuse or harassment is perpetrated by a person known by the victim, it is acquaintance rape hence there is a link between sexual abuse, sexual violence, rape, sexual harassment and acquaintance rape.

1.13 Organisation of the Book

This book is organised into 5 chapters. Each respective chapter investigated a specific area as indicated below:

Chapter 1: The Problem and Its Setting

The background and context of the study relating to factors affecting higher education students' perceptions of acquaintance rape in Masvingo of Zimbabwe are discussed. The problem statement of the study, sub-research questions, objectives, and significance of the study, theoretical framework that guided the study, assumptions, and limitations, overcoming the limitations, delimitations and key terms are also explained.

Chapter 2: Rape Culture in Higher Education

Relevant related literature that helped to display the existence of the problem is discussed. The review of related literature is guided by the sub-research questions of the study.

Chapter 3: Research Methodology

The research methodology for the study was discussed. The chapter was explained and adoption of the descriptive survey as a research design in this book was justified. The chapter also looked at techniques for selecting the research sample, sampling procedure and instrumentation (questionnaires and document analysis). Issues of reliability, validity and pilot testing were also considered in this chapter. Data collection procedures, data analysis and ethical considerations are also addressed.

Chapter 4: Rape Culture in Higher Education: Testimonies from the Field

Data from questionnaire is presented and analysed according to the sub-research questions of the study. Findings of the study are discussed in relations to the available literature under the four categories from the sub-research questions.

Chapter 5: Towards Elimination of Rape Culture in Higher Education

A summary of the findings of the book on each sub-research question is given and conclusions are drawn. Recommendations as suggestions or solutions for curbing acquaintance rape are also provided.

1.14 Chapter Summary

This chapter served as an orientation to the book. Firstly, the background to the study and the statement of the problem were outlined and then after that the research questions and research objectives were examined. This was followed by the significance of the study. The theoretical framework for the study was discussed and the limitations and delimitations of the study were also highlighted and finally organisation of the book. Key terms were then defined. The next chapter discussed the review of related literature.

Chapter 2

Rape Culture in Higher Education

2.1 Introduction

This book sought to establish factors affecting students in higher education's perceptions of acquaintance rape in Masvingo Province of Zimbabwe. Literature was reviewed based on what scholars say regarding the topic under discussion. The literature was presented under the following sub-headings derived from the book's research question: culture and acquaintance rape, gender and acquaintance rape, peer pressure and acquaintance rape as well as policy, legislation or law and acquaintance rape. The book used peer-reviewed articles in journals, dissertations, book chapters and book reviews written in English and published between 1980 and 2020 which were considered eligible for review to indicate study gaps, which the present book sought to fill in.

In the subsequent section, literature on factors affecting higher education students' perceptions of acquaintance rape in Masvingo was presented.

2.2 Culture and Acquaintance Rape

Culture is perceived to be playing a major role when it comes to interpreting acquaintance rape (Mittal, Signh & Verma, and 2017:1). Johnson and Johnson (2017:3) observe that acquaintance rape in America is under-recognised due to tacit cultural normalisation in dating relationships. Culture, just like any other social variable, affects perceptions of both perpetrators and victims of acquaintance rape positively and negatively. Flood and Pease (2006:27) note that acquaintance rape is one of the sexual victimisation crimes considered by law to be severe in America and internationally. According to World Health Organisation (2017:4), acquaintance rape occurs in institutions assumed to be safe by the public such as schools, colleges and universities where perpetrators who include peers, teachers or lecturers or any other institutional employee commit the crime due to common cultural practices which emanate from the society. In a study conducted by World Health Organisation

(2017:1) from around the globe including South Africa and Latin America, it was found that girls experience sexual harassment and abuse on the way to and from school as well as on school and university campuses. Gravelin *et al.* (2019:15) observe that in both European and African cultures, rape culture and acquaintance rape are inherently linked phenomena hence they are commonly practiced. Acquaintance rape perpetrated by school mates or college mates normally takes place in classrooms, offices, lavatories and dormitories. Acquaintance rape, although controversial and ambiguous, is more prevalent in cultures that have a general acceptance of violence (Nyul *et al.*, 2018:1). The view that acquaintance rape is under-recognised as a sexual crime due to tacit cultural normalisation in dating relationships is in line with the Social Learning Theory which guided this study in that members of the society, including both assailants and victims of acquaintance rape, perceive it as a normal dating practice (Dixie, 2017:41).

Johnson and Johnson (2017:9) carried out a study in the United States of America (Northeast, Midwest, and West districts) using a sample of 232 females and 82 males on an empirical exploration into the measurement of rape culture among acquaintances. Two-hundred and sixty-one (83.1%) participants identified themselves as exclusively heterosexual, 5 (1.6%) as homosexual and 48 (15.3%) as lying between these two extremes. The Whites constituted the largest number of participants (70.1%), 13,4% were Africans Americans, 4,8% were Asian/Pacific Islander, 2.2%, Hispanic/Latinx, 3.2% Middle Eastern and 4.1% were multiracial. All the participants were recruited using a snowball sampling from February to August of 2014. Snowball sampling technique might have the weakness that some participants might not be known. In order to counter the weakness, this study employed the random sampling technique to come up with a sample. Randomised samples in survey designs may facilitate the generalisability of study results to the target population. Johnson and Johnson's (2019:9) study in the United States revealed that sexual violence and acquaintance rape was justifiable at the cultural level as opposed to personal perceptions of femininity, individuals' perception that their peers view women as objects of acquaintance rape. Both De Leon (2013:10) and Johnson and Johnson's (2017:9) participants on acquaintance rape indicated that both ordinary people and students in institutions of higher learning's perceptions of acquaintance and that of Johnson and Johnson's (2017:9) studies were conducted at American Universities, this study used participants from three institutions in Masvingo on factors affecting higher education students' perceptions of acquaintance rape. Johnson and Johnson (2019:9) and De Leon's (2013:10) studies employed a quantitative approach.

However, for a book as the present one which is largely qualitative, quantitative approach has a weakness in unearthing the extent or context in which participants talk thus rendering the voice of participants silent as observed by Creswell and Plano Clark (2007: 9). Quantitative research uses numbers and statistics (Tichapondwa, 2013:108). Some researchers and readers might not be acquainted with statistical data. Therefore, this study employed the concurrent mixed methods approach to ensure triangulation of data sources. This practice was meant to curb the weaknesses of quantitative or qualitative approach.

De Leon (2010:10) also carried out a study on students' personal interaction and acquaintance rape perception in the United States of America, and it was found that culture does affect the perceptions of students in higher education institutions' perceptions of acquaintance rape. Both victims and perpetrators of acquaintance rape accepted rape myth, adhered to traditional views of female/male sexuality as well as perceived sexual aggression as a normal cultural practice. A survey conducted by De Leon (2013:12) in America using a questionnaire which was emailed to 500 male college students also confirmed that culturally, specific norms and social relations have a profound influence on people's attitudes and perceptions of acquaintance rape. De Leon's (2013:12) study had male participants only, this study had both male and female participants to avoid gender bias.

Students in higher education institutions influence each other in their day to day interactions depending on the symbolic classifications they make, encode or decode. Tafirei, Makaye and Mapetere (2017:6) note that some members of the society believe that African traditional culture accepts and justifies cultural practices which include forcing acquaintances to have sex with assailants and gradually becoming part of culture. They may decode situations as good for their own group whilst bad for others. Thus, Social Learning Theory has been relied upon by researchers to explain how individuals learn both good and bad behaviour (Dixie, 2017:43). This study sought to explore how culture affects higher education students' perception of acquaintance rape in Masvingo.

International, regional as well as sub-Saharan African cultural practices especially in sexual relationships tend to have a negative perception towards acquaintance rape victims. De Leon (2010), Ziera *et al.* (2002), Deming, (2017; Dixie, (2017), Okeke (2011), Vandiver and Dupalo (2012), Johnson and Johnson, (2017) and Odu and Olusegun's (2012) studies revealed that women should be responsible for preventing unwanted sexual experiences by not displaying behaviours that might mislead men. De Leon's (2013:14) findings in America concurs with Dixie's (2017:43) findings that culturally, men are perceived to have sexual needs that cannot be controlled or repressed. In dating or courtship, there is no distinction between acquaintance rape and a normal sexual relationship (Armstrong, 1989:68; De Leon, 2013:10; Vandiver & Dupalo, 2012:1; Odu & Olusegun, 2012:10; Zeira *et al.*, 2002:152; Date Rape Cases Among Women: Strategies For Support and Prevention, 2008:30). This study sought to establish whether what was found in Nigeria, the United States, and Israel and elsewhere applies to Masvingo.

De Leon (2013:13) is of the view that culturally, males view "tease" or "loose" women as openly asking for sex. If they (those women regarded as tease or loose) claim rape after the act, they would be viewed as if they would have changed the goal posts. Koss and Dinero (2010:70) also underscore that as a result, most of these males believe that most acquaintance rapes are false reports. Social norms that require women to be virgins when they marry bring about different perceptions of acquaintance rape among individuals. Dixie (2017:44) argues that acquaintance rape, although it can be viewed by others as evil, can also be perceived by individuals, perpetrators, and victims as a male's social right. That is the reason why individuals, perpetrators, and victims in institution of higher learning, just like other ordinary people, perceive it (acquaintance rape) differently. This study sought to explore whether cultural perspectives of acquaintance rape the world over apply to Masvingo.

Mittal, Signh and Verma (2017:1) note that culture is perceived to be playing a major role when it comes to interpreting acquaintance rape. According to Johnson and Johnson (2017:3), acquaintance rape is under-recognised in the United States of America due to tacit cultural normalisation in dating relationships. Culture, just like any other social variable, affects perceptions of both perpetrators and victims of acquaintance rape both positively and negatively. Flood and Pease (2006:27) contends that acquaintance rape is one of the sexual victimisation crimes considered to be severe across cultures.

According to World Health Organisation's (2017:4) studies from around the globe including Latin America, acquaintance rape occurs in institutions assumed to be safe by the public such as schools, colleges, and universities where perpetrators who include peers, teachers or lecturers commit the crime due to common cultural practices. Gravelin *et al* (2019:15) note that in American culture, rape culture and acquaintance rape are inherently linked phenomena hence they are common practised. Nyul *et al.* (2018:1) on the other hand, observe that acquaintance rape, although controversial and ambiguous the world over, is more prevalent in cultures that have a general acceptance of violence. This study sought to establish whether perceptions of acquaintance rape elsewhere such as in America are similar or different to those of students in higher education in Zimbabwe's Masvingo.

A study carried out by Vandiver and Dupalo (2012:1) in South Western United States of America through the administration of a survey to 584 college students from a large public University established that most of the students did not believe in rape myth. The rape myth acceptance perception suggests that people's views of acquaintance rape have changed considerably in recent years. Vandiver and Dupalo's (2012) study also revealed that male college students in the United States of America were more likely than their counterparts (females) to believe in rape myth. This study also employed a descriptive survey since it was the most appropriate design used to study such type of a sensitive phenomenon like people's perceptions of acquaintance rape. For example, descriptive survey is the commonest design employed by most researchers like (De Leon, 2013:12), Vandiver and Dupalo (2012:1), Koss *et al.*, (1980:3), Zeira *et al.*, (2002:152) and Ben-David & Schneider, (2005:385) who studied students' perceptions on rape myth. De Leon's (2013:13) study in the United States also found that attitudes towards acquaintance rape vary across different cultural groups and communities in any country as well as from one cultural group to the other. World Health Organisation (2005:14) underscores that acquaintance rape takes different forms in different cultural groups. Attitudes towards acquaintance rape are only meaningful within cultural contexts.

The World Health Organisation (2017:2) notes that acquaintance rape takes different dimensions in different cultures due to the traditional beliefs which reinforce patriarchal attitudes towards women and sexuality in all countries involved in the same study and others elsewhere where sexuality issues are generally taboo. Culturally, women are expected to be passive in romantic and sexual relationships. On the other hand, Hersey and Freyd (2020:1) assert that men in most European countries express their love to their partners in aggressive ways (Thacker, 2017:91; Lichter & McCloskey, 2004:344; Sellers, Cochran & Branch, 2005:380; Gravelin *et al.*, 2019:14; Dixie, 2017:16; Johnson & Johnson, 2017:2; Peters & Besley, 2018:461). The same study of the Mediterranean Institute of Gender Studies (2008:11) in America also revealed that because of such cultural confusion, victims could not even recognise the existence of acquaintance date rape. Kamal *et al.* (2010:108) underscores the fact that in most cases victims of acquaintance rape ended up blaming themselves as if they would have engaged in activities or behaviours that may have triggered the act.

Gravelin *et al.*'s (2019:15) study in America concur with Vandiver and Dupalo's study (2012:22) that a culture of silence is observed by both offenders and victims of acquaintance rape in institutions of higher and tertiary education in the southern western United States of America. Gravelin *et al.*'s (2019:4) study used 102 empirical studies on acquaintance rape through the google scholar whereas Vandiver and Dupalo's (2012:22) study used a questionnaire to gather data. This study unlike Graveline *et al.* (2019:15) and Vandiver and Dupalo's (2012:22) studies which used quantitative approach used a mixed method approach. Quantitative research approach employs survey methodologies with predetermined instruments for gathering data that can be analysed statistically. The present book used mixed methods approach to cater for ordinary readers and researchers who may have challenges understanding statistics. Bandura (1986:250) also observes that this culture of silence is learned through social learning just like any social variable. This culture of silence also creates a context whereby no-one would want to testify that he/she is either a victim or perpetrator of acquaintance rape. Although assailants do it secretly, they don't want it to be known that they are acquaintance rapists. Boswell and Spade (2010:134) assert that assailants view acquaintance rape as a social norm that meets a part of rape culture. According to the Social Learning Theory which informs the study, a culture of silence is observed by both offenders and victims of acquaintance rape in social institutions. Silencing the victims of acquaintance rape is regarded as part of cultural compliance. This in synch with Dixie's (2017:41) study in America on acquaintance rape with a sample of university students where he found that victims also practice a culture of silence. This study in part sought to establish how both perpetrators and victims of acquaintance rape perceive it according to their culture.

Research by Davis, Parks and Cohen (2006) in America shows that culture affects people's perceptions of acquaintance rape. Fisher, Daigle Cullen and Turner (2003:40) propound that women the world over seem to keep quiet about their painful and traumatic experiences at the hands of their partners even if they are fully convinced that they had been raped. Van Den Aardweg and Van Den Aardweg (1988:56) observe that culture is an umbrella embracing all the accepted traditional customs, normal attributes and behaviour practised by a particular group. Van Den Aardweg and Van Den Aardweg's (1988:56) observation concurs with what Mapolisa and Stevens (2004:18) discovered that in many societies the world over, there are cultural dictates that encourage remaining ignorant about sexual matters. Van de Bruggen and Grubb (2014:3) propound that blaming ladies for being sexually assaulted is a social norm which also affects the way males and females behave in social settings including institutions of higher learning across the globe. It is from this social norm that acquaintance rape is perceived as a normal cultural practice hence it is commonly practiced internationally, regionally and in sub-Saharan Africa including Zimbabwe (Armstrong, 1989:54). This is in line with Vandiver and Dupalo's (2012:22) observation that students in institutions of higher education in European countries view acquaintance rape as a normal cultural practice. Thus, one's cultural worldview furnishes the norms that shape individuals, perpetrators, and victims and it also affects the way they interpret or perceive other people's sexual motives. In communities and institutions of higher learning, individuals, perpetrators, and victims have different views towards acquaintance rape and this is seen when they interact and socialise with each other. The present book sought to establish whether one's cultural commitment had a bearing on how one perceives acquaintance rape.

The prevalence and acquaintance rape experiences vary internationally and regionally. Carlson, Kamimura, Trinh, Mo, Yamawaki, Bhattacharya, Nguyen, Makomenaw, Birkholz and Olson (2015:82) conducted a study among college women students in the United States of America, Japan, India, Vietnam, and China on perceptions of sexual violence; a broad category in which acquaintance rape falls, using a sample of 1136 college students. Carlson *et al.*'s (2015:82) book of 2012-2013 employed a quantitative approach which enabled the researcher to clearly describe variables. The book revealed that culture shapes attitudes of students' perceptions of acquaintance rape. This study used mixed methods approach in order to interrogate the same problem from various perspectives as well as to understand the phenomenon in detail. This study sought to establish whether what is happening in the United States of America, Japan, India, Vietnam, and China applies to Masvingo. The findings of Carlson *et al.* (2015:82) are in line with the social learning theory which guides this study. The theory postulates that individuals copy each other's behaviour as they socialise and interact with each other. In line with the Social Learning Theory and the recorded literature in the present study, Mittal et al (2017:1) point out that cultural practices and acquaintance rape, like any other social phenomenon, results from the process of normal socialisation. They also found that culture shapes the attitudes of students towards sexual violence. This study sought to establish whether what is happening in the United States, Japan, India, Vietnam, and China applies to institutions of higher education in Masvingo. Koss, Oros and Cheryl's (1980:3) study findings in America on acquaintance rape discovered that because of cultural reasons during an acquaintance rape encounter, the victim could foster misperception of the experience. For example, if the perpetrator describes the victim as a "nice girl", the victim will tend to be confused and would end up saying, "a nice girl would not be in such a situation, I am responsible for unleashing this man's uncontrollable sexual drive; this couldn't be acquaintance rape because I know this man; he is not a stranger, therefore I cannot report him". Koss *et al.*'s (1980:3) study consisted of 2016 surveys which were administered and 236 ladies who met the criterion of high victim status were identified. A sample of 68 participants was interviewed, providing the situational and attitudinal data required for the study. Interviews may be problematic with sensitive issues. This study employed a questionnaire with both open and closed-ended questionnaire items. The questionnaire enabled participants to be more truthful than they would have been in a personal interview, particularly when dealing with sensitive or controversial issues as opined by Cohen et al. (2007:317), Leedy and Ormrod, (2005:185), Nardi, (2006:72), Wiersma and Jurs, (2009:212). Johnson and Hoover (2015:1) also conducted a study in America and their study findings concur with Koss *et al.*'s (1980:3) findings that culture is a catalyst to both perpetrators and victims of acquaintance rape since it causes confusion which leads to misconception and the act to be misconstrued. In view of the functionalist perspective, this study sought to establish whether cultural confusion towards acquaintance rape among victims and perpetrators plays a significant role in higher education students' perceptions of acquaintance rape in Masvingo.

In dating relationships, females are not supposed to show their sexual interests, even their refusal is interpreted as disguised consent, whereas males should act out their sexual interests. In further support of the mentioned perception, Jozkowski and Peterson (2013:50) Frese, Moya and Magias' (2004:143) study in America on acquaintance rape using a sample of 182 psychology undergraduates (91 males and 91 females) who responded to a questionnaire and found that males view aggression towards sex and acquaintance rape as their birth right whereas females view it as a tool which is culturally used to exploit them. This study used a sample of 63 participants from a Polytechnic and two Teachers' colleges. Cultural factors tend to dissuade women or females from coming out publicly with complaints of acquaintance rape (Mediterranean Institute of Gender Studies, 2008:18). Many acquaintance rape victims (using the legal definition of rape) do not label their assaults as rape but as an interactive and normal socialisation process (Dixie, 2017:44). Mittal *et al.* (2017:1) propound that although rape victims offer quite a range of reasons for not reporting the rapists to authorities, the main reason is culture. Vandiver and Dupalo (2012:22) underscore the view that in America both males and females are equal participants in cultural practices although at different levels. Thus, one's cultural worldview furnishes the norms that shape individuals, perpetrators, and victims psychologically and it also affects the way they interpret or perceive other people's sexual motives. In communities and institutions of higher learning, individuals, perpetrators, and victims have different views towards acquaintance rape and this is seen when they interact and socialise with each other. This study sought to establish whether one's cultural commitment had a bearing on how one perceives acquaintance rape, with special reference to students in higher education in Masvingo.

At times, because of cultural reasons, there might be both similarities and differences in perceptions among individual perpetrators and victims of acquaintance rape. For example, acquaintance rape is highly blurred to such an extent that a "no" according to African culture means a "yes" to an African man, but culturally an African female cannot simply say, "yes" The African sexual consent, therefore, depends on the tone of the "no" (Armstrong, 1989:68). Tafirei *et al* (2017:6) note that since it is regarded as a normal cultural practice, therefore, the perpetrator, to a larger extent, accept it and justifies it whereas the victim takes no action about it. A study carried out by the Mediterranean institute of Gender studies (MIGS) (2008:11) investigated date acquaintance rape among young women in Cyprus, Greece, Latvia, Lithuania, and Malta through a focus group discussion. The book revealed that perpetrators and society at large have a culture of victim blaming in acquaintance rape cases. The same study found that in some cultures such as those of Cyprus, acquaintance rape is viewed as private issue and not as an issue for public consumption (Date Rape Cases Among Young Women: Strategies For Support and Prevention, 2008:30). Thus, this study sought to establish whether the perceptions of students from Cyprus, Greece, Latvia, Lithuania and Malta are the same as those in Masvingo.

According to the World Health Organisation (2017:2), acquaintance rape takes different dimensions in different cultures due to the traditional beliefs which reinforce patriarchal attitudes towards women and sexuality in patriarchal societies. Another book by the Mediterranean Institute of Gender Studies (2008:11) also revealed that because of cultural differences across cultures, victims could not even recognise the existence of acquaintance date rape. In most cases, victims of acquaintance rape ended up blaming themselves as if they would have led the perpetrators to rape them (Date Rape Case Among Young Women: Strategies For Support and Prevention, 2008:30).

A survey conducted by Zeira, Astor and Benbenshty (2002:152) in the Jewish and Arab public schools in Israel using a questionnaire and a sample of 10400 students, revealed that culture does affect both victims and perpetrators' perceptions towards acquaintance rape. According to the findings of that study, Arab boys were by far the most sexually harassed group in Israel's schools unlike their counterparts (girls) who indicated the lowest report rates. According to Arab cultural values, dealing with issues related to girls' sexuality is extremely sensitive. Shalhoub-Kevorkian (1993:630) asserts that as per their culture and social norms, the honour of the family is highly important, and the family may even resort to punishing the girl involved in a sexual relationship by death to maintain the family's good image. These values and social norms affect the way males and females interact and view sexual relationships in Arab societies.

Female students in Arab schools, by virtue of their culture, refrain from contacts that they think would result in acquaintance rape while males behave more freely. Arab boys, unlike their counterparts (girls), are targets for sexual apprenticeship, so their special sexual cultural needs are fulfilled as they interact and socialise with girls. This study sought to ascertain whether the Jewish or Arabic experiences were applicable to that of Masvingo.

Research by Mittal *et al.* (2017:1) in India with a sample of 208 participants, both males and females, responded to Young Adults' Attitudes towards *Acquaintance Rape and Rape Victims* has revealed that culturally, male participants compared to females hold lesser acquaintance rape myth but have more negative attitudes towards victims of acquaintance rape. Mittal *et al.*'s (2017:1) research participants responded to Rape Myth Acceptance Scale, Attitudes towards Victims Scale and Casual Attribution towards Sexual Violence scale. This study sought to investigate whether the Indian cultural practices and perceptions of acquaintance rape applies to higher education students' perceptions of acquaintance rape in Masvingo.

As has been alluded to earlier on, acquaintance rape is socially acceptable across the globe as men developed rape culture which assumes that men are aggressive and dominant in sexual relationships (Bryden & Mador, 2016:29). Martin (2016:30) notes that culture tends to act as a defence in acquaintance rape. Van der Van Bruggen and Grubb (2014:3) on the other hand observe that among other reasons why acquaintance rape is not reported while it's quite rampant in institutions of higher learning in America is the fact that both victims and perpetrators of acquaintance rape treat it as a normal cultural practice. According to Dixie (2017:41), this perception even delays or discourages victims from disclosing it. Cultural practices vary internationally, regionally including Zimbabwe; hence both victims and perpetrators of acquaintance rape tend to have different perceptions of this social problem.

Mediterranean Institute of Gender Studies (2008:18) opines that cultural factors tend to dissuade women or females from coming out publicly with complaints of acquaintance rape. Many acquaintance rape victims (using the legal definition of rape) do not label their assaults as rape but as an interactive and normal socialisation process. Okeke (2011:30) points out that although rape victims offer quite a range of reasons for not reporting the rapists to authorities, the main reason is culture. Both males and females are equal participants in cultural practices although at different levels. Gravelin *et al.* (2019:13) on the other hand underscores the fact that culturally, in sexual relationships males would be at a dominant level whereas the females would be at a subordinate level. The cultural "template" plays a major role in protecting group members to such an extent that even if assailants do something wrong to a group member which can be regarded as wrong by other groups, that group would justify that as normal. Berkowitz (2004:37) observes that the cultural template causes confusion to individuals, perpetrators, and victims of acquaintance rape because it is constantly amended, negotiated, revised, and reproduced. On the other hand, Lam and Roman (2009:18) also note that African traditionalists view acquaintance rape as a normal cultural practice but to modern scholars it is viewed as a social vice.

Odu and Olusegun (2012:10) also conducted a study in Nigeria (an African country) on the determinants of sexual coercion among University female students in South-West Nigeria using a sample of 1 200 sexually coerced female students sampled from nine Universities. This study involved both male and female students to avoid gender bias as has been mentioned. Odu and Olusegun's (2012:10) study also revealed that acquaintance rape is affected by cultural reasons among other social variables. This study, unlike the above (Odu & Olusegun, 2012:10), sought to explore whether what is prevailing in Nigerian institutions of higher education apply to institutions in Masvingo. This study limited its scope to establishing the position of culture in relation to higher education students' perceptions of acquaintance rape in Masvingo. Unlike Odu and Olusegun's (2012:10) study, this study employed a quantitative approach to collect data on this social problem (acquaintance rape). The quantitative research operated from the positivist paradigm which is based on the rationalistic and empiricist philosophy. In the African context acquaintance rape is taboo. In this study, the quantitative approach was found to be the most suitable method to tap what is inside participants' heads.

Oshiname *et al.*'s (2013:138) study findings in Nigeria tend to concur with earlier Nigerian findings by Odu and Olusegun's (2012:915) that forced sex by males is tolerated within the context of sexual relationships in Africa although studies on acquaintance rape are quite rare in the continent. Oshiname *et al.*'s (2013:138) study employed a cross-sectional survey which was conducted among 651 female undergraduate participants who were selected using a four-stage random sampling technique. Oshiname *et al.*'s (2013:138) participants filled in a semi-structured questionnaire which might have been weak in that participants could generalise their responses. This study employed both open-ended and closed-ended questionnaire items to curb the stated weakness of the semi-structured questionnaire items. Armstrong's (1987:68) study in Zimbabwe established that according to traditional African culture, perpetrators justify themselves for committing acquaintance rape whilst victims suffer silently and at times may not even be aware of it as a crime. Lisak *et al.* (2010:1318) contends that both perpetrators and victims perceive acquaintance rape as a culturally acceptable social practice hence they tend to justify it. African culture and perceptions which are pan-African in nature are reflected in African social and dating practices (Okeke, 2011:30).

Oltedal, Moen, Klempe and Rundmo (2004:7) argue that human beings learn to believe that the standards, principles, perspectives, and explanations that they acquire from their culture affect the way they view any phenomenon. Zeira *et al.* (2002:152) observe that cultural scaffolding of rape is a framework of attitudes that stem from and support patriarchy and provide ideational space and justification for acquaintance rape. Koss and Dinero (1988:68) observe that sexually aggressive men from diverse settings have greater hostility towards their victims, have stronger sexual dominant desires, and have more traditional attitudes towards gender roles as well as sexual relationships and greater acceptance of rape myth.

Sampson (2002:10) also notes that acquaintance rape, because of its ordinary characteristics, cannot be easily recognised across the globe since individuals naturally gravitate towards perceptions which emanate from culture that reflect their group. If acquaintance rape is committed, both perpetrators and victims view the act as a product of the group. Thus, Linton (1945:32) declares that "culture is the configuration of learned behaviours and results of behaviour whose component element are shared and transmitted by the members of a particular society".

Turner and Stets (2005:8) note that individuals react to situations and other individuals based on learnt or acquired cultural ideas, bias, and normative expectations of what is anticipated in a particular instance. Edwards, Bradshaw and Hinsz (2014:188) on the other hand, observed that behaviour therefore can be said to be dictated by what is socially or culturally acceptable or appropriate for a particular situation. Because of cultural influence, both victims and perpetrators indulge in acquaintance rape unknowingly as they try to orbit within cultural practices. Kahan (2010:4) noted that the influence of culture on human beings' perceptions of fact is stronger than any other social variables; hence, perceptions are culturally linked. Herman (1984:102) concurs with O'Sullivan (1993:78) that from a cultural point of view, those sexually active men are positively reinforced by being referred to as "studs" or "sluts".

Fanflik (2007:18) is of the view that in institutions of higher learning, in most cases, acquaintance rape takes place among acquaintances with or without their understanding of the act and without their sexual consent. Colantonio-Yurko (2018:2) reiterates that because of cultural confusion in sexual relationships among college mates, there is also no likelihood of reporting the issue to the police. Armstrong (1989:68) propounds that cultural practices in Zimbabwe tend to cover social vices such as child marriages, pledging with daughters, and payment of avenging spirits using girls and acquaintance rape as well as other unethical dating practices. In most cases all these social practices affect women and girls. Interactionists observe that culture acts as a blanket that covers both good and evil practices of a society (Dube and Tagutanazvo, 2002:25). This is in tandem with Mazrui and Mazrui's (1995:134) observation that every culture is unique and the psychology of living together is also dynamic, hence different societies view other cultural practices as strange and as a result tend to affect perceptions of observers of those cultures either positively or negatively. That is the reason why, individuals, perpetrators and victims tend to have different perceptions of acquaintance rape. The above literature that cultural practices tend to cover social vices is in tandem with the Social Learning Theory which informs this study. The theory postulates that individuals copy each other's behaviour as they socialise and interact with each other. The above literature on cultural practices also asserts that acquaintance rape, like any other social phenomenon, results from the process of normal socialisation (Mittal *et al.*, 2017:1).

Armstrong (2000:45) observes that dating tactics have no formula to follow hence they confuse partners and causes acquaintance rape to occur unwittingly. Victims fall prey to acquaintance rapists in trying to observe cultural practices. According to Boswell and Spade (2010:134), across all cultures men are viewed as initiators of sex and women as passive resisters of it. If they (women victims) let those (men) in, they would have accepted sex. Some communities even worsen the victimisation of the abused by the labels or stigmatisation they attach to the victim. Mittal *et al.* (2017:2) are of the view that from a cultural perspective, individuals and victims view acquaintance rape as a normal cultural practice which should be observed just like any other social norm.

Armstrong (2000:92) advocates that Zimbabwean Shona language, which is a product of African culture used especially in dating, is also structured in such a way that activities relating to courtship, marriage and sex protect the men (who happen to be the main perpetrators of acquaintance rape). Armstrong (1989:68) also notes that because of African cultural norms, sex is taboo to talk about especially in the presence of the opposite sex, so the victim observes silence on this matter. The passivism ascribed here by Armstrong, for him, explains how the perpetrator escapes punishment for acquaintance rape in many African societies. Thus, it was relevant for this study to explore the influences of culture on students' perceptions of acquaintance rape. Culture and human perceptions are inseparable hence it is of importance to study them together. From recorded related literature so far (De Leon, 2010; Zeira *et al.*, 2002; Johnson & Johnson, 2017; Dixie, 2017; Singh & Verma, 2017; Deming, 2017; Okeke, 2011; Vandiver and Dupalo, 2012; and Odu and Olusegun, 2012), it can be assumed that perceptions of people in general and students in particular are influenced by culture.

Related literature recorded so far indicated that acquaintance rape is perceived differently internationally, regionally as well as in sub-Saharan Africa including Zimbabwe. Students' perceptions of acquaintance rape are influenced mainly by cultural dynamics. Studies carried out in Nigeria, an African country, Europe and elsewhere indicated that both victims and perpetrators of acquaintance rape do not have knowledge about it due to patriarchal attitudes towards the problem (Sellers, Cochran & Branch, 2005:379; Johnson & Johnson, 2017:1; Mediterranean Institute of Gender Studies (2008:11; Dolan, 2019:1; Singh & Verma, 2017:1; Zeira, 2002:152; Odu & Olusegun, 2012:10).

This section discussed literature on how culture affects people's perceptions of acquaintance rape. One key culturally related aspect is gender. The next section dealt with how gender affects students' perceptions of acquaintance rape.

2.3 Gender and Acquaintance Rape

Internationally, regionally and locally, acquaintance rape seems to be perceived not only on cultural terms but also on gender basis. The World Health Organisation (2017:2) observes that for a large proportion of young women, the first sexual intercourse is forced. Data obtained from the same study by the World Health Organisation (2017:2) suggests that the younger the age of the victim, the higher the probability that their first sexual intercourse is acquaintance rape. According to the World Health Organisation (2017:2) multi-country study, some women reported that their first sexual intercourse was forced, hence it was acquaintance rape, at rates in the range of less than 1% in Japan to nearly 30% in rural Bangladesh. In studies with both males and females, the prevalence of reported rape or sexual abuse has been established to be higher among the female gender. In Lima, Peru for example, the number of young women reportedly forced into sexual initiation by a male acquaintance was (40%), four times greater than for males (11%) abused by female acquaintances. World Health Organisation (2017:3) also noted that females are targets of intolerance, chauvinism and acquaintance rape in the education system which hinders their access to participation in higher education system. In light of the foregoing, this book sought to establish whether the Japanese, Bangladesh or Peru scenarios described above apply to Masvingo.

Acceptance of sex-role stereotype is perceived to have a negative impact on acquaintance rape. Hills and Pleva (2020:77) observe that gender roles together with cultural connotations are thought to play a fundamental role in what happens in sexual relationships. Gravelin *et al.* (2019:6), in their study conducted in America found that females in their sex-role stereotyping groups blame victims more than males for their victimisation. Deming's (2017:14) study in the United States of America employed a questionnaire and established that females in these sex-role stereotyping groups feel that victims would have given the perpetrator the wrong idea, and also would have given the victim more responsibility for her situation than females in low sex-role stereotyping groups if raped by acquaintances. Gerger, Kley, Bohner and Siebler's (2007:17) study in America employed a 30 item self-report scale measuring the acceptance of modern myth about sexual aggression and a sample of 1279 participants and established that acquaintance rape victims blame can be twofold; that is, characterological blame (blame attributed to a stable factor like personality) and behavioural blame (blame attributed to a changeable factor, for example, the victims' actions and reactions). According to Mazrui and Mazrui (1995:134), acquaintance rape in institutions of higher learning takes place within the psychology of living together. Because males are always given preferential treatment by members of the society even in sexual relationships, these sexual crimes are not taken seriously. Kathryn, Feltey and Ainslie (2016:229) conducted a study using a quantitative approach and a sample of 378 persons which was generated from teachers and students from rural, urban and suburban high schools. Participants from Kathryn *et al.*'s (2016:229) study were from a mid-sized, mid-western metropolitan area in the United States of America. This study employed a mixed method approach with a sample of 63 participants comprised of students, academic and non-academic staff from three institutions of higher education from Masvingo which were conveniently selected because of their proximity to the researcher. The participants in this study were from urban, peri-urban, mining, resettlement and rural areas. Kathryn *et al.*'s (2016:229) study confirmed the assertion that males are more likely than females to support acquaintance rapists or sexually coercive behaviour across situations.

Johnson and Johnson's (2017:4) study in the United States of America found that the female gender is a target of acquaintance rape, sexual assault and molestation. Johnson and Johnson (2017:4) collected data from 314 participants including both males and females who were selected using snowball sampling from February to August of 2014. Snowball sampling technique has a challenge that participants might not want to disclose their lived experiences especially acquaintance rape survivors. In this study the researcher used a random sampling technique to select students and convenient sampling technique to select the three institutions of higher education. Participants represented all the geographical regions of the United States of America (i.e., Northeast, Midwest, South, and West districts). Two-hundred and sixty-one (83.1%) participants identified themselves as exclusively heterosexual, 5 (1.6%) as homosexual and 48 (15.3%) as lying between these two extremes. The whites constituted the largest number of participants (70.1%), 13.4% were Africans Americans, 4.8% were Asian/Pacific Islanders, 2.2%, Hispanic/Latinx, 3.2% Middle Eastern and 4.1% were multiracial. Human differentiation on the basis of gender, just like culture, is a fundamental phenomenon that affects virtually every aspect of people's daily life (Bussey & Bandura, 1991:1). Culture and human beings' historical background in which sexuality is defined or centred upon is a gendered foundation that maintains separate rules for males and females' behaviour (Hird & Jackson, 2001:32). Tafirei *et al.* (2017:6) observe that human society, particularly in patriarchal societies, has always been characterized by female marginalization, as evidenced by the teachings of famous philosophers as far back as Aristotle who remarked that being female by virtue means lacking some qualities that males possess.

Ben-David and Schneider's (2005:385) study in America revealed that rape in general, and acquaintance rape in particular, should not be viewed as a deviant sexual act but as an aggressive way for males to sexually control females. This, however, assumes that perpetrators of acquaintance rape are only men and not women. Ben-David and Schneider's (2005:385) survey sample consisted of 150 university students who filled in a questionnaire on students 'perceptions of acquaintance rape. Gravelin *et al.*'s (2019: 13) study in the United States of America also established that society is arranged in such a way that men are bread winners and as such, they have social, political, and economic powers to control every family member especially their wives and children. The World Health Organisation (2007:3) observed that studies on men and boys have shown how inequitable gender norms influence how males interact with their partners. Deming's (2017:5) study in the United States of America concurs with Thacker's (2017:93) study that the social structure gives men powerful positions while relegating women to be subordinates of males. It is the main reason why females are the main victims of acquaintance rape and while males are the main perpetrators. Tichapondwa (2013:126) observe that questionnaires are not time consuming and that they enable researchers to collect large quantities of data. Most researchers such as Deming (2017:5), Thacker (2017:93) among others used questionnaires in their studies on acquaintance rape hence the use of the questionnaire in this study is justified.

Armstrong (1989:68) observes that even in courtship and sexual advances, men are socially privileged such that they are the ones that initiate a date. Cook *et al.* (2001:17) concur with Dumont *et al.* (2003:103) on that ladies are mostly perceived as stereotypical rape victims, even if they report their assailants, they cannot be believed due to gender stereotyping. Dumont *et al.* (2003:103) on the other hand points out that men learn to act out their sexual interest and are encouraged not to control their sexual urges in courtship. According to Frese *et al.*'s (2004:144) study in Israel, women are perceived as sexual objects whose function is to satisfy men's sexual needs and as such sexual coercion is regarded as a normal and acceptable social practice in role behaviour. Thus, Jewkes (2012:23) notes that "sexual harassment, a term under which acquaintance rape falls, regardless of its form, is related to the sexist male ideology of male dominance and male superiority". Tangri, Burt and Johnson (1982:33) opine that society's perception of females as an inferior sex and the gender stratification that emphasises sex role expectation introduces and maintains acquaintance rape in social institutions. The view that acquaintance rape should not be viewed as a deviant sexual act but as an aggressive and antisocial tool for male control over females is in tandem with the theory of social learning that informs the study. The theory emphasises the fact that members of the society realise their gender roles and societal members' expectations from societal practices hence they see no harm in acquaintance rape.

Gravelin et al (2019:4) conducted a study in America on blaming the victims of acquaintance rape based on individual, situational, and socio-cultural factors, using dissertations and theses published from December 2017 (inclusive) to 2019. Additional articles were obtained by conducting forward and backward searches utilising reference sections of retrieved articles as well as earlier literature reviews through Google Scholar. The approach obtained 137 articles which were then assessed for fit according to their inclusion criterion. The study's review was restricted to studies of lay observers. Only studies of victim blaming in cases involving female victims and male assailants which were most often depicted via a written or visual scenario were automatically included in their study. Their study exposed participants to a vignette/scenario/description of an acquaintance rape, then the observer assessed victim blaming. 102 empirical studies on acquaintance rape that had at least one measure of victim blame, as defined above, were located. Their main goal was to identify key factors that have been considered as predictors of victim blaming and found that females are less likely to blame victims of acquaintance rape as compared to males. This study endeavoured to establish whether the scenarios prevailing in some parts of the globe apply to students from Masvingo.

The findings in a study by Ben-David and Schneider (2005:385) in Israel with a sample of one hundred and fifty Israeli students on Rape Perceptions, Gender, Role Attitudes, and Victim Perpetrators of Acquaintance rape showed that both perpetrators and victims have different perceptions of acquaintance rape scenarios and punishment given to rape committed by a neighbour, an ex-boyfriend and a current life partner. According to Gravelin *et al.* (2019:4), a connection was found between gender role attitudes and gender stereotype. Significant gender differences were also found in gender role attitudes which revealed that females tend to hold more egalitarian attitudes towards acquaintance rape than their male counterparts. Gravelin *et al.*'s (Ibid) findings concur with Ferrao, Goncalves, Giger and Parreira's (2016:241) findings that females tend to hold more liberal views on gender roles than males do. Ferrao *et al.*'s (2016:241) findings on the connection between gender and rape perceptions indicated that there was a significant gender difference in the measures of perception of the appropriate punishment for acquaintance rape offenders. There was also no significant gender difference in the perceptions of both victims and perpetrators of acquaintance rape. According to Cairney's (2012:319) study findings in the United States of America, gender differences found on the perception of the situation or happening were like those found by other researchers who indicated that females tend to evaluate acquaintance rape more seriously than males do. What it means is that because of social norms, victims (who in most cases are females) of acquaintance rape suffer silently. This study sought to establish whether gendered social norms affect students in higher education's perceptions of acquaintance rape in Masvingo.

Xenos and Smith (2001:1103) also conducted a Melbourne-based survey of 608 adolescents and young adults from both secondary schools and universities in Australia using a questionnaire and found that males were more blaming of rape victims than females. Most males in Xenos and Smith's (2001) study had greater beliefs that they had a right of sexual access to their partners especially if they are in a long-term sexual relationship which involves more formal commitments. In this study, the sample was similar to Xenos and Smith's (2001:1103) study sample which was composed of both males and females. The combination of both males and females was to avoid gender bias. David and Lee (1996:788) also note similar gender differences in perceptions towards acquaintance rape in their study among 244 secondary school students aged between fourteen and sixteen years in Newcastle using a questionnaire. This study, as has been mentioned before also used a questionnaire because of the fact that, it is the most commonly used research tool. Johnson and Johnson (2017:9), De Leon (2010:10), Ben-David and Schneider

(2005:385), Deming (2017:14), Odu and Olusegun (2012:10), Zeira *et al.* (2002:152), Tafirei *et al.* (2017:6), Dixie, (2017:44), Carlson *et al.* (2015:82) among other researchers utilised a questionnaire in their studies which focused on acquaintance rape. According to DeJudicibus and McCabe (2001:40), adult males from America, unlike females, are also blamed targets of acquaintance rape and sexual harassment. This study sought to establish whether the Australian and American scenarios above are applicable to Masvingo.

Zeira *et al.*'s (2002:151) study in Israel observe that sexual harassment, a broad term in which acquaintance rape falls in, is primarily directed at females. In a study conducted by Ajuwon, Olaleye, Faromoju, Ladipo and AkinJimoh (2001a) at Ibadan University in Nigeria on sexual coercion of University students, it was found that females are the main victims of sexual coercion and acquaintance rape due to gender stereotyping. Kamal, Shaikh and Shailkh's (2010:109) study in Pakistan found that when individuals, perpetrators and victims interact, they classify their experiences, encode or decode situations and as such that is where males interpret and misinterpret females' actions sometimes resulting in acquaintance rape. A cross-sectional survey with convenience sampling was conducted among male and female students of Quide-e-Azam University, Islamabad. Kamal *et al.*'s (2010:108) study employed a structured, self-administered, anonymous and pre-tested questionnaire with closed-ended questions. This study utilised a descriptive survey to describe, explain and explore factors affecting higher education students' perceptions of acquaintance rape in Masvingo of Zimbabwe. Abbey, Helmers, Jilani, McDaniel and Beribourich (2021:749) note that males (more so, often than their counterparts) view certain cues such as wearing revealing clothing, agreeing to a secluded date location, for example a man's room or the beach, drinking while dating as well as tickling the man as evidence that women are interested in having sex with them. According to Boswell and Spade's (2010:137) study in Palestine using interviews with open-ended questionnaire items about gender relations on campus, their attitudes about acquaintance rape, and their own experiences on campus, it was found that, acquaintance rape is mostly committed during the night, especially during college functions like parties and dances. Due to over-excitement and misinterpretation of the social problem (acquaintance rape), individuals and perpetrators misconstrue females' actions and end up raping them. Oshiname *et al.*'s (2013:142) study in Nigeria on knowledge and perception of date rape among female acquaintance undergraduates of a Nigerian university also established that many victims of acquaintance rape (undergraduate young women) perceive it as a dating practice which is socially acceptable and justified. Oshiname *et al.*'s (2013:146) study also established that the perception of acquaintance rape as a social variable has the potential of making acquaintance rape victims not to acknowledge their own experiences as rape. This study sought to establish if what was found in most Nigerian Universities apply to students in higher education institutions in Masvingo. In a similar study, Polaschek and Gannon's (2004:299) in America established that males perceive females to be constantly sexually receptive. Unlike Oshiname *et al.*'s (2013:146) study in Nigeria which used the close ended questionnaire items only to produce quantitative data, this study used both open and closed- ended questionnaire items and produced both quantitative and qualitative data. Mertens (2009:304) opined that mixed methods involve the application of both quantitative and qualitative approaches to answer study questions in a particular problem as well as that might be part of a larger study programme. Mixed methods enabled the quantitative and qualitative approaches to complement each other in a single study.

The gendered ideology of male dominance over females brings about different perceptions between both male and female perpetrators and victims towards acquaintance rape. According to Miller and Marshall (1987:38) observe that, "males' sexuality is viewed as more natural, acceptable, and uncontrollable than females' sexuality, many males and females excuse acquaintance rape by affirming that males cannot control their natural urges". From a gender perspective, males think about sex 6 to 15 seconds on average. Thus, sex is regarded as important to males and is considered as a reflection of their masculinity by both genders in the society. If the male gender does not express any desire for sex, it becomes a societal concern. Women on the other hand are not expected to talk about their sexual pleasure or their sexual desires. McCabe, Tanner and Heiman (2010:252) argue that females are culturally expected to limit their sexual inclinations. As human beings interact and socialise with each other, they acquire priorities, skills, traits, norms and self-perceptions which characterise each sex. It is from this base, that males and females have different perceptions towards acquaintance rape. The Nigerian study by Oshiname, Ogunwale and Ajuwon (2013:137) establishing knowledge and perceptions of acquaintance date rape among female undergraduates of a Nigerian university using participants who were selected using a four-stage random sampling technique, found that male dominance in sexual matters is quite rampant in most Nigerian societies. Oshiname *et al.*'s (2013:137) Nigerian study also found that the scenario of male dominance in sexual matters is dictated by gender, perceptions and attitudes which promote females' differences to males in decisions on sexual matters. This study sought to establish if male dominance in sexual matters which is quite rampant in most Nigerian societies is applicable to Masvingo.

Person, Dhingira and Grogan (2018:7) concur with Peters and Besley's study in America (2019:459) that in most African social institutions, males are likely to engage in acquaintance rape because they have negative attitudes towards females especially if they apply traditional masculinity and male privilege views. This study sought to explore whether what was found among European victims of acquaintance rape on blaming victims exists among Africans with special reference to students in higher education institutions from Masvingo and whether this influenced the students' perceptions of acquaintance rape.

Hay-Yahia (2003:534) observes that there is also a relationship between adherence to conservative gender norms and tolerance for acquaintance rape among men in a wide variety of communities and countries, both western and non-western. Perceptions are of central concern in relation to acquaintance rape. Anderson, Sampson-Taylor and Herman (2004:78) concur with Anderson, Cooper and Okamura (1997:295) that individuals, perpetrators and victims of acquaintance rape in institutions of higher learning have different perceptions of acquaintance rape. On the other hand, Berkowitz (1992:176) concur with Anderson, Cooper and Okamura (1997:295) that boys and young men endorse more rape supportive beliefs hence they justify the occurrence of acquaintance rape as both a cultural and social practice. Stalan and Finn (2000:11) note that male police officers make decisions regarding the arrest of acquaintance rapists based on abstract rules of the justice system whereas female police officers give perpetrators of acquaintance rape preferential treatment. The present study sought to establish whether gender affects the perceptions of both victims and perpetrators of acquaintance rape in institutions of higher education in Masvingo.

Haj-Yahia's (2003:540) study in China found those gender-role attitudes and norms structure males and females' attribution of responsibility, blame, and affective responses to victim sympathy.

Given the fundamental relationship between attitudes of acquaintance rape and attitudes towards gender, factors shaping attitudes towards acquaintance rape cannot be considered in isolation from factors shaping gender and sexuality in general. According to Santrock (2005:264), all known societies across the globe recognise biological differentiation and use it as the basis for social distinctions. In any society, the process of crafting gendered human beings starts at birth.

Viewed in this way, acquaintance rape is perceived by the society as men's game hence it is regarded as a necessary evil. Edwoldt, Monson, Langhirichsen-Robbing (2000:808) note that the belief that a woman's sexual consent is derived automatically from an intimate heterosexual relationship continues to persist among acquaintances as well and that is the main reason why it is viewed as normal. This perception expresses itself in many legal systems that have not yet acknowledged acquaintance rape as a crime. This study sought to establish whether gender-role perceptions of societies in America and European countries of acquaintance rape can also apply to Masvingo. Katz, Carion and Hilton (2002:94) are of the view that males and females attribute acquaintance rape to different views centred on gender stereotyping.

Presented literature so far assumed that both males and females blame victims of acquaintance rape (Lambert & Raichel, 2000:853) for their misfortunes. Simonson and Subich (1999:12) note that gender-role beliefs have a significant influence on both males and females' perceptions of acquaintance rape. Thus, Suprakash, Ajay, Murthy and Biswajit's (2017:2) study in India found that individuals, perpetrators and victims of acquaintance rape perceive gender as a major factor that triggers acquaintance rape. Demographics of acquaintance rape in Suprakash *et al.*'s (2017:2) study were obtained from crime records, hospital data, non-governmental organisations and surveys. Suprakash *et al.,* (2017:2) indicated that their data sources underestimate the actual magnitude of the problem of acquaintance rape. This study, similar to Suprakash *et al.*'s (2017:2) study also utilised document analysis, data from open-ended and closed-ended questionnaire items.

Traditional perceptions of gender are not only associated with tolerance for violence against victims but also support male acquaintance rapists, at least, from a traditional perspective. Deming (2017:8) contends that the best attitudinal predictor of acquaintance rape may be a measure combining the attitudes that describe a hostile form of masculinity or patriarchal ideology whereby women are expected to be submissive to men. Patriarchal values and norms run high within different social groups, especially in patriarchal societies, and it is from this perception that males are often reported as having sexually assaulted females. Van der Bruggen and Grubb's (2019:459) study in Israel also established that in all societies, to a greater degree, ladies and girls are subjected to physical, sexual and psychological abuse across all cultures. Women and girls are a soft target for acquaintance rape. Van der Bruggen and Grubb (2014:3) concur with Peters and Besley (2019:459) that the presence of acquaintance rape in the society is difficult to locate because of its patriarchal nature hence society assumes that it is non-existent since it occurs in private spheres. This study sought to establish whether gender influences the perceptions of both perpetrators and victims of acquaintance rape and their decision making process when evaluating it.

Okeke (2011:39) conducted a study in Nigeria on sexual harassment using a stratified random sample of 397 male faculty staff and administrators from a state university, and established that males, unlike females, perceive more situations as being sexually or potentially sexually accommodative and as a result view acquaintance rape as being normal and appropriate for courtship. For example, "positive attitudes of acquaintance rape were also noted to be indicators of acquaintance rape acceptance by most college students". Societal perceptions are gender-oriented and that is the main reason why perceptions tend to differ between males and females. In a similar approach of study in which Okeke (2011:39) employed a questionnaire, this study also used a questionnaire as a research tool to cover as many participants as possible. In this study, the social norm gap was covered by consulting authorities or studies across the globe. According to Schuller, McKimme, Masser and Klippenstine (2010:764), acquaintance rape seemed to have a bias towards females as victims. Unlike previous studies by Oshiname *et al.* (2013:137), Odu and Olusegun (2012:915), Carlson et al (2015:82) and Okeke (2011:1), this study included both males and females with different life experiences. As has been alluded to earlier, males perceive acquaintance rape as a normal cultural dating practice whereas females are in confusion as to whether it is socially accepted or not (Oshiname *et al.*, 2013146). This study sought to establish in part how gender affects the perceptions of students in higher education institutions in Masvingo.

In all the recorded studies in this study, females view acquaintance rape in institutions of higher learning as part of college life (De Leon, 2013; Ben-David & Schneider, 2005; Sampson, 2002; Okeke, 2011; Kahan, 2010; Zeira et al., 2002; Finn, 1977; Russo, 2000; Kamal et al., 2010; Frese et al., 2004). Frese et al (2004:155) assert that females therefore view males as having social rights to enjoy sex from both sexual partners as well as acquaintances. The present study sought to establish if what was found in European and Asian countries (Gravelin *et al.* (2019:4); Beere *et al.*, 1984; King & King, 1990; Manson & Lu, 1988; Simonson & Subich, 1999; Cainey, 2012; De Leon, 2013; Sampson, 2002; Kahan, 2010; Zeira *et al.*, 2002; Finn, 1997; Russo, 2000; Kamal *et al.*, 2010; Frese *et al.*, 2004) and Nigeria, an African country (Okeke, 2011;Oshiname *et al.*, 2013) applies in Masvingo.

In sub-Saharan Africa, Zimbabwe in particular, Mutekwe, Modiba and Maposa's (2012:115) study in Zimbabwe also revealed that because of cultural factors, girls are the most victims of sexual abuse (a term in which acquaintance rape falls), and boys are the main perpetrators of acquaintance rape. Mutekwe *et al.*'s (2012:115) study used a sample of 40 participants who were purposively selected from high schools. Data was gathered through observations and focus group discussion sessions. Mapfumo, Shumba and Chireshe's (2007:15) study on the same problem found that besides boys, male young teachers are also perpetrators of acquaintance rape in high schools. Mapfumo *et al.*'s (2007:15) study used 118 high school girls who voluntarily participated. Similar to Mapfumo *et al.*'s (2007:15) study which used a descriptive survey, this study also adopted a survey design to collect data through a questionnaire. This study also employed a survey and gathered original, factual and attitudinal data from the three institutions of higher education in Masvingo of Zimbabwe. So, it seems that, acquaintance rape stretches from high schools to institutions of higher learning.

The section discussed literature on how gender influences one's perceptions of acquaintance rape, especially in social settings where people live in large numbers. Geographical, cultural, gender, age (peer), time, policy, legislation or law implementation gaps were highlighted. A key aspect related to gender is peer pressure. The next section discussed how peer pressure influences students' perceptions of acquaintance rape.

2.4 Peer Pressure and Acquaintance Rape

There are various factors which influence students' perceptions of acquaintance rape, internationally, regionally and locally. Peer pressure is one such factor which influences adolescents' perceptions towards acquaintance rape in most colleges and universities. Lightfoot and Evans (2000:1160) also conducted a study on acquaintance rape from a university in the New Zealand and found that due to social learning, most adolescents have been sexually abused by those peers who have been sexually abused by acquaintances during their childhood within social contexts. This study also employed the social learning theory to investigate factors affecting higher education students' perceptions of acquaintance rape in Masvingo. Human beings are found in social groups, and one such important group is the peer group at an institution of higher education. According to Lev-Wiesel (2004:199), peers normally suffer from peer pressure and it affects the way they perceive acquaintance rape. For Gwartney-Gibbs *et al* (1987:276) the influence and consequence of acquaintance rape to both perpetrators and victims of acquaintance rape depends to a large extent on how peers view it.

According to Sexual Offences in England and Wales: year ending March 2017 Statistics Report (2018:22), 38% of 61125 victims of acquaintance rape reported that the offender(s) were under the influence of alcohol. The same proportion of victims (38%) said they were under the influence of alcohol. In the same report, other victims reported that the offender was under the influence of drugs (8%) while others were under the influence of drugs they had chosen to take (2%). In addition, 6% of victims reported that they thought that the offender had drugged them during the last incident of rape or penetration (including attempts) they had experienced. Victims and perpetrators of acquaintance rape are prevented from resisting acquaintance rape due to physical and mental incapacity induced by drugs or alcohol. Consent may not be obtained in situations where the victim is intoxicated. The perpetrators interpret non-verbal communication, silence, passivity, or lack of resistance as consent due to drugs and alcohol abuse. Research by Walker, Hester, Mc Phee, Williams, Bates and Rumney (2019:1) in England in 2010 and 2014 also found that rapes against younger women and girls included quite several assaults by peers (friend or fellow students). The results indicated that acquaintance rape is prevalent among peers. The findings were pertinent to this study.

Bohner, Siebler and Schmelcher (2010:287) also conducted a study in Germany using a sample of male university students on social norms and the likelihood of raping: perceived rape myth acceptance of others affects men's rape proclivity and it was found that, "if males are told that others in their peer group had a high level of acceptance of rape myths, their own rape proclivity (in this case, how aroused they would be in certain situations of sex and else-where where peer cultural coercion and how likely they would be to behave like that) increased. As has been mentioned earlier on, this study sample also included both males and females to avoid gender bias. Bohner *et al.* (2010:144) note that similar social dynamics operate in institutions of higher learning. Dixie (2017:45) asserts that male peers perceive rape culture as part of male peer groups. Mittal *et al.* (2017:2) are of the view that acquaintance rape can also be committed by young male urban gangs which apply peer group dynamics to sexually assault females whom they know. This book sought to establish whether the German scenario tallies with those factors which influence the perceptions of students in higher education institutions in Masvingo.

A book by Do and Mark (2020:1), using a sample of 6 159 women and men enrolled in 32 higher education institutions across the United States of America using an online questionnaire, revealed that since the age of 14 years, 27, 5% of college ladies had experienced an acquaintance rape from their peers and 7.7% of college males admitted that they had committed such an act. This book also employed a questionnaire since it was suitable to gather data from participants from a wider geographical area about their perceptions, knowledge and beliefs about acquaintance rape. Most of such assaults committed in institution campuses were perpetrated by boyfriends, friends, or acquaintances of the victim, with more than 59% occurring on a date. Participants in this study also perceived peers as having peer pressure and using peer norms to commit acquaintance rape. According to Dixie (2017:42), the impact of peer pressure on acquaintance rape cases can lead to detrimental consequences to all parties involved, that is, influencing how they think and how they should behave and interact with others socially, and what they expect from others, and what others may expect from them. This study sought to establish if the above scenario applies to Masvingo.

According to De Leon (2013:18), a large body of quantitative and qualitative research indicates that male peer support is a powerful determinant to men's actions. Dekeseredy, Donnermeyer, Schwartz, Tunnell and Hall (2007:295) conducted a study in Ohio in America using a qualitative approach and found that rural men relied much on their fellow male friends and neighbours, including police officers to support their violent patriarchal status. This study employed mixed methods approach in order to triangulate data sources, methods and theories. Dekeseredy *et al.* (2007:301) also found that male sexual abusers who happen to receive male peer support also adhered to the ideology of public patriarchy. This study sought to investigate if the American scenario stated above is also applicable to students of Masvingo.

It has been alluded to earlier that there is a lot of rape culture, especially at fraternity parties at colleges and universities (Peters & Besley, 2018:458) where males mistreat females, that is why they abuse them sexually. Boswell and Spade (2010:139) propound that male peers in fraternity pledges tend to view female students at college bars as being morally loose hence they treat them as targets for hooking up. Sleath and Bulls (2017:1) observed that when peers commit acquaintance rape under the influence of alcohol and drugs, both perpetrators and victims may not be able to give an account of what would have transpired. Boswell and Spade (2010:135) used a mixed method approach of using observations of interactions between male and female students at fraternity parties and bars, formal interviews as well as informal conversations. Sampson (2002:3) used a cross-sectional survey and Jewkes (2012:7) used internet literature search on published papers or reports on acquaintance rape. Rhodes' (2019: v) study in America used an online questionnaire and participants were randomly assigned to one of four versions of a vignette where a man and a woman were at a party together where they answered research-created questions pertaining to the behaviour of the people in the vignette and societal attitudes about sex and alcohol. Finn's (1997: vii) book in the United States of America used telephone interviews with administrators, programme coordinators and other staff at more than thirty colleges and universities on acquaintance rape. Finn's (1997) study revealed that both victims and perpetrators of acquaintance rape perceive acquaintance rape as part of adolescence peer culture. This study employed the mixed methods approach since it is methodologically eclectic, therefore in this study, the researcher managed to triangulate quantitative and qualitative approaches in a single study. Acquaintance rape, being a sensitive issue but of great importance, meant that this study was planned to establish the factors affecting higher education students' perception of acquaintance rape in Masvingo.

De Leon (2013:14) conducted a study in America on examination of students' personal interactions and rape perceptions among peers and found that individual students, perpetrators, and victims of acquaintance rape observe how their peers behave in intimate relationships during college life and offenders (who happen to be peers as well) would provide an initial learning of behavioural alternatives which are "appropriate" for these sexual relationships. Armstrong *et al.* (2006:483) observe that some male peers perceive their girlfriends as replacements for a hook-up, so they don't see acquaintance rape as a social vice. Bridges (1991:295) concurs with Edwoldtet *et al.* (2000:1178) that if those who commit acquaintance rape are not reported by the victims, significant others who also happen to be peers would view the offender as a sexual hero resulting in false and rape-supportive beliefs among peers that acquaintance rape is regarded as an extreme and appropriate version of traditional male-female sexual interaction (Ben-David & Schneider, 2005:388). The presented literature so far indicates that peer pressure does influence the perceptions of students in both high schools and institutions of higher learning. Thus, of relevance to this study are the factors affecting higher education students' perceptions of acquaintance rape in Masvingo.

According to Santrock (2005:351), "one of the most important functions of peer groups is to provide a source of information and life experience about the world outside the family". Lev-Wiesel (2004:200) reasons that dating skills are not taught at home but among peers. From peer groups, adolescents receive feedback about their abilities such as dating and convincing ladies to engage in sexual intercourse. Deviant peers, through interaction and socialisation with significant others, would represent positive gratifications for the individual than the ordinary person that would learn to value behaviour that are imposed by a group. On the other hand, Kaplan, Johnson and Bailey (1987:227) observe that both perpetrators and victims of acquaintance rape are more likely to accept, justify and engage in acquaintance rape when they happen to have frequent and close contact with significant others who accept and justify acquaintance rape or aggressive sexual behaviour. Sampson, (2002:3) notes that college life, just like peer groups, is socially viewed as full of promiscuity and acquaintance rape. This study sought to ascertain whether what was prevailing in America at Ohio State University was also taking place in institutions of higher education in Masvingo.

Dixie (2017:42) observes that in the United States of America among male peer groups, if an individual does not apply violence on a female partner, this is perceived as being sexually weak. Gwartney-Gibbs *et al.*'s (1987:276) study in the United States found that females in a sexually aggressive peer group indicated rates of sustaining sexual abuse and sexual violence 20% more of the total sample of 1120 participants as compared to those without such a peer group. The influence of peers on this male dominated subject (acquaintance rape) in Gwartney-Gibbs *et al.*'s (1987) study in America was only significantly associated with sustaining sexual aggression rather than abuse or violence. This study sought to establish whether the situation revealed in America on acquaintance rape applies to students in higher education's perceptions of acquaintance rape in Masvingo. The literature presented above is in line with the theory of social learning which underpins the present study because dating and courtship practices are associated with sexual aggression which emanate from the society and common social practices. On the other hand, Dixie (2017:45) observes that peer pressure among some peers has also been known to influence males' attitudes towards both sexual intercourse and acquaintance rape. The present study sought to establish whether peer pressure influences students' perceptions of acquaintance rape in Masvingo.

Santrock (2005:351) notes that most students in higher education institutions are adolescents and have strong needs to be liked, loved, and accepted by friends and large peer groups. Peers' interactions usually result in pleasurable feelings when accepted or extreme stress and anxiety when excluded or rejected. In a study carried by Armstrong, Hamilton and Sweeney (2006:483) from a large University in Midwestern India through ethnographic observation involving 55 women who happened to be single and childless, it was found that peer pressure may affect acquaintance rape. This study sample consisted of 63 participants. Most of these undergraduate students were upper-middle class with few responsibilities other than their college work. All the peers interviewed believed in going out, having fun, and drinking a lot, always partying and meeting guys. They also believed that as part of a peer group, they were supposed to hook up with guys. Both male and female university peers tried to give up that part of peer life but could not manage due to peer pressure. Armstrong *et al.*'s (2006:483) study also revealed that both males and females wanted to be accepted into their peer groups.

Boswell and Spade's (2010:143) study which was conducted in America concurs with Carlson, Kamimura, Trinh, Mo, Yamawaki, Bhattacharya, Nguyen, Makomenaw, Birholz and Olson's (2015:83) study which was conducted in the United States, Japan, India, Vietnam and China on perceptions of violence against women among college students that peer groups are influenced by peer pressure and situational norms of both male and female college students to perceive a college or a university as a place for acquaintance rape. Boswell and Spade's (2010:143) study used the qualitative approach because it collected data from limited cases or individuals which means that the study findings were not generalised to the large population as advised by Tichapondwa, (2013:143). Females in both Greek and Asian institutions of higher learning who are at great risk are those whom fraternity brothers (male peer groups) do not personally know by name. Boswell and Spade (2010:143) further concur with Olusegun (2012:916) that these fraternity brothers (male peer groups) refer them (female acquaintances) as faceless victims as well as nameless acquaintances, not friends hence they sexually attack them freely. The above findings that peer groups are influenced by peer pressure are in line with the theory of social learning that informs this study. Bussy and Bandura (1999:5)'s theory maintains that individual societal members act according to their gender and peer groups, so members of a particular gender tend to have similar perceptions towards social issues.

Acquaintance rape, just like in Europe, America, Asia, Australia, as well as in the sub-Saharan Africa, including Zimbabwe is also influenced by peer pressure. Seller, Cochram and Branch (2005:379) contend that it has been observed for quite a long time that if a male partner is challenged or is denied sex by his sexual partner, he would seek support from his male peers or male social group. Male peer-support was found to be a very common practice in the United States. The advice the male perpetrator gets from his peer group is to sexually fix the partner. Okeke's (2011:28) study in Nigeria on sexual harassment, a broad term in which acquaintance rape belongs, found that female victims of acquaintance rape are blamed by the peer group if they report the assailant to the police. Okeke's (2011:28) study employed a quantitative approach. This study employed the mixed method approach as Tichapondwa (2013:143) argues, a lot of studies focus only on reporting the mean and forget or ignore to interpret the rest of the indices that make clear understanding of the distribution more completely. Mixed methods approach provided comprehensive study results from the applied varied methods of collecting data on factors affecting students' perceptions of acquaintance rape in Masvingo. Victims of acquaintance rape would be said to have deviated from the social norm of being docile and submissive. Okeke (2011:28) observes that peers in Nigerian societies are socialised to believe the rigid orientation of male aggression towards females, a concept which is quite common in Nigerian institutions of higher learning. This study sought to establish in part whether male peer-support theory applies to Masvingo.

Partying also is a way of college life. Participants in Armstrong *et al.*'s (2006:488) study in Zimbabwe also revealed that they did what their peers were doing to fit in, be popular as well as have friends. Partying was also used as a primary method to meet men on the campus. According to Armstrong *et al.* (2006:488), universities and colleges make possible "heterosexual peer cultures" and further revealed that it is also possible to breed a "culture of romance" in campuses. Thus, Social Learning Theory emphasises both negative and positive influence of peers on adolescents' development and adolescent peer culture as a corrupt influence that undermines societal norms, parental values, and control. Gravelin *et al.* (2019:10) observe that during parties, women are pressurised to wear scant, sexy clothing and as a result this exposes them to acquaintance rape by their acquaintances.

Akers and Jennings' (2009:103) study in America using a questionnaire established that as students interact and socialise with each other, role models within peer groups or those with high social status (like sons and daughters of politicians and prominent businessmen) or those with high academic competence or those with proximity to resources are in most cases targets for observational learning. From a social learning point of view, prominent people in the society are likely to be admired by most ordinary people hence their actions are copied and acquaintance rape is not exceptional. Dekeseredy *et al.*'s (2007:296) study in America also found that individuals within peer groups are viewed as role models hence the dating tactics and strategies they apply in sexual relationships are admired by peers and copied as well. Koss, Dinero, Seibel and Cox's (1988:19) study in America concurs with Bridges's (1991:293) study on that in these institutions of higher learning rape by acquaintances as compared to those by strangers are less likely to be regarded as real rape and that victims also perceive these scenarios in the same way. This study sought to establish if the above-mentioned perceptions of acquaintance rape also apply to Masvingo.

According to Muray (2018:5) males should also have sexual experience with multiple partners and if there is a lack of interest or if a man fails to engage in sexual activity, he may receive disapproval from his peers. This may lead to questioning the heterosexual man's masculinity and sexual orientation. Thus, to avoid putting their masculinity or sexual orientation in question, men engage in frequent acts of sexual activity. Gravelin *et al.* (2019:13) also observes that the perception of male dominance in all spheres of life is a common practice in communities where peers are grouped together, especially colleges and universities.

Related literature recorded so far in this study indicated that internationally, regionally, in the Sub-Saharan Africa and locally, perceptions of students of acquaintance rape in institutions of higher learning are influenced by peer pressure. Studies conducted by Frese et al (2004:149), Sampson (2009:13), Finn (1987:1), Walker *et al.* 2019:1, Sexual Offences in England, and Wales; year ending March 2017 Statistics Report 2018:22; Rhodes 2019: v) concur that peers depend much on alcohol consumption hence they resort to rape culture. This study sought to establish whether the Nigerian, Israel, United States, English, Wales, Japanese, Indian, Vietnam, Chinese, Greek, and Asian scenarios apply to Masvingo.

Having discussed literature on peer pressure and acquaintance rape, the next section discusses how policy, legislation or law influences students' perceptions of acquaintance rape.

2.5 Policy, Legislation or Law and Acquaintance Rape

Factors which influence perceptions of acquaintance rape among college students stretch from culture, gender, peer pressure, policy, legislation and law among others (Human Rights Watch, 2017:2). Poor or lack of implementation of policies which protect students in higher education institutions is one of the main causes of acquaintance rape. As students interact and socialise they would not know courtship boundaries. Johnson and Johnson (2017:2) observe that absence or limited policies guiding students in higher education institutions' sexual behaviour together with cultural practices confusion, gender stereotype and peer pressure lead to courtship confusion hence they end up committing acquaintance rape. Flintort (2010:250) concurs with Sampson's (2002:15) quantitative study that acquaintance rape is quite rampant in most colleges and universities across the globe, and it remains a hidden crime. According to Kahan's (2010:11) quantitative study in America, "women's rights groups argued that women are being punished for the exercise of sexual autonomy by laws and societal attitudes that licensed men to impose unwanted sex on women who engage in supposedly suggestive behaviour or who had engaged in consensual sexual relations on other occasions with other men. Sampson's (2002:4) study in the United States of America also established that there are so many reasons as to why the crime is not reported and courts are also not taking it seriously. Eboe-Osiji (2012:146) also notes that many acquaintance rapists are not even tried in courts.

In exploring literature sources, studies conducted by the Mediterranean Institute of Gender Studies (2008:32) in Cyprus, Greece, Latvia, Malta, and Lithuania indicated that there are no legislative acts or policy documents which specifically differentiate acquaintance rape from other forms of sexual violence. What it means is that the justice system in all the nations does not have prescribed procedures to deal with acquaintance rape. Russo's (2000:5) study in Australia established that governments have neither common approaches nor any policy mechanism to combat acquaintance rape hence both victims and perpetrators of acquaintance rape perceive it (acquaintance rape) as just a hidden crime. Some of the victims and perpetrators do not even know the existence of acquaintance rape. As has been suggested earlier, lack of policies specifically for acquaintance rape in institutions of higher education enable students not to have limits in terms of their cultural values, cultural practices, norms, folkways and common thoughts. Findings from Oshiname *et al.*'s (2013:146) study in Nigeria concur with those from Ben-David and Schneider's (2005:387) study in Israel that victims perceive both the acquaintance rape and even the punishment given to the offender as less of rape and, in the mind of the victim, it is perceived as less violating the victim's rights as well as having less psychological damage.

According to the American Association of University Women, Policy Documents and Reports (2015:145), many cases of acquaintance rape and attempted assaults are never reported and if reported they are not consistently counted as official. Because of the perception that acquaintance rape is not perceived as rape, this discourages or delays its disclosure. Page (2008:388) also observed that individuals, perpetrators, and victims of acquaintance rape tend to have negative attitudes towards the law and as such they view reporting their assailants as just mere waste of time. This study sought to establish whether the findings of the Mediterranean Institute of Gender Studies (2008:320) on how policy, legislation or law affects perpetrators of acquaintance rape also apply to Masvingo.

Bondestam and Lundqvist (2020:402) conducted a study in the United Kingdom using a quantitative approach with a sample of 5562 published articles without geographical limits around the globe on sexual harassment (a term in which acquaintance rape falls) in institutions of higher education. This study employed a mixed methods approach to curb the weakness of the single study method approach that is of both qualitative and quantitative approach. Bondestam and Lundqvist (2020:402) established that more than half of the students and faculty who participated confirmed that victims of acquaintance rape do not report to management. Bondestam and Lundqvist (2020:402) used the following databases: ERI (Educational Resources Information Centre), ERC (Education Research Complete), Web of science, Core collection, Gender studies, Google scholar, Scopus and Sociological abstracts. The present study used the following databases: Taylor and Francis, Wiley online, Routledge, Jstor, Google scholar and Sage publication. Database sites are searched basing on area of study and the particular researchers' study objectives as advised by Mertens (2009:99).

According to the Mediterranean Institute of Gender Studies and police documents (2008:32), acquaintance rape cases are difficult to prosecute due to victim credibility in the absence of evidence. Bohner *et al.* (2009:293) note that victims of acquaintance rape in America themselves also have limited knowledge on the authenticity of the crime. From the above stated background, administrators in institutions of higher education also do not put in place strict policy pertaining to acquaintance rape and sexual crimes. Flood and Peace's (2006:48) quantitative study in the United States of America also established that policy, legislation or law is too far ahead of societal attitudes and societal perceptions towards acquaintance rape. Stakeholders in education and training are products of patriarchal society, hence it is not easy to coin or implement policies, legislations or laws specifically for acquaintance rape because they regard such a move as deviating from a cultural practice. Policies which guard against acquaintance rape are not easy to implement because of patriarchal minds among members of the society (Deane, 2018:89). The crime is also committed in private places hence there is lack of evidence. Roe (2004:5) points out that even if evidence is there, victims of acquaintance rape often refuse to testify. Victims and perpetrators of acquaintance rape perceive policy as there in theory. Scattered policies might be found in documents but institutions of higher education might not be implementing those policies, hence those policies do not be serve any purpose in protecting victims of acquaintance rape. In most cases, acquaintance rapists take long to be tried in courts and, as a result, victims may develop psychological trauma during trial, and may also lack confidence in the justice system. According to Van der Bruggen and Grubb (2014:528), victims of acquaintance rape are also vulnerable to societal blame since they tend to lack both social and institutional support. Victims of acquaintance rape regard policy as a tool which cannot protect them at all.

Russo's (2000:1) study in Australia established that acquaintance rape is a controversial and ambiguous crime such that its victims/ survivors, offenders as well as professionals in the criminal justice system have negative attitudes towards it. Michalski (2004:667) asserts that both victims and perpetrators of acquaintance rape as well as professionals in the justice system view it as a normal social dating norm and, as a result, reporting rates to the police tend to be exceptionally low and only a few acquaintance rapists are successfully prosecuted. This study sought to establish whether low acquaintance rape statistics on police documents from Australian higher education institutions apply to institutions in Masvingo province. Peters and Besley's (2018:) study in the United States of America concurs with Dixie's (2017:164) study that there are no policies governing sexual crimes no empirically based police interventions in institutions of higher learning, and so perpetrators of acquaintance rape do not regard it as a crime. Koss *et al.*'s (1988:18) study in America concurs with Ben -David and Schneider's (2005:387) study in Israel that rapes by acquaintances are also unlikely to be regarded as rape by both perpetrators and victims. Oshiname *et al.*'s (2013: 138) study in Nigeria revealed that forced sex by male acquaintances is tolerated within the context of dating relationships in Africa although research on this phenomenon is quite rare.

Stubbs (2003:14) observed that the criminal justice system in any nation has an important symbolic role in shaping community perceptions of what is perceived to be legitimate or illegitimate, legal, or criminal behaviour. In a similar vein, Walker *et al.* (2019:6) notes that acquaintance rape cases are viewed by judges and prosecutors as difficult to investigate. In a study on the impact of policy, legislation, or law on sexual violence in America, Salazar (2005:13) established that the existence of legal sanctions has an impact on attitudes towards .violence against women in general and acquaintance rape in particular. Salazar's (2005:13) telephone survey of 973 participants demonstrated that perceptions of criminal justice policies impacted on attitudes towards justice responses and had effects on victim-blaming attitudes in relation to acquaintance rape. This study sought to establish whether the application of the legal system in Masvingo affects students' perceptions of acquaintance rape.

Sleath and Bull (2017:1) conducted a study in the United Kingdom on "Police perceptions of rape victims and the impact on case decision making: A systematic review". In their study Sleath and Bull (2017:1) used twenty-four articles published between 2000 and 2016 and found that some of acquaintance rape investigating officers instead of sympathising with acquaintance rape victims displayed negative attitudes towards the victims. Most of the articles used quantitative methodologies to access police perceptions of victims or their acceptance of rape myth. Only five studies used qualitative methods but the predominant methodology was to examine perceptions of victims using a vignette of a rape scenario followed by questionnaire on blame or credibility as well as items related to police decision making, decision to authorise the case and perception of guilt. The study also found that victims of acquaintance rape were blamed more than victims of stranger rape. This study employed the mixed methods approach to investigate whether students in higher education in Masvingo perceive victims of acquaintance rape as blameworthy.

Internationally, regionally and locally acquaintance rape in institutions of higher learning is also viewed differently due to differences in the implementation of policy, legislation or law. Presence or absence of policies, legislations or law has a bearing on students' perceptions of acquaintance rape. According to Sampson's (2002: iii), research findings in the United States of America as well as police practices and operations in America, the United Kingdom, Canada, Australia, New Zealand, the Netherlands and Scandinavia, the police are finding problems in dealing with acquaintance rape cases. Eboe-Osiji (2012:147) states that the failure of both law and the justice system to protect individuals and victims of acquaintance rape enables society to view the law as a useless tool. Anderson (2010:644) observes that rape law often condemns females who are not chaste and at the same time excuses males who act with sexual entitlement. Rape law the world over so far acts as a significant site for the valorisation of female chastity and constraint and, on the other hand, gives males powers and freedom. Roe (2004:2) reiterates that societal knowledge that is obtained from the criminal justice system offers no protection to potential victims hence they remain in abusive situations. Carlson *et al.* (2002:15) observed that acquaintance rape remains a major problem to college students since there are no policies at colleges and universities which protect students. Individuals, perpetrators, and victims of acquaintance rape view rape laws as useless government tools which are non-functional. This study sought to establish whether the perceptions of students in European countries and the world over apply to students in Masvingo.

According to *Right To Be Free From Rape: overview of legislation and State of Play in Europe and International Human Rights Standard* (2018:10), currently there is no international or regional human rights instruments or standards which provide a definition of consent and State Parties to (for instance, the Istanbul Convention) enjoy a margin of appreciation in this regard. There are several attrition studies from other regions which provide insight into how different criminal justice systems handle cases of sexual violence and offer points for comparison with the countries researched within this study. The studies reviewed focus on New Zealand, South Africa, the United States, and several European countries. Each features a multimethodological approach including quantitative and qualitative research methods and applies a tiered approach to understanding attrition: first locating attrition points during the various stages of the criminal justice process and then exploring how attrition occurs.

Karjane, Fisher and Cullen (2002:137) conducted a study in the United States of America on what colleges and universities are doing about acquaintance rape in institutions of higher education using a sample of 2 500 high schools, all historically black colleges and universities and all tribal colleges and universities. The study found that there are policies formulated from Federal laws that protect students and among these laws is the Campus Sexual Assault Victims' Bill of Rights of 1992. Both public and private non-profit institutions of higher education in the United States of America which enrol the majority of students are the most likely to have a written sexual assault (a broad term in which acquaintance rape falls) response policy. According to Karjane *et al.'s* (2002:137) study, a formal policy should address all forms of sexual assault (including acquaintance rape) on campus as a statement of the institution's commitment to recognise and deal with the problem. The study also found that victims of acquaintance rape may be embarrassed or fear reprisal and those who may have been drinking before the assault might fear sanctions for violating institutional policy on alcohol use. This study sought to establish whether the absence of policy which guards against students' behaviour on acquaintance rape in the United States of America applies to students in Masvingo.

Dixie (2017:36) investigated the position of consent as a factor in sexual assault prevention in the United States of America and found that defining sexual consent is a critical factor in determining what constitutes acquaintance rape. In the justice system, the need for proof that a person engaged in sexual intercourse without a partner's consent is very necessary, but an assailant cannot be convicted for acquaintance rape without evidence of force or threats. A victim's verbally saying "no" is subject to interpretation in a court of law. Kahan's (2010:729) study in America concurs with Dixie's (2017:36) study in the United States of America that it is common for defence lawyers to inform the jury that the statement "no" does not always mean "no" to some people, and it can sometimes be interpreted as a "maybe", also known as token resistance. This study sought to establish whether the scenario in the United States applies to Masvingo.

According to Cairney's (2012:297) study in the United States of America, the reform goal of eliminating resistance and non-consent requirements in rape statutes is appropriate in strange rape cases but prevents the successful prosecution of acquaintance rapists. This part of the reform itself seems to protect the perpetrators of acquaintance rape rather than the victim. Individuals, perpetrators, and victims of acquaintance rape view courts as unnecessary institutions when it comes to trial of acquaintance rape cases. Bryden and Lengnick's (1997:199) study in the United States of America also established that college students, especially males also regard rape laws as playing a limited role in acquaintance rape cases hence they do not see the importance of consent in sexual relationships. Bryden and Lengnick (1997:199) also observed that rape laws are not formulated in line with societal perceptions and reality; hence acquaintance rapists escape justice. Institutions of higher and tertiary education should be frontliners in policy implementation, but they are giving this social phenomenon negligible attention. Peters and Besley's (2018:460) study in the United States of America also established that instead of serving as a way through which policy results are realised, college administrators act as partners in committing acquaintance rape. Campus police officers and college administrators also fear that too much attention on the problem may lead students' guardians and parents thinking that acquaintance rape occurs more often at their institutions than at others. This study sought to establish in part whether the effect of policy, legislation, or law to students' perceptions towards acquaintance rape the world over applies to Masvingo.

Skinneder, Montgomery and Garret (2017: xi) conducted a study in the Asia-Pacific region which sought to analyse how the varying criminal justice systems in Thailand and Vietnam responded to reported cases of rape and sexual assault, and to identify the key institutional factors associated with the disposition of cases in these two countries. The study found that acquaintance rape cases can be fabricated or condemned during trial at every stage of the justice process. The study also found out that females reporting cases of rape in Thailand and Vietnam by acquaintances encountered significant societal, legal, institutional policies, legal and cultural practices acting as barriers to justice. Those justice barriers were also found to inhibit reporting of sexual crimes as well as reducing the likelihood that a female will persist in redress through the criminal justice system. The study also established that the police, prosecutors, and judges are not immune to biases and stereotypes towards sexual violence, hence had positive attitudes towards the offences, victims of acquaintance rape and the alleged perpetrators. The study further established that the criminal justice system service providers are not systematically held responsible for providing rights-based, victim-centred services as well. In light of such international literature, this study sought to determine, in part, whether policy, legislation, or law have resulted in either positive or negative perceptions of acquaintance rape among students in higher educational institutions in Masvingo.

Human Rights Watch research (2017:2), in its study conducted in India found that there are still persistent gaps in enforcing the laws, relevant policies, and guidelines specifically for victims of sexual violence in general and acquaintance rape in particular. The in-depth research covered 21 cases, 10 involving girls under 18 years at the time of the incident. Research by Indian organisations and more than 65 Human Rights Watch interviews with acquaintance rape victims, their family members, lawyers, civil society activists, advocates, doctors, forensic experts, government and police officials found out that the criminal justice system does not treat victims and their families with sensitivity, dignity and without discrimination. This study sought to establish whether the way policy, legislation or law was enacted in students in higher education in Masvingo's perceptions of acquaintance rape.

According to World Health Organisation (2017:4) in a 2014 study by Palemo, Black and Peterman in India on masculinity and intimate partner sexual abuse (a broad category in which acquaintance rape falls), it was found that 38% of 2250 people who were surveyed were not aware of laws on sexual violence against women. Interestingly, women participants who were also unaware of the law, or regarded the law as inappropriate were 1.3 to 1.5 times more likely to experience intimate partner sexual violence or acquaintance rape. Men who were unaware of the law were 1.5 times more likely to perpetrate intimate partner sexual violence or acquaintance rape. Thus, this study sought to investigate if the Indian scenario applies to Masvingo.

In both studies by the *Right To Be Free From Rape* (2018:12) in 2005 in Australia and South Africa on women's decision to report sexual assault by acquaintances and service responses, the victim of sexual assaults in those cases that were not captured by police statistics were never reported. They were also extensively under-reported, and only one in nine women who had been raped by an acquaintance reported to police. A recent survey in Europe found that in total, victims had reported the most serious incidents of partner sexual violence to the police. Thirteen percent of these sexual violent cases were the most serious incidents of acquaintance rape (*Right to Be Free from Rape*, 2018:12). The relationship between the victim and offender may constitute one of the biggest impediments to reporting given that most women are sexually assaulted by men they know. International literature recorded so far suggests that the likelihood of a victim reporting to police decreases as the relationship distance between victim and offender decreases. Skinneder *et al.* (2017:13) observed that police in most acquaintance rape cases are most likely to be notified of sexual assaults perpetrated by strangers followed by estranged partners or known non-intimate offenders. Thus, this study sought to find whether the Australian and South African contexts apply to students' perceptions of acquaintance rape in Masvingo.

Roe's (2004:2) 'qualitative study findings in America concur with those from Odu and Olusegun's (2012:919) study in Nigeria that individuals, perpetrators, and victims have no faith in the justice system hence they view acquaintance rape as a minor crime. According to Rape and Sexual Assault: A Renewed call to Action (2014:17), there is also a fraught relationship between the criminal justice, policies and law reform versus legislation and societal attitudes towards acquaintance rape in America. As such, policy, legislation, or law does not mitigate the cruelty of perpetrators of acquaintance rape. Odu and Olusegun's (2012:919) descriptive study in America also established that failure of laws and policies to protect individuals from acquaintance rapists brings about societal negative attitudes towards acquaintance rape.

Walker *et al.*'s (2019:12) study in America observed that the justice system discriminates against acquaintance rape victims at each stage of trying acquaintance rapists. Thus, Chireshe and Makura (2013:4) observed that policies and outcomes are influenced by the immediate context in which they are implemented. Viewed in this way, the justice system itself is weak and corrupt in nature such that its outcomes are biased, hence individuals, perpetrators and victims of acquaintance rape do not trust it and view it as useless. Doshi (2014:6) observes that institutions of higher learning the world over do not have strict and observed policies which prohibit acquaintance rape. This study sought to find out whether policies, legislations or law in higher education institutions affect students' perceptions of acquaintance rape in Masvingo.

According to Bryden and Lengnick's (1997:197) qualitative study in America, prosecutors are also afraid of losing acquaintance rape cases which may taint their records and that is the reason why they are excessively reluctant to prosecute acquaintance rapists. When acquaintance rapists are prosecuted, in most cases, the system puts the victim rather than the defendant on trial. Gerger *et al.* (2007:422) note that the justice juries, like other practitioners in the Justice Juries Legal System, are motivated by the same biases, and in most cases, they tend to blame the victims and acquit rapists. Thus, this study sought to establish whether American higher education students' perceptions of acquaintance rape tally those from Masvingo.

Schoeukopf's (2012:9) and Churchill's (2012:2) studies concur that victims of acquaintance rape on the other hand also see it as unnecessary to report their assailants since they know that no one would believe them. As such, they see silence as a safe way of protecting their dignity. This book sought to explore, in part, how legislation, policy or law affects the perceptions of students in Masvingo.

Deane (2018:93) observes that in South Africa, a sub-Saharan country, perceptions and attitudes around how seriously acquaintance rape issues are treated play a fundamental role in how resident students in institutions of higher education view the importance of policies which protect students against acquaintance rape. According to the Civil Service Commission Circular Resolution Number 01-1940, Philippines, with other international states of the world, have reaffirmed, through the Vienna Declaration and Programme of Action and the Beijing Declaration and Platform for Action to respect human rights including acquaintance rape. On the same note, it has committed itself to fulfilling its duty to encourage as well as promote universal respect for, and observance and protection of all human rights as well as fundamental human freedoms for all in accordance with the Charter for the United Nations (in which Zimbabwe is a member). In the same vein, other instruments which are related to human rights and international law such as the Vienna Declaration and Programme of Action highlights that all forms of rape are incomparable with the dignity and worth of the human being and must be eradicated by means of legal measures and through national action. So, every institution of higher learning across the globe should have policies to curb acquaintance rape. Section 4 of the South African Republic, Act Number 6713 clearly provides norms of personal conduct for both public officials and students to observe when performing official duties. It also caution citizens to be always respectful of the rights of others, the law, good morals, good customs, public policy, public order, public safety as well as public interest at all times. According to the United Nations Human Rights Code of Conduct, one of the objectives of the Sexual Offences law in South Africa is to afford the complainants of sexual offences a maximum legal protection and to minimise the trauma of the judicial process.

Application of policies and laws specifically for acquaintance rape is not only limited to European, American, Asian countries but also to sub-Saharan African countries. Deane (2018:90) observes that in South Africa, the implementation of policies, legislations or laws that protect victims of acquaintance rape are affected by traditional beliefs and values of a large portion of South Africans which regulate the view of male perpetrators and legitimise the right of males to exercise their power over females.

Armstrong (1989:73) underscores that the perception that acquaintance rape is ignored affects how individuals in different set-ups interact and socialise with each other. According to Zeira *et al.* (2002:163), in Zimbabwe, or Africa as a whole, the law of consent is not respected because of the confusion between traditional and modern law. Mooney and Sacacht (2007:114) noted that 80% of all rape cases are likely not to be reported and most difficult to prosecute is acquaintance rapes. In Armstrong's (1989:69) study in Zimbabwe, interviewed women from Harare, Bulawayo, Chitungwiza, Chiweshe, Glendale, Gokwe, Dzivarasekwa and other parts of the country revealed that under Shona customary law, the offence of rape also consists of sexual intercourse with a woman or girl without her consent. This law of consent is also subjective in nature due to cultural reasons.

There are Zimbabwean pieces of legislation that have a bearing on the book. These include the Sexual Offences Act (Chapter 9.21), 2001 and the Domestic Violence Act (Chapter 5.16), 2007. The following sections highlight relevant sections of the Acts. The Domestic Violence Act (2007), Chapter 5.16 criminalises sexual offences. Although the Act does not specifically mention the term acquaintance rape, it refers to sexual abuse which involves perpetrators who are known to the victims (acquaintances). Potential victims, according to Section 2, subsection 1 of the Act, include the following: a current, former or estranged spouse, a child-biological, adopted or step, which has been living with the perpetrator, one who cohabits with the perpetrator or is/has been in an intimate relationship with the perpetrator. By implication, therefore, the sexual abuse, including rape in the context of the Domestic Violence Act, involves people known to complainants. When such rape occurs, it is acquaintance rape.

The Sexual Offences Act (Chapter 9.21) criminalises rape, incest or indecent assault. Section 8, subsection 1 of the Act criminalises non-consensual sexual acts including rape but is not confined to offenders known to victims. Thus, the Act does not specifically refer to acquaintance rape but makes inferences. Given that there are pieces of legislation in Zimbabwe that have a bearing on acquaintance rape, such laws may have an influence on societal perceptions of acquaintance rape. In view of this, the current study sought to find out whether Zimbabwean laws on sexual offences influence Masvingo higher education students' perceptions of acquaintance rape.

Du Toit (2017:465) notes that in Zimbabwe, implementation of policies, legislations or laws that protect students from acquaintance rape is also affected by the limited scope of Section 65(1) in the Zimbabwean Criminal Code in light of the country's obligations under the international human rights law and standards. The Case for Reform: Criminal Law and Sexual Violence in Zimbabwean (2020:9) observes that the scope of human protection that Section 65(1) offers is severely restricted in nature since it fails to prescribe other non-consensual invasive sexual acts that amount to acquaintance rape. These shortcomings are as follows; non-consensual penetration of another person with a penis, non-consensual vaginal, anal or oral penetration of a sexual nature of another person with objects or body parts other than the penis and same-sex rape, that is, men who rape other men, and women who rape other women and non-consensual, invasive sexual assault constituting rape of sexual minorities, such as gender non-conforming individuals, including transgender persons.

The case for reform: Criminal Law and Sexual Violence in Zimbabwe (2020:10) for institutions of higher education to be able to formulate policies which protect students against acquaintance rape certain implementations should be done. From an examination of the international jurisprudence on the crime of acquaintance rape and rape in general, the language of Section 65(1) of the Rape Criminal Code should include a clearly revised definition of rape and acquaintance rape.

In most institutions of higher education, policies on acquaintance rape and the definition of sexual consent should be clearly indicated in the rules governing acquaintance rape. European culture and African cultural gaps were displayed as literature on policy, legislation and law on acquaintance rape was laid down in the present book. Persistent gaps in the application of the relevant policies, legislations, guidelines and laws aimed at justice for victims of acquaintance rape should be applied fairly by the justice system internationally.

It should be reiterated that law, policy or legislation affects both victims and perpetrators' perceptions of acquaintance rape. Human behaviour is socially guided by the laws of the land. Since human behaviour is guided by the laws of the land, knowledge of the law and its implementation may have a bearing on perceptions of acquaintance rape. The next subheading presents the summary of the chapter.

2.6 Chapter Summary

This chapter reviewed the body of knowledge of experts in both educational and social psychology on issues concerning students' perceptions of acquaintance rape. The literature review displayed international, regional, local and time gaps which were covered in this book.

The chapter was executed under the following subheadings: Culture and acquaintance rape, gender and acquaintance rape, peer pressure and acquaintance rape and policy, legislation or law and acquaintance rape. The next chapter, Chapter 3, discussed the research methodology followed in this book.

Chapter 3

Research Methodology

3.1 Introduction

The main thrust of this book was to establish factors affecting students in higher education's perceptions of acquaintance rape in three institutions of higher education in Masvingo. This chapter discusses the research methodology that was followed in the book. Specifically, the chapter discusses the philosophical worldview or paradigm, the research approach, the research design, the sample and sampling procedure. The chapter further discusses the research instrument, validity and reliability, pilot testing, data collection procedures, data analysis and ethical considerations.

3.2 Philosophical Worldview or Paradigm

According to Creswell and Plano (2007:21), all researchers are encouraged to have a foundation for enquiry, and they must also be aware of the implicit paradigms (worldviews) they bring to their studies. A paradigm is a viewpoint, framework or simply a worldview which is based on human beings' philosophical assumptions about the social world and the epistemologies used to direct and interpret book material study (Babbie, 2007:43; Creswell, 2007:19; Mertens, 2012:8). According to De vos, Strydom, Fouche and Delport (2011:513), in social sciences the study material is individuals or groups of people who are viewed in different ways based on different paradigms.

This book employed the positivist paradigm. For Rossman and Rallis (2014:46), positivism is directly associated with the idea of objectivism. Mertens (2012:10) contends that positivism is based on the rationalistic, empiricist philosophy that originated with Aristotle, Francis Bacon, John Locke, Auguste Conte and Immanuel Kant. Positivism is a philosophy which adheres to the views that only "factual" knowledge gained through observation (the senses), including measurement, is trustworthy (Cohen, Manion & Morrison, 2007:18; Denscombe, 2010:120). Positivism was relevant to this book since it explored factual knowledge on factors affecting higher education students' perceptions of acquaintance rape in Masvingo.

Positivism entails that it is possible to deduce universal laws to explain both human and social phenomena in the same way as they are applied in sociology, physics, chemistry or biology (Parahoo, 2006:39; Kumar, 2012:14). Collins (2010:38) notes that positivism has an atomistic, ontological view of the world that comprises discrete, observable elements and events that interact in observable, determined and regular manner. Thus, in their operations, positivist researchers adopt scientific methods that systematise the knowledge generation process, that is, with the help of quantification to enhance precision in the description of parameters (Henning, *et al.*, 2014:71). Emphasis is on measurement of objective reality that exists in the society (Creswell, 2009:8; Fraenkel & Wallen, 2006:433). This book was also based on empirical evidence which is related to positivism to establish the factors affecting students' perception of acquaintance rape in higher education institutions in Masvingo.

Empirical evidence can apply in the mixed methods approach which can be employed by the researcher to inquire about the problem through observing and recording data, entities, events or relationships that appear to the researcher's senses when he/she studies a particular aspect of the world (Locke, Silverman & Spirduso, 2004:23; Parahoo, 2006:41). This book used mixed methods approach. Empirical scientific evidence was appropriate in this book because the researcher obtained what participants felt based on their culture, gender, peer groups and policy, legislation or laws in institutions of higher education.

Parahoo (2006:39) notes that positivists believe in the unity of science. What it means is that the scientific method used in natural sciences should be equally applied appropriately to the study of social phenomena. Educational psychology is a social science (De vos *et al.*, 2011:4; Dunne, Pryor & Yates, 2009:135; Shastri, 2008:6), hence positivist epistemology is also quite appropriate in this study which is in Educational Psychology. Kim (2010:5) notes that epistemology is a set of beliefs about knowing using methodology which involves interviewing as well as observing participants in their natural environments to capture the reconstructions participants use to interpret the meaning of the world. Positivism was followed in this book as it helped the researcher to deduce acquaintance rape by providing knowledge on the factors affecting students in higher educations' perception of acquaintance rape in Masvingo. People's perceptions are the ones that predict with precision the probability of a social event or phenomenon to happen. In this case, the higher the degree of certainty, the more scientific the knowledge on which prediction would be based (Locke et al., 2004:133; Parahoo, 2006:39). This book may also enable both victims and perpetrators of acquaintance rape to be aware of the factors which influence their perceptions of acquaintance rape as they socialise and interact with each other in sexual relationships.

In line with the narrated views on positivism, this book obtained triangulated data which was a product of quantitative, qualitative methods and data sources in a single book. Corroborated and convergence results were also obtained from different approaches on the same problem (factors affecting students in higher education's perceptions of acquaintance rape in Masvingo). In this book, the positivist researcher was detached and objective as well as neutral as he studied aspects of social life. Mixed methods approach was also used as it was realised that positivism alone is not enough. The research approach is discussed in the following section.

3.3 Research Approach

A research approach is the whole research design that includes the researcher's assumptions, the whole process of inquiry and the type of collected data as well as the meaning of research findings (Parahoo, 2006:48; Mertens, 2009:309). Positivist worldview is best addressed by the mixed methods approach (De vos *et al.*, 2011:63; Parahoo, 2006:48; Dunne *et al.*, 2009:41; Denscombe, 2010:132). Thus, this study employed the mixed methods approach to corroborate data on factors affecting students in higher education's perceptions of acquaintance rape in Masvingo. Positivist researchers use mixed methods approach to study as well as to predict patterns of human behaviour (Babbie & Mouton, 2002:21; Locke *et al.*, 2004:132). Locke *et al.* (2004:132) observe that mixed methods research approach has the capacity to describe, predict as well as to explain both social and psychological phenomena. This is not to undermine the complexity of human behaviour, which by any standard is more complex than just items subjected to empirical laboratory testing. The researcher applied mixed methods research approach by seeking answers, explanations and predictions about factors affecting higher education students' perceptions of acquaintance rape in Masvingo. As will be explained later in this chapter, the factors were obtained from the perceptions of students themselves, college administrators and non-academic staff who work with students. The mixed methods research approach is discussed in the following paragraph.

3.3.1 The Mixed methods research approach

As has been alluded to earlier in this book, Social Learning Theory advocates that individuals should be studied in situ. As such, this book deploys the mixed method approach to gather data on the extent to which culture, gender, peer pressure, policy, and legislation influence students in Zimbabwe's institutions of higher learning's perceptions of acquaintance rape. According to De Vos, Strydom, Fouche and Delport (2011:435), mixed methods research include the combination of techniques or methods of collecting and analysing quantitative and qualitative data. In other words, mixed methods approach include both qualitative and quantitative features as complimentary in the design, data allocation and analysis of a given book (see also, Tichapondwa, 2013). In this book, the researcher triangulated data from open-ended questionnaires, closed-ended questionnaires and document analysis. In this study the researcher employed the mixed methods research approach, to investigate, collect and analyse data as well as to integrate the findings and drew inferences using both quantitative and qualitative approaches or methods in a single book or program of inquiry. Against the grain, this study adopted a mixed methods research approach as it was seen suitable for the study of 'Factors affecting students in higher education's perceptions of acquaintance rape in Masvingo of Zimbabwe' and capitalised the strength of both quantitative and qualitative approaches (Creswell & Clarke, 2007, 2007:22) Quantitative research approach involves looking at amounts or quantities of one or more variables of interest. Quantitative researchers try to measure variables in some ways using commonly acceptable measures of the physical world or carefully designed measures of psychological characteristics or behaviours (Leedy & Ormrod, 2010:94; Parahoo, 2006:49).

McMillan and Schumacher (2010:12) and Wiersma and Jurs (2009:118) concurred that quantitative approach is associated with research questions that deal with the inter-relationships among variables, predictability of certain outcomes as well as the comparison of specific groups. According to Tlali (2017:119), perceptions are internalised processes whereby both victims and perpetrators sense the world and situations around them differently as they interact with each other. Everyone perceives acquaintance rape differently. Individuals' personal judgments are also different. Thus, this study therefore measured psychological characteristics, interrelationships and variables governing sexual relationships as well as how both victims and perpetrators perceive acquaintance rape with special reference to such factors as culture, gender, peer- pressure and policy, legislation or law. According to Taylor, Sinha and Ghoshal (2009:5), the results of quantitative research denote methods that generate data comprising numbers. In line with the point raised by Taylor et al. (2009:5), quantitative approach seeks to produce data comprising figures and is easy to work with. Since quantitative data can be easily summarised, it also facilitates communication of findings (Chireshe, 2006:87; Creswell & Plano Clarke, 2007:22; Morgan, 2007:48) hence the methods facilitate comparison. With the quantitative approach, the researcher collected data from many participants, settings or geographical locations, situations and times and then compared the findings (Taylor, 2000:164; Bryman, 2004:8).

Using the mixed methods approach, this book compared data obtained from different settings internationally, regionally and sub-Saharan Africa including Zimbabwe on factors affecting students in higher education's perceptions of acquaintance rape in Masvingo and information was displayed thematically according to the stated variables.

Mertens (2013:309) observes that specific mixed methods approaches are defined by the ordering of the application of the quantitative and qualitative methods simultaneously or sequentially. Qualitative and quantitative data collection methods can be applied in parallel or sequential form. In this study mixed methods approach was applied sequentially. Teddlie and Tashakhori (2009:69) note that mixed methods can involve the conversion of qualitative data to a quantitative form or vice versa. Mixed methods also include multilevel design in which quantitative data are collected at one level of an organisation (for example student level) and qualitative data are collected at another level (for example administrator level). In this study, the multilevel design was applied by collecting quantitative data from students, non-academic staff who work with students and administrator's closed-ended questionnaire items and qualitative data from open-ended questionnaire items from the pilot study to the final study. Literature review for this study was also captured globally, regionally and sub-Saharan Africa. In part, the study compared the factors that affect both victims and perpetrators' views in line with their cultural practices, gender, peer-pressure and policy, legislation or law.

Since perceptions which have to do with rape are interpreted and predicted within a cultural context (Russo, 2000:1; Carlson *et al.*, 2015:18) in sexual relationships, acquaintance rape in particular, both victims and perpetrators should be able to predict their acquaintances' behaviours as they interact with each other. In this study, the researcher was interested in the factors that affect both victims and perpetrators' perceptions of acquaintance rape.

Frankel and Wallen (2006:433) also observe that quantitative research assumes that there exists a reality out there, existing independent of human beings and waiting to be discovered thus making it the task of science to discover the nature of that reality and how it works. This is to say the present book explored the existence of a phenomenon (acquaintance rape) among social institutions (institutions of higher learning) as well as how the affected groups (victims and perpetrators) perceive it. The other assumption of mixed methods research approach is that accurate statements about the way the world really is can be arrived at through research investigation (Leedy & Ormrod, 2005:95; Bryman, 2004:8). This book sought to establish the reality of the world through focusing on the factors that affect students in higher education institutions' perceptions of acquaintance rape in Masvingo.

However, quantitative research approach has its own weaknesses of the context or settings in which people talk, thus rendering the voice of participants silent. It can also be further noted that personal biases and interpretations of quantitative researchers are seldom discussed as they are in the background (Creswell & Plano Clark, 2007:9). To counter the highlighted weaknesses, this book deployed the qualitative element in the mixed methods approach to examine the problem in detail so that data collected on open-ended questionnaire items were informal and relaxed which encouraged subjects to participate in such a sensitive area. In this study as part of triangulation, the researcher also employed a few open- ended questionnaire items with spaces provided for the justification of participants' responses. Triangulation is a technical system which is employed studies using multiple forms of data collection tools such as questionnaires, document analysis, observations or interviews to investigate a problem (Tichapondwa, 2013:110). Most studies may employ more than one data collection method leading to the development of different datasets. Results from those datasets are analysed independently, but would need to be analysed independently as well as compared to each other in some way. Tichapondwa (2013:132) observes that document analysis is unobtrusive as well as non-reactive hence it yielded enough data about the values, perceptions and beliefs of participants in their natural settings. Document analysis complemented the questionnaire in the data collection process and helped to answer questionnaire items that were not addressed by quantitative and qualitative elements of the mixed methods approach. In this study document analysis filled in gaps that might have been left open by other data collection strategies (Tichapondwa, 2013:132).

From open-ended questionnaire items, the researcher got accurate and unbiased data from participants (Terrell, 2012:277). The other reason for including a few open-ended questionnaire items was to ensure that participants justified and elucidated on the content left out in the closed ended questionnaire items. From questionnaire items, participants responded as they wished with regard to the factors affecting higher education students' perceptions of acquaintance rape in Masvingo.

The shortcomings of qualitative research approach in the mixed methods research approach such as that: data could be collected from few cases or individuals, which means that research findings could not be generalised to a larger population, the research quality could be heavily affected by the researcher's skills and it could not be easily well understood as compared to quantitative research were encountered by document analysis. Creswell and Plano Clarke (2007:9) note that, strength of the mixed methods research is that it offsets the weaknesses of both quantitative and qualitative research.

The methodology employed in this book was mainly mixed. The major task of this book was to explore the factors affecting higher education students' perceptions of acquaintance rape in Masvingo. The next sub-heading discusses the research design.

3.4 Research Design

A research design is a plan, structure and strategy of investigation employed by the researcher to obtain answers to research questions or research problems (Kumar, 2012:94; Burns & Grove, 2009:211). According to Tlali (2017:92), a research design can be explorative (to get more insight into the problem), a descriptive survey (to describe a phenomenon) or casual (to test the cause and effect of variables).

A good or appropriate research design enables a researcher to meet his/her research aims and objectives with easy. In most practical cases, the selection of the research design depends largely on the researcher's beliefs and values, resources available, how accessible the participants are and whether the study is ethically sound (Polansky & Waller, 2010:94). This study used a descriptive survey design which was primarily mixed methodological in nature to explore the factors affecting higher education students' perceptions of acquaintance rape in Masvingo. The adopted descriptive survey which was used is discussed below.

3.4.1 Descriptive Survey Design

According to Kumar (2012:10), a descriptive survey, "attempts to describe systematically a problem, situation, service or programme, phenomenon, or provides information about, say, the living conditions of a community, or describes attitudes towards an issue". A descriptive survey justifies current practices as well as makes judgments which would develop theories which would be used in research. This study employed the descriptive survey to provide a clear picture on the factors that affect higher education students' perception of acquaintance rape in Masvingo. Descriptive survey involves information acquisition among groups of people regarding their characteristics, attitudes, opinions, actions or previous experiences by asking participants questions while they jot down their responses (Leedy & Ormrod, 2010:18; Babie & Mouton, 2001:249; Neuman, 2003:35). The descriptive survey design was relevant for this book since it sought to establish participants' perceptions, attitudes and opinions on the factors affecting students in higher education's perceptions of acquaintance rape in Masvingo.

The descriptive survey design is a common design associated with acquaintance rape. (De Leon, 2013:12; Vandiver & Dupalo, 2007:1; Ben-David & Schneider, 2005:385; Kamal *et al.*, 2010:108; Mapfumo *et al.*, 2007:15; Sampson,2002:3). Researchers such as the Illinois Coalition against Assault (1993:2) used a survey on the 11to14-year-olds to establish the prevalence of acquaintance rape at Rhode Island Rape Crisis Centre. Ziera *et al.* (2002:154) also applied the survey on college campuses to study acquaintance rape and sexual assault. Carlson *et al.* (2012-2013) also used the survey design on acquaintance rape. Ben-David and Schneider (2005) also conducted a study in Israel on undergraduate male and female students on Rape perception, Gender Role Attitudes, and victim-perpetrator acquaintance using a survey. Thus, this study employed the descriptive survey to establish the factors affecting higher education students' perceptions of acquaintance rape in Masvingo.

The main function of descriptive survey in research is to investigate the problem at a large scale using a large population by surveying a sample of that population (Fink, 2002:15; Delport, 2005:166). In this study, the descriptive survey was useful in exploring the factors affecting students' perceptions of acquaintance rape of a particular population (students in institutions of higher education). A survey is naturally designed to provide a clear picture of a prevailing situation as it naturally manifests itself (Burns & Grove, 2009:201). A survey has a general characteristic, that is, it is descriptive in nature, explanatory as well as exploratory (Tlali, 2017:72). Thus, this study sought to establish the factors affecting higher education students' perceptions of acquaintance rape in Masvingo with special reference to their culture, peer pressure, gender and policy, legislation or law governing sexual relations. There is no any other method to expose students in higher education's perceptions of acquaintance rape besides a descriptive survey.

In this study, the descriptive survey guided the methods, approaches and decisions the researcher made during his study and set the logic which he used to explore the factors affecting higher education students' perceptions of acquaintance rape in Masvingo. In this case, the descriptive survey was "fit for purpose" (Denscombe, 2010:99). In this study, a survey produced original data which was an accurate portrayal or a clear account of the characteristics of the problem (Polit & Hungler, 2009:179). This study attempted to provide accurate accounts of participants' views, beliefs as well as knowledge on the factors that affect students' perceptions of acquaintance rape in higher education institutions in Masvingo.

According to Polit and Beck (2004:50), a survey design was selected particularly for this study because of its high degree of representativeness as well as the ease with which the researcher would obtain participants' opinions towards the problem under study. Leedy and Ormrod (2010:179) observe that a descriptive survey does not involve the changing, or modification of situations. The researcher gathered information on factors affecting the perceptions of acquaintance rape in higher education institutions in Masvingo and presented it as it was obtained without altering and filtering it. Ramalinga (2005:24) observes that survey research involves the gathering and quantification of data which becomes permanent sources of information. A descriptive survey was also found to shield active intervention on the part of the investigator, that is, avoid the production of researcher bias. In this book, participants who included principals, vice-principals, hostel wardens, assistant hostel wardens, disciplinary chairpersons, nursing sisters and students responded on factors affecting higher education students' perception of acquaintance rape in Masvingo. This study did not change or modify participants' behaviour, situations in higher education institutions in Masvingo or perceptions of acquaintance rape but simply gathered data pertaining to the problem under study.

Even though the descriptive survey has its own strengths, the use of survey in studies has its own weaknesses (Chimhenga, 2014:59). Participants who responded in this study were aware that they were under study and could have produced biased data as suggested by Leedy and Ormrod (2010:188). There might have been a likelihood of collecting relatively superficial data basing on the complexities like contradictions of human action, behaviour and perceptions. Surveys rarely probe deeply into the complexities like contradictions of human action, behaviour and perceptions. From the researcher's point of view, the strengths of a descriptive survey outweighed its weaknesses hence it was found to be the most appropriate design to be used in this book. The above-mentioned limitations of the descriptive survey as mentioned above in the discussion were mitigated using strategies revealed in the ways to overcome limitations discussed in Chapter 1, section 1.10.1. The next section discusses the population which was surveyed in this book.

3.5 Population

When a researcher is conducting a survey, s/he would be collecting data from part of the population. Polit and Beck (2006:258) advocate that population refers to a well-defined set of people, animals, objects, or events that have certain specified properties. Thus, population refers to the whole group of individuals from which a sample is drawn and to which research results can be generalised (McMillan & Schumacher, 2010:489). It refers to a group which the researcher would like to make inferences.

This book's target population comprised all students and all administrators from all the seven institutions of higher education from Masvingo in teachers' colleges, universities and a polytechnic. The target population may not be manageable due to its location, size, distribution and other practical issues such as money, time as well as personal. For this stated reason, the target population for this study was scaled down to three institutions of higher education in Masvingo which was manageable (Johnson & Christensen, 2011; 218) and was also rich with necessary data to answer the study's major research question which read as: What are the factors that affect students in higher education institutions' perceptions of acquaintance rape in Masvingo of Zimbabwe? College administrators and non-academic staff were directly involved with students hence they were in a position to provide relevant information on the factors affecting higher education students' perceptions of acquaintance rape in Masvingo. So, the results were over generalised to the three institutions of higher education in Masvingo. The population in this was heterogeneous as it included principals, vice principals, hostel wardens, assistant hostel wardens, nursing sisters, disciplinary chairpersons, genders, different types of colleges, different qualifications and experience and students from different age groups, some of whom could have been victims of acquaintance rape. The population in this study was drawn from rural, urban, peri-urban, church owned, government teachers' colleges and a polytechnic from Masvingo.

In the next section, the research sample for this book is discussed below.

3.6 Sample and Sampling Procedure

A sample is a representative for a study whose characteristics exemplify the large group from which it was selected (Taylor et al, 2009:48; Patton, 2016:244; Denzin & Lincoln, 2001:370). The sample for this study was drawn from three institutions of higher education from Masvingo province. This study focused on students in higher education because they are a rich source of data on the pertinent issue. These three institutions of higher education were conveniently selected because of their proximity to the researcher (Neuman, 2006:225) as well as the availability of research assistants. The main sample was approximately 10% of the target population. According to Davis and Sutton (2004:151), convenient sampling involves selecting participants purely on the basis that they are conveniently available to the researcher. Leedy and Ormrod (2010:212) advocate that in convenient sampling, the researcher selects participants because of their easy availability or access. In this study, convenient sampling was used because of its low cost and easy to use in gathering data from the available participants. Like in any ordinary province in Zimbabwe, these institutions of higher education range from government, church owned, rural, mining compound, resettlement area peri-urban and urban, hence it was a very rich sample to provide research data. In all institutions of higher education, participants were randomly selected to control the biased information that could have been obtained as a result of convenient sampling of the institutions of higher education.

The sample for this book consisted of 63 participants made up of 3 principals (1 male and 2 females), 3 vice principals (1 male and 2 females), 3 hostel wardens (1 male and 2 females), 3 assistant hostel wardens (1 male and 2 females), 3 nursing sisters (1 male and 2 females), 3 disciplinary chairpersons (1 male and 2 females) and 45 students (12 males and 33 females) from the three out of the seven educational institutions in Masvingo. The age range of students was from 17 years to 50 years. The three educational institutions were conveniently selected for the purpose of this book. The number of female participants is higher than that of males because there are more female students and workers in the studied institutions of higher education.

Participants were randomly selected from the three educational institutions out of the seven institutions of higher learning in the province using a table of random numbers. Randomised samples in the survey designs normally facilitate the generalisability of study results to the target population. In this study, the researcher sought to select a sample that was truly representative of the target population in order to use the results obtained from the sample to make generalisations about students' perceptions of acquaintance rape in the three randomly sampled institutions of higher education in Masvingo. Leedy and Ormrod (2005:199) advise that the sample should be carefully chosen that, through it, the researcher is able to observe all the characteristics of the total population in the same relationship.

The instrumentation of the book is discussed below.

3.7 Instrumentation

This book employed a questionnaire with both closed-ended and open-ended items for triangulation's sake, as data collection tool. The selection of data collection method depends upon the purpose of the book, the resources available and the skills of the researcher, these factors were carefully considered. The questionnaire is explained below.

3.7.1 Questionnaire

According to Labovitz and Hagedon (2017:70), a questionnaire is "… a research instrument comprising of a series of questions that are filled in by participants themselves". It can be used to obtain information concerning beliefs, values, facts, opinions, views as well as intentions from participants (Leedy& Ormrod, 2005:94; Babie, 2009:292).

A questionnaire, unlike other research instruments, is the most generally used instrument in research because of its advantages which surpasses other research tools (De vos *et al,* 2011:180; Cohen *et al,* 2007:317). Wilkinson and Birmingham (2003:10) noted that questionnaires are the most effective, cheap and efficient way of obtaining participants' views and opinions from a larger number of participants in a well-structured way. In this study, a questionnaire was chosen as a data-gathering instrument because it had the capacity to capitalise on the unique ability of human beings to communicate at a rather more sophisticated and private level (Polit & Hangler, 2009:192). Both acquaintance rape and its related variables (culture, gender, peer pressure and policy, legislation or law) need to be treated in a private and confidential manner, a characteristic which a questionnaire possesses. It was also found to be a cheap, easy, fast and efficient method to obtain views and opinions from many participants from the three conveniently sampled institutions of higher education within a short period of time while the researcher, with the assistance of .assistant researchers, waited for participants to fill in the questionnaire. Denscombe (2010:146) noted that a questionnaire also has got the potential to supply social researchers with exact figures (where these are requested). Green and Browne (2005:109) note that a questionnaire has the potential to reduce researcher biases because each research question is structured uniformly. In this book, a questionnaire was considered an appropriate tool for data gathering because it was understood to be straightforward method of obtaining quantitative data, sensible and information from a substantial number of people at the same time thereby reducing biases. And, as a way of minimizing questionnaire bias (Dunne *et al.,* 2009:44; Mouton, 2012:103) in this book, the researcher included open-ended questions to allow participants to write their own responses (Wiersma & Jurs, 2009:204; Nardi, 2006:72) as well as closed-ended questionnaire items to provide participants with standardised responses from which they selected.

More importantly, a questionnaire was also considered to be a very powerful method when sorting information, opinions and attitudes (Taylor *et al.*, 2009:87). In this study, a questionnaire was used to tap rich data from participants pertaining to factors affecting higher education students' perceptions of acquaintance rape in Masvingo.

Data obtained using a questionnaire is also easy to test for reliability and validity (Mouton, 2012:100; Brink, 2009:148; Denscombe, 2010:159; Best & Khan, 2006:16). Different categories of participants completed different instruments. De vos *et al.* (2011:186) observed that a questionnaire can also be refined or validated during the study it was designed for and may be used as a basis of future study. To ensure reliability and validity in this book, the researcher made sure that responses for closed-ended questionnaire items were consistent for all participants and that information generated would be quantified and compared (Cohen *et al.*, 2007:321; Wiersma & Jurs, 2009:204).

A likert scale was used for the structured items to allow for fairly accurate assessment of participants opinions as propounded by McMillan and Schumacher (2016:198) and Cohen *et al.* (2007:323). Taylor *et al* (2009:2000) define a likert scale as a series of gradation levels or values that describe various degrees of something. All the items have 5-point likert scales which were used: SA-Strongly Agree; A-Agree; N-Neutral; D-Disagree and lastly S.D- Strongly Disagree. In this book, the likert scale was chosen because it provided great flexibility since the descriptors on the scale varied to fix the nature of the question or statement.

In fact, the likert scale was a useful device for the book since it enabled the researcher to build a degree of sensitivity and differentiation of responses while still generating numbers.

The design of the questionnaire was guided by research objectives and literature review. Examples of questionnaire items which were derived from the literature are shown in Table 3.2.

Table 3.1 A grid on literature study authors

Item	Author (s)
Influence of culture on acquaintance rape	Flood & Pease (2006:27); Ben-David & Schneider (2008:385); Russo 2000:1); Armstrong (1989:68); Boswell and Spade (2010:134); Frese, Moya and Magias (2004:143); Okeke (2011:30); Kottack (2009:58)
The Influence of Gender on acquaintance rape	Ben-David & Schneider (2008:385); Okeke (2011:34); Matchen and DeSoza (2000:295); McAmslan (2004:749); Boswell & Spade (2010:137); Taylor & Mouzoz (2006:6)
Influence of peer pressure on acquaintance rape	Jewkes (2012:221); Sampson (2002:120); Lev-Wiesel (2004:199); De Leon (2013:18)
Influence of Policy, Legislation or law on acquaintance rape	Kahan (2010:11); Page (2008:389); Roe (2004:2); Cairney (2012:297)

Source: Compiled by Author, 2023

Validity is discussed in the next paragraphs.

3.7.2 Validity

According to Leedy and Ormrod (2010:28), validity is the measurement instrument which measures what the instrument is intended to measure. Wiid and Diggins (2015:85) elaborate that validity determines whether the research measures what it is supposed to measure and perform as per research objectives. This concurs with Patton's (2016:140) conceptualization that validity is a demonstration that the evidence for the obtained results reported is sound and when the argument made by researchers are based on the obtained results is strong. Taylor *et al* (2009:158) underline that in quantitative research validity is a requirement and lack of it renders the book to be worthless. In this study, the researcher had a clear idea about the problem under study and selected a research tool that was suitable to obtain information relevant to the specific problem (Tlali, 2017:86). Denzin and Lincoln (2005:10) note that validity in quantitative research can be addressed through honesty, depth, participants approached as well as the extent of triangulation and the objectivity of the researcher. In this study, validity was ensured through accurate recording, presentation, analysis and interpretation of the data obtained.

Validity was also achieved through the researcher's careful sampling, appropriate instrumentation as well as appropriate statistical treatment of data. The researcher also enforced the validity of the instrument using criterion Jury validation (external validity) where an expert in research (supervisor) scrutinised the relevance of the questionnaire items that is with special reference to objectives of the current study. The principals, vice principals, hostel wardens, assistant hostel wardens, nursing sisters and disciplinary chairpersons from the three institutions of higher education are heterogeneous in nature, hence it enabled them to be suitable representatives of different settings in terms of perceptions of acquaintance rape of students in the province. The random sampling procedure employed to select students in institutions of higher education within the province enhanced the validity of the research design of this study.

To ensure that errors of any nature in the data gathering instrument was up to standard before distributing the questionnaire, construct validity was carefully considered and a pilot study conducted to check on the general validity that would ensure reliability. Creswell, Ebersohn, Eloff, Ferreira, Ivankova, Janson, Neuwenhuis, Pieterson, Plano-Clark and Van der Westhuizen (2010:35) advised researchers that in all research cases, it is essential that newly constructed instruments in their semi- final form be tested before being administered in the main study. Questionnaire items in this study, measured higher education students' perceptions of acquaintance rape in Masvingo. The following subheading discusses reliability.

3.7.3 Reliability

According to Denscombe (2010:106), both validity and reliability are the cornerstones for evaluating social research designs. In reliability, there is consistency, constancy, dependability, accuracy or precision with which an instrument measures the target population's attributes (Burn & Grove, 2005:374). A study is said to be reliable if the same results are reproduced repeatedly using the same research instrument of measurement or methodology. In simple terms, what it means is that the administering of the same instrument by the same researcher or different researchers using the same instrument on people of the same characteristics under the same conditions would provide the same results (De vos *et al.,* 2005:163). To achieve this, in this study, the researcher pre-tested the questionnaire through pilot testing. The researcher also achieved reliability in this study by developing the questionnaire in consultation with the supervisor.

Items which were regarded as unclear by the supervisor were also corrected accordingly.

The researcher carried out pilot testing to increase the research instrument's reliability and practicability as suggested by Kumar (2012:181) and Cohen et al. (2007:341). The following subheading looked at reliability analysis of questionnaire items.

3.7.4 Reliability analysis

Each part of the questionnaire had various question items relating to a topic. For instance, Part 2 had 11 question items all relating to culture and acquaintance rape, Part 3 had 3 question items all relating to gender and acquaintance rape, while part 4 and part 5 had 9 question items each. It proved cumbersome to perform chi- squared tests of independence on each of the question items. Therefore, the question items were aggregated in each of the parts. Since Likert scale data is ordinal in nature, the aggregation was carried out via the mode function. The mode represents the most frequent item in a list of items. The result was an aggregated variable representing the modal response for each student in each of the parts 2 to 5. However, before the aggregation was done it was necessary to measure the internal consistency of the question items in each of the parts through a reliability analysis.

Reliability analysis was carried out for the question items in each of the parts 2, 3, 4 and 5 of the questionnaire. Specifically, the Chronbach (alpha) model for internal consistency was used. The alpha model is used to measure the extent to which the question items in a Likert scale instrument are measuring the same construct. An alpha value of above 70 is considered good internal consistency.

3.8 Training of Research Assistants

The researcher of this study was assisted by three research assistants who were conveniently selected from the three institutions of higher education in Masvingo to collect data from participants. These research assistants were chosen because they have technical skills in research. The conveniently selected research assistants had some research experiences and were lecturers in institutions of higher educations. Training of research assistants was done so as to improve reliability of the results of the study. The trained research assistants together with the researcher collected data for this study. The researcher explained the objectives of the study and their ethical responsibilities to participants. Ethical issues discussed during training of research assistants in this study included confidentiality, anonymity, informed consent, harm to respondents and privacy. The training session of research assistants also included the sampling procedures to be used for selecting participants as well as the administering of the questionnaires for the study. Research assistants were also used in the pilot study to test validity and reliability of research instrument used for data collections. The following subheading discussed the pilot study.

3.9 Pilot Study

Pratt and Loizos (2003:59) defines a pilot study as a mini version of the main book (feasibility book) as well as a pre-testing process of a particular research instrument. This understanding is reinforced by Silverman (2016:45), who notes that a pilot book is a smaller version of a large book that is conducted to prepare for that book. A pilot study was conducted since it was found to be an essential component of this survey. The main objective of pilot testing in this study was to standardise the data collection tool (questionnaire). Davis and Sutton (2004:177) contend that the pilot study allows a preliminary data analysis and ensures that the data collected answers the main research question. The pilot study was also used to check how well the proposed research design would work as advised by Denscombe (2010:106).

McMillan and Schumacher (2016:195) note that a pilot study helps the researcher to work out some of the procedural bugs. A pilot test helped the researcher to reduce the number of unanticipated problems as he (the researcher) was afforded the opportunity to redesign parts of the study to curb difficulties that the miniature study revealed. In further support of the above- mentioned point of view by McMillan and Schumacher (2016:195), Creswell (2006:9) also notes that pilot study would provide the researcher with the opportunity to discover ideas, approaches and clues that he/she might not have foreseen before the pilot test. According to Creswell (2006:10), such ideas and clues would increase the chances to produce quantitative data that is close to the main study since the pilot study would also permit the researcher to evaluate the usefulness of the data. The whole process of pilot testing would enable the researcher to make some alterations during the data collection process so that the data to be obtained in the main study would be analysed more efficiently (Spratt *et al.*, 2004:12; Davis & Sutton, 2004:177). In short, one major advantage of conducting a pilot study in this study was that it afforded me the opportunity to project the direction and outcome of the research.

It was also carried out to eliminate some ambiguous items, establish whether there were problems in administering the questionnaire as well as anticipating and amending any logical and procedural difficulties regarding the study. The pilot testing questionnaire item for non-academic staff under "Section B" that was on culture and acquaintance rape had a double barrel meaning and ambiguous since it read like this "What are the effects and causes of acquaintance rape on culture to students in higher education?" It was corrected to read: "Write comments on how culture affects students' perceptions of acquaintance rape." Participants and institutions used in the pilot study were not the same as those involved in the main study but were from Masvingo province. In this study, assistant researchers and the researcher visited the three conveniently sampled institutions of higher education and administered the questionnaires. Participated students filled in the questionnaire in their classrooms while the assistant researchers and the researcher were therein present to prevent cheating. College staff also filled in their questionnaires in their respective offices and assistant researchers and the researcher then collected the questionnaires. The next sub-section presents the sample of pilot testing.

3.9.1 The Sample

The sample for the pilot study consisted of 33 participants made up of 3 principals (1 male and 2 females), 3 vice principles (1 male and 2 females), 3 hostel wardens (1 male and 2 females), 3 assistant hostel wardens (1male and 2 females), 3 nursing sisters (1 male and 2 females), 3 disciplinary chairpersons (1 male and 2 females) and 15 students (7 males and 8 females) from three institutions in Masvingo which were different from the three institutions in the main study from the same province. The number of female participants in this study was more than that of males because there are many female students and workers in institutions of higher education in Masvingo. Both students and college staff's home background range from rural, urban, peri-urban, mining compounds and resettlement areas. This sample was approximately 10% of the target population in institutions of higher education in Masvingo

(Kombo & Tromp, 2009:50). The researcher employed convenient sampling to select the participants of the pilot study who were within the reach of the researcher. The pilot study sample shows biographical data grid for participants from the selected three institutions of higher education from Masvingo.

The participants were given the opportunity to make comments on the questionnaire and their comments were then considered and necessary modifications were done before the main study was carried out. After carefully analysis and evaluation of the questionnaire for this study, it was reproduced.

Nardi (2006:95) advocates that the participants involved in the pilot study are not to be part of the final sample the final sample the reason being that they would have already seen the questionnaire. If they are involved in the main study for the second time could bias the results. Nardi (2006:95) further advises researchers that, for the pilot study, the questionnaire should be distributed with all the same procedures intended to be followed in the actual data collection phase. As has been apprised earlier, in this study, the participants who were involved in the pilot study were not part of the final sample in order to avoid bias in the final results.

The next subheading presents the data collection procedures.

3.9.2 Data collection procedure

The pilot study was done with a sample similar in characteristics to the main study sample of students in the three institutions of higher education selected for this book. After being cleared by the UNISA ethics committee, permission to undertake the study was also sought from the permanent secretary of the Ministry of Higher and Tertiary Education, Innovations, Science and Technology Development. The letter of permission to carry out the study was also handed to principals of respective institutions of higher and tertiary education. The researcher, with the assistance of assistant researchers, distributed questionnaires to principals, vice-principals, wardens, assistant wardens, disciplinary chairpersons, nursing sisters and students at their institutions in their respective offices and classrooms. Questions and format of the questionnaire were the same for student participants, academic staff and non-academic staff in both the pilot study and the main study. Other participants (students) filled in the questionnaire while the assistant researchers and researcher were waiting to avoid bias and cheating. The assistant researchers together with the researcher moved around institutions administering and collecting data for the pilot study.

The guiding information to participating students, college administrators and non-academic staff was as follows: The questionnaire sought to ask participants' opinions on the factors affecting higher education students' perceptions of acquaintance rape in Masvingo. The participants were notified that they were selected to participate in this study because they are the very people who know what is taking place in institutions of higher education. They were also told that they have a rich source of information pertaining to students in higher education institutions' perceptions of acquaintance rape. Participants were further instructed not to write down their names on the questionnaire for ethical reasons. Besides, participants were informed that there were no "right" or "wrong" answers but the researcher was only interested in their opinions. More importantly, participants were informed that the information was gathered would be treated as strict and confidential information. They were also requested to complete the questionnaire as honestly as possible. After completion of the questionnaire, the researcher thanked participants for taking their time to complete the survey. The next subheading presents data collection procedure in the main study.

3.10 Data Collection Procedure: Main Study

3.10.1 Questionnaire Administration

The questionnaires were personally distributed by the research assistants and the researcher to participating students, administrators and non-academic staff at their respective institutions. The research assistants and the researcher orally explained the purpose of the study to the research participants. The instructions given to the participants were the same as given during the administration of the pilot study. Questionnaires in the main study were collected by both the research assistants and the researcher.

3.11 Data Analysis

Kombo and Tromp (2009:86) explain that data analysis involves examining what has been collected in survey or experiments and making some deductions and some inferences. Data analysis includes uncovering the underlying structures, extracting important variables, detecting any anomalies and testing some underlying assumptions. It also helps the researcher to have a plan which would help him to begin thinking about how he/she would answer the research questions for the problem which she/he is gathering the data for. With such an analysis plan, the researcher would be ready to slice through the data and glean some messages.

In this study, data from all the questionnaires was aggregated and presented in a Spreadsheet which was fed into Statistical Package for Social Sciences (SPSS) version 16 to produce statistical information. This software was adopted for its simplicity in application and also for its suitability in the social sciences. The SPSS performed an x^2-test and Simple Linear Regression analysis to evaluate relationships between each predictor variables and the response variable. In this case, the predictor variables were culture, gender, peer pressure and policy, legislation or law. The response variable was acquaintance rape. The x^2-test sought to measure whether there was association or relationship between each of the predictor variable with acquaintance rape. The coefficient of determination, R^2, sought to establish the amount of variation on acquaintance rape explained by each predictor variable (culture, gender, peer pressure and policy, legislation or law). In this study, descriptive statistics in the form of both absolute values and percentiles were used to describe findings.

The x^2-test adopted in this study sought to address the objective of evaluating the degree of association between each of the predictive variables (culture, gender, peer pressure and policy, legislation or law) and the predicted variable (acquaintance rape). The coefficient of determination, R^2 was used to explain variations in acquaintance rape explained by changes in culture, gender, peer pressure and policy, legislation or law.

Both statistical measures (i.e., the x^2-test and R^2) used in this study sought to address objectives 1.5.1.0, 1.5.1.1, 1.5.1.2 and 1.5.1.3. The significance was predetermined at 0.05 and this α -value was compared with the p-value for each predictive variable to determine the significance of each variable or lack of it.

The qualitative data was screened and coded then content analysed the qualitative data using excerpts from open-ended questionnaire items as they were presented by participants' perceptions. In this study, excerpts from college administrators, non-academic staff and students were relevant as they captured participants' perceptions on factors affecting students' perceptions of acquaintance rape. Data from closed-ended questionnaire items was also decoded to produce meaning. Such information permitted the researcher to reveal participants' perceptions of acquaintance rape based on their culture, gender, peer pressure and policy, legislation or law. The following subheading discussed coding.

3.11.1 Coding

After data was collected using a questionnaire, it was coded in a form that allowed it to be subjected to computer analysis. In research, coding is the process whereby raw data is transformed into standardised and quantitative form. The process of coding involves assigning numbers (or codes) to observations so the gathered data was then converted into numerical codes. Burns and Grove (2005:455) advocate that, when coding research responses from rating scales, the responses are converted into a series of score. The assigned number or score to an observation is called a code. In the study, each individual participant was termed a case. Every case had a number representing that particular individual's score for each variable or measure. In this study, each individual participant or case had a serial number. Each item also on the questionnaire was assigned a column number for identification. For recording purposes, the serial number for each case was captured first, followed by the column number for each item. Responses for each questionnaire item were also assigned codes. Then, the code for each item was entered against each column number.

3.11.2 Statistical Analysis

In this study, the researcher used the Statistical Package for the Social Sciences (SPSS) version 16 which performed both the descriptive and inferential statistical analyses for several reasons. The Statistical Package for the Social Sciences (SPSS) consists of a wide variety of statistical procedures which include that it can easily handle large sets of research data, multiple variables as well as missing data points. The Statistical Package for Social Sciences can also present all research results in an easy to read and manageable table format. In this study, the Statistical Package for Social Sciences also tested for characteristics such as kurtosis that might have violated the assumptions on which parametric statistical procedure was based and was also speedy in completion of statistical tasks. The statistical package for the social sciences also allowed the researcher to summarise and display data in tables. In this study, the researcher had total control of the analysed data and knew what, when, how, where and why calculations were being calculated.

One way frequency tables were calculated to answer each and every questionnaire item as an initial step in the exploratory analysis. This initial step was undertaken by the researcher to validate data as well as to correct or remove spurious responses. One way frequency tables on biographical variables were also calculated to describe the sample population. Combined two-way frequency tables were calculated to answer all multiple response questionnaire items to reduce analysed output as a result it produced compact results which were of manageable proportions. The following subheading discusses content analysis.

3.11.3 Content Analysis

In this study, content analysis was employed to analyse data from the very few open-ended questionnaire items because it produced a relatively systematic and comprehensive summary of the produced data set as a whole. In this study, the researcher examined data from the few open-ended questionnaire items for recurrent instances which were systematically identified across the data sets and grouped together thematically.

3.11.4 Variables

The dependent variables in this study were perceptions of participants and the independent variables were culture, gender, peer pressure and policy, legislation or law. The way that these independent variables affected students in higher education's perceptions of acquaintance rape in Masvingo was established.

3.12 Ethical Considerations

Throughout the study, guidelines and rules empirical research were observed to produce unbiased data. Participants have a right to refuse to participate in any study, for instance if they think or even suspect that the study goes against their cultural, religious or social beliefs. Fraenkel and Wallen (2011:23) advise researchers that, "human subjects have the right to choose the extent to which and manner in which they will share or withhold information about their behaviour, attitudes, or opinions". In this book, it was important for the researcher to carry out his study in an ethical manner where principles of informed consent, harm to participants, anonymity and confidentiality were carefully considered. The next sections focus on the ethical standards that were followed in this study to ensure that the safety and rights of all participants who were randomly selected were observed, respected and protected as well. Hardcopies of filled in questionnaire items in this study were locked in the researcher's cupboard in his office and would be destroyed after five years. Electronic data was also saved in his computer with codes so that no-one would not get access to it. The following ethical issues are discussed next

3.12.1 Permission

Permission to carry out this book was sought from the University of South Africa's research ethical clearance committee. An ethical clearance certificate was granted for the period 2019/06/12 to 2024/06/12. In this study, permission for both pilot testing and final research was also obtained from the Ministry of Higher and Tertiary education, Science and Technology Development as well as from the four respective institutions of higher learning. Permission to carry out a study makes the research authentic as well as possible to conduct (Asford & LeCroy, 2010:35; Christians, 2005:144; Denscombe, 2010:74).

3.12.2 Informed Consent

According to Asford and LeCroy (2010:35), informed consent is a process whereby participants give consent to participate in a research after obtaining honest information about its procedures, risks and benefits (if any). The researcher also informed his participants about the purpose of his study as well as made participants aware of the risks which could be encountered in the study. The researcher made sure that participants were free to make decisions as to whether they wanted to participate or not. Participants were also given the right to withdraw at any point of the study (Best & Khan, 2015:45) especially if they think that their rights were violated. In other words, they needed to have informed consent (McMillan & Schumacher, 2006:33).

3.12.3 Confidentiality

Patton (2016:412) propounds that confidentiality means that the public would not have access to participants' data or names in the possession of the researcher and that no one can match research information with that of a participant. In this study, participants were protected from other persons or readers from settings where private information might have exposed them. In this study, since the researcher used questionnaires, data from questionnaire items was saved in the computer with secret password only known by the researcher. Questionnaire item scripts were kept under lock and key. McMillan and Schumacher (2010:122) advocate that " confidentiality can be ensured if no one has access to individual data or to the names of participants except the researcher or researchers." In this study, numbers, pseudonyms or codes were used instead of participants' names to conceal their identities. Participants were also told that the data would be used for academic purposes only not for any other use and that hard copies (filled questionnaires) would be destroyed after five years

3.12.4 Anonymity

In research, participants have rights to have their identity remaining anonymous (Christian, 2005:145). The conditions of anonymity apply to the collection of data by means of research tools (Mouton, 2012:243). In this study, it was also the researcher's obligation to keep participants' identity and responses private. Participants were also promised that the obtained information would not be revealed to the public (Urombo, 2000:28; Denscombe, 2010:54).

3.12.5 Harm to Participants

Patton (2016:274) points out that in any study, participants need to be protected from psychological, physical, social, emotional and spiritual harm or from potential harm of any nature. Babie (2007: 27) advises that if participants are not protected in research, there are chances that they can be psychologically, physically or emotionally harmed. In research of disciplines such as humanities and social sciences, harm to participants can be in the form of irritation, anger, negative labelling, invasion of privacy as well as damage to personal dignity (Urombo, 2000:120) and integrity. In this study, the researcher ensured that participants were not exposed to harm by avoiding questions which were relating to how they experienced acquaintance rape. Further, participants who displayed signs of psychological harm due to the sensitivity of the topic were referred to registered psychologists for psychological counselling.

3.13 Chapter Summary

This chapter discussed the research methodology which was used by the researcher. The research paradigm, research approach, research design, quantitative design, sample and sampling procedure as well as ethical issues were discussed. The chapter also examined the instruments used which were the questionnaire. The chapter also established the validity and reliability, pilot testing, data collection procedure and data analysis. The next chapter will present, analyse and discuss findings of the empirical research.

Chapter 4

Rape Culture in Higher Education: Testimonies from the Field

4.1 Introduction

As noted earlier, this book sought to investigate factors affecting higher education students' perceptions of acquaintance rape in Masvingo Province. The previous chapter discussed the methodology employed in the book. In this chapter, data generated from the empirical study is presented and discussed in the context of the four sub-research questions which guided this study (see section 1.4 of chapter 1).

The next section presents biographical variables of research participants of this study which constituted principals, vice-principals, hostel wards, assistant hostels wardens, nursing sisters, disciplinary chairpersons and students randomly selected from three out of the seven institutions of higher education in Masvingo. These biographical variables of research participants portray as well as convey the research context in which data was gathered in this study.

4.2 Biographical Variables of the Research Participants

Table 4.1 below presents the biographical data of students who participated in this study.

Table 4.1 Biographical variables of students (N=45)

PARTICIPANTS	BIOGRAPHICAL VARIABLE	VARIABLE DESCRIPTION	FREQUENCIES
Students	Gender	Male	12(26.7%)
		Female	33(73.3%)
		Total	**45(100%)**
	Age Range	17-20	3(6.7%)
		21-30	33(73.3%)
		31-40	7(15.6%)
		41-5O	2(4.4%)
		51-60	0(0%)
		Total	**45(100%)**
	Highest Academic Qualification	Ordinary Level	(75.6%)
		Advanced Level	(24.4%)
		Total	**45(100%)**

	Level At Institution	National Certificate National Diploma 1st year	15(33.3%)
		National Diploma 2nd year	15(33.3%)
		Higher National Diploma	0(0%)
		Total	**45(100%)**
	Institution Attended	Teachers' College (gvt)	15(33.3%)
		Polytechnic (gvt)	15(33.3%)
		Teachers' College (Church owned)	15(33.3%)
		Total	45(100%)
	Location of Origin	Urban	4(53.3%)
		Peri-Urban	6(13.3%)
		Mining Compound	0(0%)
		Resettlement Area	4(8.9%)
		Rural	11(24.4%)
		Total	**45(100%)**
	Residential status at College	Non-resident	18(40%)
		Resident	27(60%)
		Total	**45(100%)**
	Tribe	Karanga	26(57.7%)
		Korekore	2(4.4%)
		Manyika	3(6.7%)
		Ndau.	2(4.4%)
		Ndebele	2(4.4%)
		Nyanja	0(0%)
		Shangani	3(6.7%)
		Zezuru	7(15.6%)
		Total	**45(100%)**

Source: Author, 2023

Table 4.1 shows that there were more female students than male students in this study as can be seen in Figure 4.1.

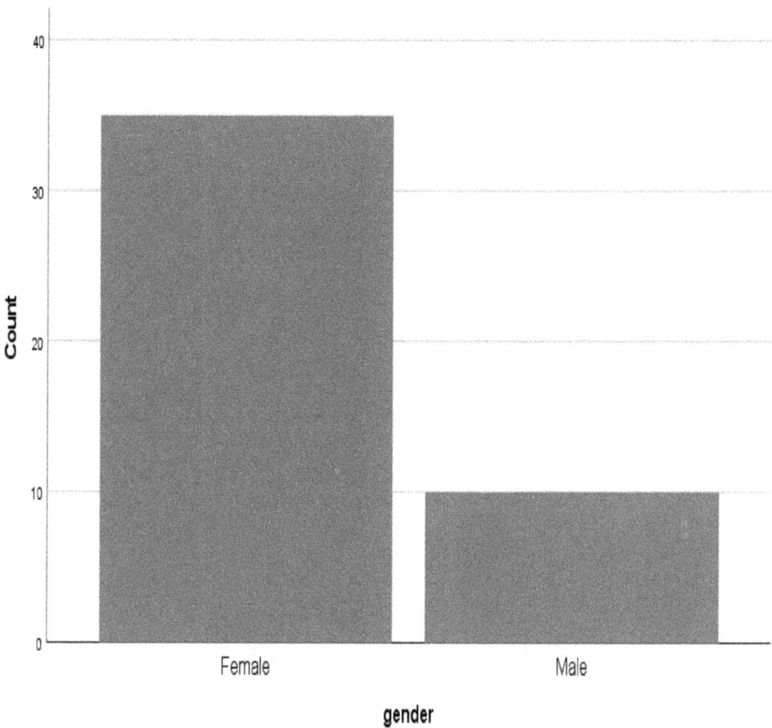

Figure 4.1 Gender distribution of student participants
Source: Author, 2023

The majority of the participating students were in the 21 to 30 years age range and the minority was in the 17 to 20, 31 to 40 and 41 to 50 years age range (Figure 4.2).

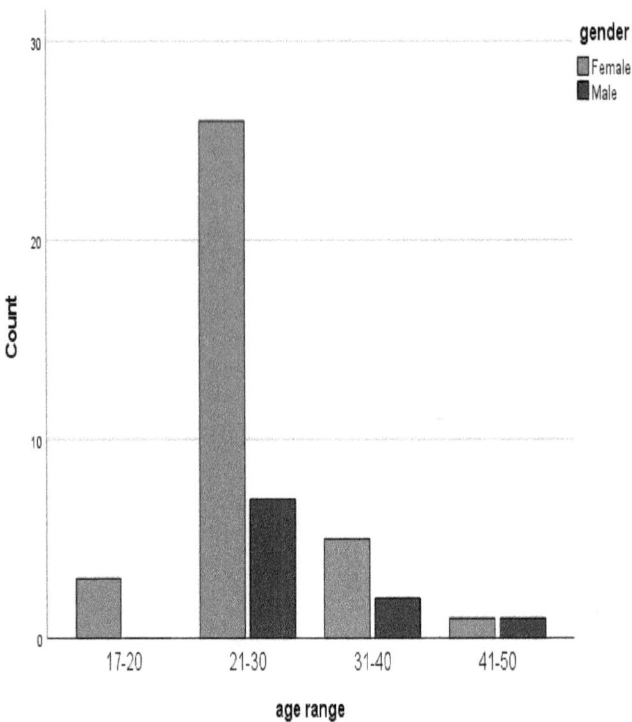

Fig 4.2 Distribution of student participants by age
Source: Author, 2023

The table further reveals that participating students also had varied professional qualifications since they were in both Polytechnics and Teachers' colleges. 15% had National Certificates and 15% had National Diplomas, and 15% had Higher National Diplomas (Fig. 4.3).

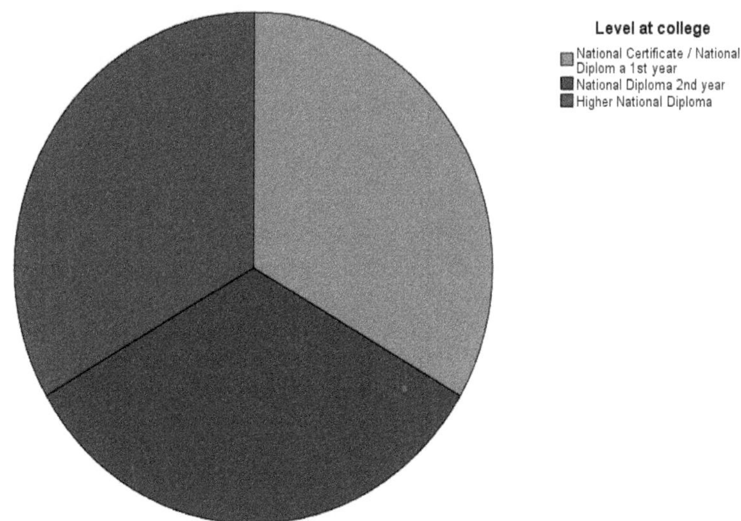

Figure 4.3 Distribution of student participants by programme

Source: Author, 2023

Students who participated in this study were both non-resident and resident; 40% were non-resident and 60% were resident students as illustrated in Fig 4.4. Of the 45 participants, 25% had an urban background, 53.3% peri-urban, 13.3% mining compound, 8.9% resettlement area and 24.4% had a rural background.

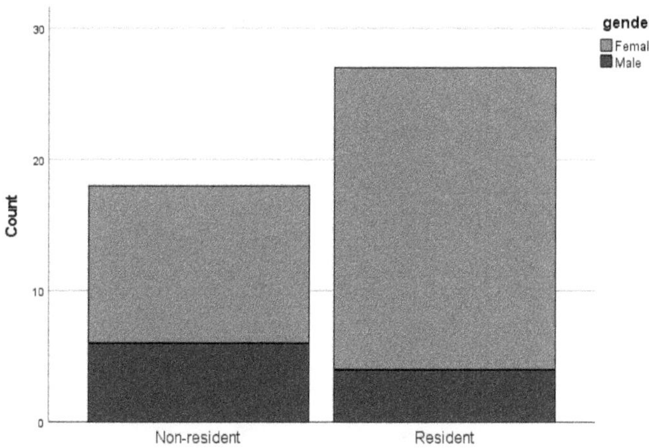

Figure 4.4 Distribution of student participants by resident status

Source: Author, 2023

Participants who participated in this study were of the following ethnic groupings; Karanga (57.7%), Korekore (4.4%), Manyika (6.7%), Ndau (4.4%), Ndebele (4.4%), Nyanja (0%), Shangani (6.7%) and Zezuru (15.6%) as illustrated in Fig. 4.5.

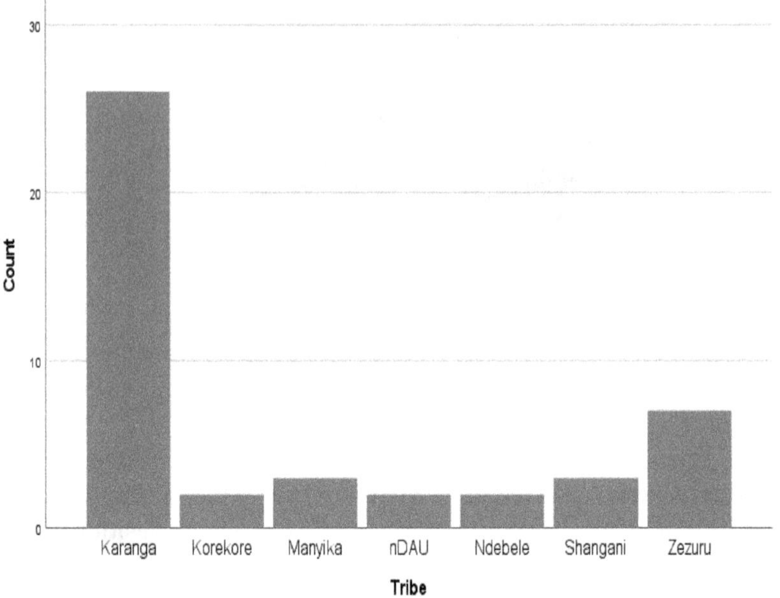

Figure 4.5 Distribution of student participants by ethnic grouping

There were also an equal number of participants in this study, (33.3%) from a government Teachers' college, a government polytechnic, and a church owned Teachers' college, respectively (Figure 4.6).

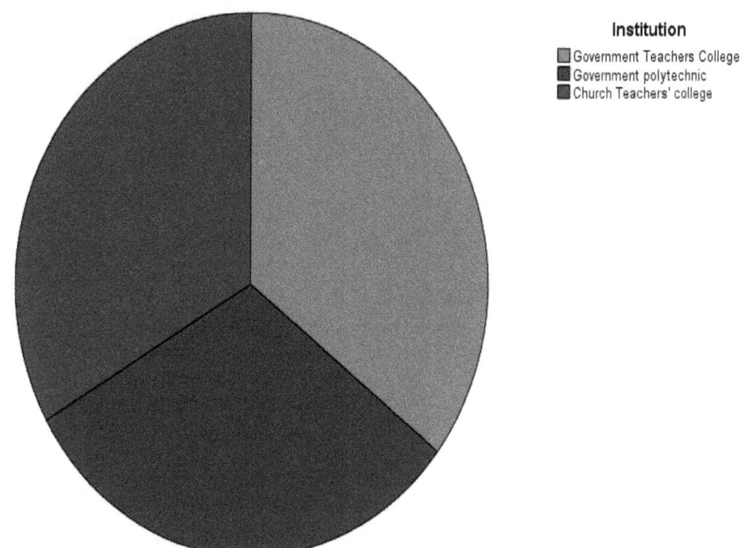

Figure 4.6 Distribution of student participants by institution
Source: Author, 2023

Only 31.7% of students had Advanced level certificates while 68.3% had Ordinary level certificates.

Table 4.2 Biographical variables of college administrators and non-academic staff (N=18)

PARTICIPANTS	BIOGRAPHICALVARIABLE	VARIABLE DESCRIPTION	FREQUENCIES
Academic And Non- Academic Staff	**Gender**	Male	11 (61.1%)
		Female	7 (38.8%)
		Total	**18 (100%)**
	Age range	17-20	0 (0%)
		21-30	2 (11.1%)
		31-40	14 (77.7%)
		41-50	2 (11.1%)
		51-60	0 (0%)
		Total	**18 (100%)**
	Professional qualification	National Certificate	**5 (27.7%)**
		National Diploma	6 (33.3%)
		Higher National Diploma	1 (5.6%)
		BA, BED,BSC	3 (16.6%)
		MA, MED, MSC, MPHIL, DED, PHD	3 (16.6%)
		Total	**18 (100%)**
	Institution working at	Teachers' College (gvt)	**15 (33.3%)**
		Polytechnic (gvt)	15 (33.3%)

		Teachers' College (Church owned)	15 (33.3%)
		Total	**18 (100%)**
	Experience at institution of higher learning	1-5 years	**3 (16.6%)**
		6-10 years	3 (16.6%)
		11-15 years	6 (33.3%)
		16-20 years	1 (5.5%)
		21-25 years	2 (11.1%)
		26-30 years	3 (16.6%)
		31 + years	0 (0%)
		Total	**18 (100%)**
	Location of origin	Urban	**9 (50%)**
		Peri-urban	4 (22.2%)
		Mining Compound	2 (11.1%)
		Resettlement Area	0 (0%)
		Rural	3 (16.6%)
		Total	**18 (100%)**
	Ethnic Group	Karanga	**13 (72%)**
		Korekore	0 (0%)
		Manyika	0 (0%)
		Ndau	1 (5.5%)
		Ndebele	0 (0%)
		Nyanja	1 (5.5%)
		Shangani	0 (0%)
		Zezuru	3 (16.6%)
		Total	**18 (100%)**

Table 4.2 presents the biographical variables of principals, vice principals, nursing sisters, hostel wardens, assistant hostel wardens and disciplinary chairpersons who participated in this study. Table 4.2 shows that there were more male college administrators and non-academic staff (61.1%) than females (38.8%). The majority of college administrators and non-academic staff were in the 31 to 40 (77.7%) years range and a few were in the 41 to 60 (11.1%) years range. The table also indicates that the majority of college administrators and non-academic staff fell in the 11 to 20 (33.3%) years range and 1 to 10 (33.3%) years range and a minority was in the 21 to 30 (27.7%) years range of experience in institutions of higher education. Sixteen point six percent (16.6%) of the college administrators and non-academic staff had first degrees and sixteen point six (16.6%) had Masters Degrees as well. None of the college administrators and non-academic staff had Doctorate degrees. Only one percent (1%) of the non-academic staff and college administrators had Higher National Diplomas, twenty five (25%) had National Diplomas and twenty one (21%) had National Certificates.

The following section provides information on the extent to which culture affects students' perceptions of acquaintance rape in higher education institutions in Masvingo.

4.3 Culture and Acquaintance Rape

The first sub-research question presented in section 1.4.1 of Chapter 1 explored the extent to which culture affects higher education students' perceptions of acquaintance rape in Masvingo. The findings of this sub- research question are presented in Table 4.3.

nd Students' perceptions of acquaintance rape (N=63)

Aspects	Responses							Total
	SA	**A**	**N**	**D**	**S D**			
1. lturally ladies nt sex no tter how ey get it.	3(16.7%)	8(44.4%)	3(16.6%)	3(16.7%)	1(5.6%)			18(10
2. If a oman is raped an quaintance, ciety will say at the victim serves it.	4(22.2%)	12(66.7%)	2(11.1%)	0(0%)	0(0%))			18(10
3. Women o wear vealing othing are king for sex.	7(38.9%)	9(50%)	0(0%)	2(11.1%)	0(0%)			18(10
4. Females o claim to ve been ed, do so to aw public ention.	5(27.8%)	3(16.7%)	3(16.7%)	4(22.2%)	3(16.7%)			18(10
5. It is lturally rrect for ales to rape eir quaintances.	6(33.3%)	5(27.8)	1(5.6%)	3(16.7%)	3916.7%)			18(10

annot by she ıt by	2(11.1%)	8(44.4%)	3(16.7%)	3(16.7%)	2(11.1%)			18(100%)
emales ːaped nces ıow its	3(16.7%)	7(38.9%)	2(11.1%)	1(5.6%)	5(27.8%)			18(100%)
ollege ınce ms ʾe a ɔ	2(11.1%)	9(50%)	4(22.9%)	2(11.1%)	1(5.6%)			18(100%)
ɔrcing ıll that no lly ːt.	2(11.1%)	5(27.8%)	2(11.1%)	8(44.4%)	1(5.6%)			18(100%)
ictims ntance ʾrve a ʃ	5(27.8%)	9(50%)	2(11.1%)	2(11.1%)	0(0%)			18(100%)
ıl	**39(21.7%)**	**75(41.7%)**	**22(12.2%)**	**28(15.6%)**	**16(8.9%)**			**180(100%)**
male force	0(0%)	1(2.2%)	0(0%)	18(40%)	26(57.8%)			45(100%)

111

female students for sex.								
12. A "No" on sexual advances from a female is taken as a "yes".	6(13.3%)	11(24.4%)	9(20%)	13(28.9%)	6(13.3%)			45(
13. Males and females learn dating tactics from acquaintances.	8(17.86%)	25(55.6%)	5(11.1%)	4(8.9%)	3(6.7%)			45(
14. Male students normally hook-up female students in college bars.	10(22.2%)	16(35.6%)	6(13.3%)	10(22.2%)	3(6.7%)			45(
15. Females are passive participants whereas males are aggressive for sex.	9(20.5%)	10(22.7%)	4(9.1%)	13(29.5%)	8(18.2%)			44(
16. Forcing a woman for sex is culturally normal.	3(7.0%)	6(14.0%)	3(7.0%)	15(34.9%)	16(37.2%)			43(
17. Members of the society including	16(36.4%)	16(36.4%)	3(6.8%)	3(6.8%)	6(13.6%)			44(

tance ctims do ort tance ators.							
. lly, an tance is arded as	7(16.3%)	9(20.9%)	2(4.7%)	15(34.9%)	10(23.3%)			43(100%)
. Victims ators of tance at it as	8(17.8%)	14(31.1%)	4(8.9%)	10(22.2%)	9(20%)			45(100%)
Victims aintance blamed bers of iety.	10(22.7%)	14(31.8%)	3(6.8%)	11(25.0%)	6(13.6%)			44(100%)
. If a d sex woman he can at she have ted.	8(18.2%)	8(18.2%)	5(11.4%)	12(27.3%)	11(25%)			44(100%)
tal	85(17.5%)	130(26.7%)	44(9.0%)	124(25.5%)	104(21.4%)			487(100%)

113

The first column of Table 4.3 represents the participants. The second column represents aspects or statements stated on the questionnaire section B (See Appendix J). The third column up to the fifth column represent the level of agreement and disagreement on various aspects or statements from "strongly agree, agree, disagree to strongly disagree" on participants' responses on the extent to which culture affects higher education students' perceptions of acquaintance rape in Masvingo. The eighth column represents totals. The last column, that is the ninth column, represents the Chronbach's alpha calculation.

Table 4.3 shows that the alpha value for staff was very high at .853 while that for students was moderately high at .672. This shows that the 10 question items for staff were attuned to each other to a very high degree and therefore an aggregate variable that is representative for responses by staff on culture and acquaintance rape was computed. The 11 questionnaire items for students were also to an acceptable degree in agreement and so an aggregate variable that is representative for responses by students on culture and acquaintance rape was also computed.

Chi-square tests of independence were done to establish the patterns of responses of both staff and students' demographic variables with respect to the aggregate variables on culture and acquaintance rape. In all cases, 0.05 was used as the level of significance. Table 4.4 shows a summary of chi- square tests of independence results between various students' demographic variables and aggregate students' perceptions of culture and acquaintance rape.

There was no difference between male and female students with regards to their perceptions on culture and acquaintance rape, $X^2(4, N = 45) = 2.396, p = .663$. There was also no difference in the perceptions of culture and acquaintance rape: by students' age range, $X^2(12, N = 45) = 10.661, p = .558$; by students' level at college, $X^2(8, N = 45) = 10.180, p = .253$; between resident and non-resident students, $X^2(4, N = 45) = 2.491, p = .646$; and by institution, $X^2(8, N = 45) = 4.258, p = .833$.

Table 4.4 Summary of chi-square test of independence results between various students' demographic variables and aggregate students' perceptions of culture and acquaintance rape

Variable	H_0	X^2	df	Sig.	Significance
Gender	There is no difference in perceptions of culture and acquaintance rape between males and female students	2.396	4	.663	Not significant
Age	There is no difference in perceptions of culture and acquaintance rape between different student age ranges	10.661	12	.558	Not significant
Level at college	There is no difference in perceptions of culture and acquaintance rape by student level at college	10.180	8	.253	Not significant
Resident status	There is no difference in perceptions of culture and acquaintance rape by students' resident status	2.491	4	.646	Not significant
Institution	There is no difference in perceptions of culture and acquaintance rape by student institution	4.258	8	.833	Not significant

Table 4.5 shows a summary of chi-square test of independence results between various staff members' demographic variables and aggregate perceptions of culture and acquaintance rape.

There was significant difference in the perceptions of culture and acquaintance rape between male and female staff members, X^2(4, N = 18) = 14.393, p = .006. There was, however, no difference in the perceptions of culture and acquaintance rape between staff members of different age ranges, X^2(8, N = 18) = 8.669, p = .371; by staff members' work experience, X^2(20, N = 18) = 22.114, p = .334; and between staff members working at different institutions of higher learning, X^2(8, N = 18) = 3.686, p = .884.

Table 4.5 Summary of chi-square test of independence results between various staff members' demographic variables and aggregate perceptions of culture and acquaintance rape

Variable	H_0	X^2	df	Sig.	Significance
Gender	There is no difference in perceptions of culture and acquaintance rape between males and female staff members	14.393	4	.006	Significant
Age	There is no difference in perceptions of culture and acquaintance rape by age of staff members	8.669	8	.371	Not significant
Experience	There is no difference in perceptions of culture and acquaintance rape between staff members of different working experiences	22.114	20	.334	Not significant
Institution	There is no difference in perceptions of culture and acquaintance rape by institution of staff member	3.686	8	.884	Not significant

The subsequent section presents qualitative findings of this study on the participants' (principals, vice principals, hostel wardens, assistant hostel wardens, nursing sisters, disciplinary chairpersons and students) responses on the extent to which culture influences students in higher education institutions' perceptions of acquaintance rape in Masvingo.

4.3.1 Participants' responses on culture and acquaintance rape

4.3.1.1 College Administrators' responses

College administrators revealed that culture positively affects students in higher education institutions' perception of acquaintance rape in Masvingo. The participants revealed that culture encourages acquaintance rape as a way of protecting relationships. All participants also revealed that African culture treats women and girls unfairly with regards to acquaintance rape. For example, African culture does not allow women to open on sexual relationships, prohibits revealing of sexual activities and protection of perpetrators of acquaintance rape as well as blaming them for causing rape.

The following extracts confirm the above:

> *Culture encourages acquaintance rape by mandatory silence as a way of protecting relationships* **(Principal 01).**
>
> *Culture does not allow women to open on sexual issues* **(Vice Principal 01).**
>
> *Zimbabwean African culture treats woman unfairly by assuming that they are responsible for acquaintance rape* **(Principal 02).**
>
> *Culture seems to condone acquaintance rape* **(Vice Principal 02).**
>
> *Culture encourages acquaintance rape by the way it handles such cases* **(Vice Principal 03).**

4.3.1.2 Non-academic staff's responses

Like the administrators, non-academic staff also revealed that, culture may affect the perception of students in higher education institution's perceptions of acquaintance rape.

The following extracts confirm the above:

> *A married woman cannot report acquaintance rape according to African culture* **(Hostel Warden 01).**
>
> *Culture shapes the way people perceive issues and tend to hide acquaintance rape issues* **(Hostel Warden 02).**
>
> *Women, culturally, perceive men as the dominant sex and therefore may give in to their sexual demands* **(Hostel Warden 03).**
>
> *Sex is a woman's duty according to African culture* **(Assistant Hostel Warden 001).**

Most rape victims do not report acquaintance rape because sexual issues are taboo according to African culture **(Assistant Hostel Warden 002).**

African societies are patriarchal in nature therefore women are always to blame if acquaintance rape occurs **(Assistant Hostel Warden 003).**

According to Karanga culture, a woman or girl cannot openly consent to sex, so a "no" means "yes" depending on the tone of the "no". If it is low tone, it means go on, and if it is high tone, it means a real "no" **(Nursing Sister 01).**

Culture tends to favour men, hence it gives perpetrators advantages and blames victims of acquaintance rape **(Nursing Sister 02).**

Culturally, males are expected to initiate the sexual act, and if a woman does so, they are regarded as prostitutes **(Nursing Sister 03).**

African cultural beliefs and practices protect acquaintance rapists, so its existence in society cannot be recognised; even if it occurs, it is not taken seriously **(Disciplinary Chairperson 01).**

Ladies feel exposed if they report acquaintance rape cases and would be blamed for it **(Disciplinary Chairperson 02).**

Usually, acquaintance rape issues are not openly discussed **(Disciplinary Chairperson 03).**

4.3.1.3 Students' responses

As was the case with administrators and non-academic staff, students' responses also revealed that culture has an influence on students' perceptions of acquaintance rape in Masvingo. The following extracts confirm the above:

Acquaintance rape is a crime in other cultures not African culture **(Student 001)**

Acquaintance rape is a social vice **(Student 003)**

In some societies, it is regarded as a crime or taboo to force a woman to have sex with a man. But according to African culture, it is regarded as a normal cultural practice **(Student 002)**

Culture really affects acquaintance rape since African beliefs lead perpetrators to commit acquaintance rape **(Student 006)**

Culture does not view acquaintance rape as rape since ladies and women are regarded as reproductive tools **(Student 005)**

Culture is a complex whole of norms, values, ethics, mores, folkways; it affects acquaintance rape **(Student 010)**

Victims of acquaintance rape preserve their dignity by not reporting acquaintance rapists **(Student 007)**

Victims of acquaintance rape do not report acquaintance rapists to protect their relationships **(Student 004)**

Males take advantage of culture to rape females at will **(Student 008)**

Culturally, women are not allowed to refuse sex when asked or forced to have sex by their husbands or partners **(Student 009)**

In life or even in sexual relationships, males are regarded as majors or superior whilst females are regarded as inferior hence, they have subordinate roles, so they don't dictate the pace in sexual relationships **(Student 011)**

Some cultures, especially African culture, take advantage of female gender and as a result they force them to have sex with them without their consent **(Student 02)**

The way women dress, talk and act entice men to commit acquaintance rape, so they are to blame if raped by acquaintances **(Student 013)**

Society regards acquaintance rape victims as loose if they are raped by acquaintances **(Student 015)**

Society always blames male rapists but females in most acquaintance rape cases entice men, hence they are to blame **(Student 016).**

The following sub-section presents the extent to which gender influences the perceptions of higher education students' perceptions of acquaintance rape in Masvingo.

4.4 Gender and Acquaintance Rape

The second sub-research question posed in section 1.4.2 of chapter 1 examined the extent to which gender affect students in higher education institutions' perceptions of acquaintance rape in Masvingo. Table 4.6 presents the responses by staff and students on gender and perceptions of acquaintance rape in Masvingo.

nder and students' perceptions of acquaintance rape (N=63)

Aspects	Responses					
	SA	**A**	**N**	**D**	**S D**	**Tota**
1. Females claim quaintance rape if they e spotted.	4(22.2%)	10(55.56%)	2(11.1%)	2(11.1%)	0(0%)	18(1(
2. Women are raped their acquaintances e to patriarchal sons.	7(38.9%)	6(33.3%)	3(16.7%)	1(5.6%)	1(5.6%)	18(1(
3. Rape culture nong males is a mmon college practice.	5(27.8%)	2(11.1%)	4(22.2%)	6(33.3%)	1(5.6%)	18(1(
4. Male gender reotype supports male ists.	3(16.7%)	10(55.6%)	2(11.1%)	3(16.7%)	0(0%)	18(1(
5. Male perpetrators sconstrue the victims' tions.	5(27.8%)	10(55.6%)	2(11.1%)	1(5.6%)	0(0%)	18(1(
6. Acquaintance ists view acquaintance e as part of college e.	5(27.8%)	5(27.8%)	7(38.9%)	1(5.6%)	0(0%)	18(1(
7. Both male and male genders tend to me rape victims.	5(27.8%)	9(50%)	2(11.1%)	2(11.1%)	0(0%)	18(1(
8. Male students n't view acquaintance e as a social vice?	3(16.7%)	10(55.6%)	3(16.7%)	2(11.1%)	0(0%)	18(1(
9. College ministrators do not	2(11.1%)	5(27.8%)	5(27.8%)	6(33.3%)	0(0%)	18(1(

t acquaintance ctims.						
. College strators treat tance rape victims titutes	2(11.1%)	9(50%)	3(16.7%)	4(22.2%)	0(0%)	18(100%)
otal	**41(22.8%)**	**76(42.2%)**	**33(18.3%)**	**28(15.6%)**	**2(1%)**	**180(100%**
. Most female tance rape victims erred to as slut.	13(28.9%)	10(22.2%)	3(6.7%)	10(22.2%)	9(20%)	45(10%)
. Gender ype enables man to n per perpetrators aintance rape.	8(18.2%)	16(36.4%)	10(22.7%)	6(13.6%)	4(9.1%)	44(100%)
. Perpetrators of tance rape are ted by society.	3(6.8%)	7(15.9%)	5(11.4%)	16(36.4%)	13(29.5%)	44(100%)
otal	**24(18.1%)**	**33(24.8%)**	**18(13.6%)**	**32(24.1%)**	**26(19.5%)**	**133(100%**

Table 4.6 shows that there was high internal consistency with regards to responses on perceptions of gender and acquaintance rape as shown by the computed alpha values for both staff, ($\alpha = .812$) and students ($\alpha = .795$). As a result, the 10 question items for staff were aggregated into a single representative value. This was also done for the 3 question items for students.

Chi-square tests of independence were conducted to establish the patterns of responses of both staff and students demographic variables with respect to the aggregate variables on gender and acquaintance rape. 0.05 was used as the level of significance. Table 4.7 shows a summary of chi- square tests of independence results between various students' demographic variables and aggregate students' perceptions of gender and acquaintance rape.

Table 4.7 Summary of chi-square test of independence results between various students' demographic variables and perceptions of gender and acquaintance rape

Variable	H_0	X^2	Df	Sig.	Significance
Gender	There is no difference in perceptions of gender and acquaintance rape between males and female students	2.427	4	.658	Not significant
Age	There is no difference in perceptions of gender and acquaintance rape between different student age ranges	17.528	12	.131	Not significant
Level at college	There is no difference in perceptions of gender and acquaintance rape by student's level at college	10.350	8	.241	Not significant
Resident status	There is no difference in perceptions of gender and acquaintance rape by students' resident status	4.444	4	.349	Not significant
Institution	There is no difference in perceptions of gender and acquaintance rape by student's institution	5.551	8	.697	Not significant

There was no difference in perceptions on gender and acquaintance rape: between male and female students $X^2(4, N = 45) = 2.427$, p = .658; by students' age range, $X^2(12, N = 45) = 17.528$, p = .131; by students' level at college, $X^2(8, N = 45) = 10.350$, p = .241; between resident and non-resident students, $X^2(4, N = 45) = 4.444$, p = .349; and by institution, $X^2(8, N = 45) = 5.551$, p = .697.

Table 4.8 shows a summary of chi-square test of independence results between various staff members' demographic variables and aggregate perceptions of gender and acquaintance rape.

Table 4.8 Summary of chi-square test of independence results between various staff members' demographic variables and aggregate perceptions of gender and acquaintance rape

Variable	H_0	X^2	df	Sig.	Significance
Gender	There is no difference in perceptions of gender and acquaintance rape between males and female staff members	3.770	3	.287	Not significant
Age	There is no difference in perceptions of gender and acquaintance rape by age of staff members	10.286	6	.113	Not significant
Experience	There is no difference in perceptions of gender and acquaintance rape between staff members of different working experiences	15.927	15	.387	Not significant
Institution	There is no difference in perceptions of gender and acquaintance rape by institution of staff member	4.582	6	.598	Not significant

There was no difference in the perceptions of gender and acquaintance rape: between male and female staff members, $X^2(3, N = 18) = 3.770$, p = .287; between staff members of different age ranges, $X^2(6, N = 18) = 10.286$, p = .113; by staff members' work experience, $X^2(15, N = 18) = 15.927$, p = .387; and between staff members working at different institutions, $X^2(6, N = 18) = 4.582$, p = .598.

The subsequent section presents participants' responses on open-ended questionnaire items on the influence of gender on students in higher education institutions' perceptions of acquaintance rape in Masvingo.

4.4.1 Participants' responses on gender and acquaintance rape

Just like on culture as a factor which affects students in higher education's perception on acquaintance rape, on gender, participants also came up with different views on the subject. Data from open-ended questionnaire items also confirmed that college administrators, non-academic staff and students had different perceptions of acquaintance rape on the effects of gender on students in higher education institutions in Masvingo. College administrators, non-academic staff and students who participated in this study seemed to suggest that gender plays different roles on students in higher education's perceptions of acquaintance rape.

4.4.1.1 College administrators' responses

College administrators in this book revealed that gender affects students in higher education's perceptions of acquaintance rape in Masvingo.

The following excerpts confirm the above:

> *Male ego and masculinity are advantageous on victim blaming* (**Principal 01**). *Society is patriarchal in nature hence males tend to force females especially acquaintances into sex* (**Vice Principal 03**).
> *Male acquaintance rapists are socially accepted and justified* (**Principal 02**).

4.4.1.2 Non-academic staff's responses

Non-academic staff in this study revealed that gender affects students in higher education's perceptions of acquaintance rape in Masvingo.

The following extracts confirm the above:

> *Males control females in sexual relationships giving them advantages over them* (**Disciplinary Chairperson 01**).

Male gender stereotyping perceives females as objects for sex, so when a female is raped by an acquaintance society sees it as a normal practice **(Disciplinary Chairperson 02).**

There is always territorial supremacy among men and women as such, force is always applied for men to get sex **(Disciplinary Chairperson 03).**

Males are socialised to believe that females should be passive recipients in sexual relationships **(Hostel wardens 03).**

Females' actions at times are suggestive for sex, so failure to have sex with them shows males' weaknesses **(Hostel warden 02).**

Some acquaintances force or threaten female victims resulting in acquaintances rape due to male gender stereotype **(Hostel warden 01).**

Males are aggressive for love and females are passive resistors in love and sexual relationships, that's why acquaintance rape is socially accepted and justified **(Assistant hostel warden 002).**

Males at times provide financial aid to females hence when raped by acquaintances they regard that as compensation for the aid provided **(Assistant hostel warden 003).**

Men are socially and culturally considered as bulls that can sleep around with women at will while women play a subservient role. The mass media highlights males as sexual athletes **(Assistant hostel warden 001).**

Male gender gets advantages in sexual relationships because African culture tends to give preferential treatment to males **(Nursing sister 01).**

Because of gender stereotyping, males are expected to initiate as well as force a sexual act hence acquaintance rape does not exist in African culture **(Nursing sister 03).**

According to African culture, females don't have sexual rights **(Nursing sister 02).**

4.4.1.3 Students' responses

Data from students' responses from open-ended questionnaire items also revealed that males are favoured in sexual relationships, thus gender affects students in higher education's perceptions of acquaintance rape in Masvingo.

The following extracts confirm the above:

Males have advantages over females in sexual relationships because African culture tends to favour males **(Student 001).**

Female acquaintance rape victims are labelled as such so that they are the ones who are blamed in cases of acquaintance rape **(Student 002).**

Males are the ones who are active in love affairs and practice more sexual activities hence their actions are justified even in love affairs **(Student 003).**

Culturally male are believed to have more power over the females **(Student 004).**

Society blames women or ladies if acquaintance rape occurs **(Student 005).**

African culture favours males at the expense of females **(Student 014).**

Males themselves feel that they are a dominant species hence they feel that they have the right to demand or force females for sex **(Student 007).**

Males have the power to ask for sex whenever they want it **(Student 008).**

Females have no right to decide for sexual intercourse **(Student 009).**

Culturally females are not allowed to display their feelings for sex **(Student 045).**

Males have been regarded by society as being superior and this cuts across all spheres of life **(Student 011).**

Males are the main perpetrators of acquaintance rape while females are the main victims **(Student 016).**

Male gender dominates in most spheres while females are always given negative labels especially in acquaintance rape cases **(Student 013).**

Males regard themselves as natural leaders, so they are above all things including customary and English-Dutch laws **(Student 017).**

Males are more powerful than women physically, that's why they overpower women even in sexual relationships **(Student 021).**

Males are more powerful than women physically, that's why they overpower women even in sexual relationships **(Student 034)**

The society is patriarchal in nature **(Student 036).**

Most males drink and smoke drugs and watch pornographic videos so they possess raping tactics so females can be easily raped by their acquaintances quite unaware **(Student 019).**

Having presented the college administrators, non-academic staff and students' responses to open-ended questionnaire items on how gender affects the perceptions of higher education students' perceptions of acquaintance rape in Masvingo. Thus, the following section presents how peer pressure influences the perceptions of higher education students' perception of acquaintance rape in Masvingo.

4.5 Peer Pressure and Acquaintance Rape

The third sub-research question posed in section 1.4.3 of chapter 1 examined the extent to which peer pressure affects the perceptions of students in higher education' perceptions of acquaintance rape in Masvingo. Table 4.9 presents the responses by staff and students on peer pressure and perceptions of acquaintance rape in Masvingo.

pressure and students' perceptions of acquaintance rape (N=63)

Aspects	Responses				
	SA	**A**	**N**	**D**	**S D**
1. Male peers w acquaintance e as a dating tics.	4(22.2%)	5(27.8%)	5(27.8%)	2(11.1%)	2(11.1%)
2. Acquaintance e is associated h college ctions.	6(33.3%)	4(22.2%)	2(11.1%)	3(16.7%)	3(16.7%)
3. Acquaintance e is associated h alcoholism.	2(11.1%)	6(33.3%)	5(27.8%)	2(11.1%)	3(16.7%)
4. Male and ale peers accept e myth.	4(22.2%)	5(27.8%)	4(22.2%)	2(11.1%)	2(11.1%)
5. Acquaintance e is a hidden ne due to peer ssure.	3(16.7%)	5(27.8%)	6(33.3%)	4(22.2%)	0(0%)
6. Patriarchal ctices normally ses acquaintance e.	6(33.3%)	8(44.4%)	3(16.7%)	3(16.7%)	1(5.6%)
7. Peer support powerful tool for rs' actions.	3(16.7%)	4(22.2%)	5(27.8%)	2(11.1%)	4(22.2%)
8. Perpetrators acquaintance rape	8(44.4%)	4(22.2%)	3(16.7%)	2(11.1%)	1(5.6%)

receive positive ratification.					
9. Acquaintance rape is quite rampant among adolescent peers.	6(33.3%)	7(38.9%)	2(11.1%)	4(22.2%)	29(11.1%)
10. Peers influence have positive attitudes towards acquaintance rape.	3(16.7%)	7(38.9%)	6(11.1%)	1(5.6%)	1(5.6%)
Total	**45(25%)**	**54(30%)**	**41(22.8%)**	**25(13.9%)**	**15(8.3%)**
26. Adolescents are very much interested in sex hence they indulge in acquaintance rape.	9(20.5%)	20(45.5%)	5(11.4%)	6(13.6%)	4(9.1%)
27. Rape culture is the main cause of acquaintance rape.	2(4.5%)	17(38.6%)	4(9.1%)	17(38.6%)	4(9.1%)
28. I learn about sex, dating, tactics from my peers.	5(11.4%)	12(27.3%)	5(11.4%)	11(25.0%)	11(25.0%)
29. Peers force their partners to have sex with them.	0(0%)	9(20.5%)	5(11.4%)	18(40.9%)	12(27.3%)
30. Peers are pressured to have	7(15.9%)	20(45.5%)	3(6.8%)	10(22.7%)	4(9.1%)

o as to be ted by others.						
1. Male and le peer groups ice rape culture.	5(11.4%)	11(25%)	5(11.4%)	15(36.4%)	7(15.9%)	4
2. Boys can be d to rape in to remain part e peer group.	3(6.8%)	16(36.4%)	2(4.5%)	13(29.5%)	10(22.7%)	4)
3 .Acquaintance is associated delinquent .	5(11.6%)	18(41.9%)	9(20.9%)	5(11.6%)	6(14%)	4
4.Male peer- ort is the main of intance rape	7(16.3%)	16(37.2%)	9(20.9%)	5(11.6%)	6(14.0%)	4
otal	**43(10.9%)**	**39(35.4%)**	**47(12%)**	**100(25.4%)**	**64(16.3%)**	**4**

Table 4.9 shows information at administrators and non-academic staff and participated students' level of contribution and findings on the influence of peer pressure on higher education students' perceptions of acquaintance rape. There was high internal consistency with regards to responses on perceptions of peer pressure and acquaintance rape as shown by the computed alpha values for both staff, (α = .646) and students (α = .899). As a result, the 10 question items for staff were aggregated into a single representative value. This was also done for the 9 question items for students.

Chi-square tests of independence were conducted to establish the patterns of responses of both staff and students' demographic variables with respect to the aggregate variables on peer pressure and acquaintance rape. 0.05 was used as the level of significance. Table 4.10 shows a summary of chi square tests of independence results between various students' demographic variables and aggregate students' perceptions of peer pressure and acquaintance rape.

Table 4.10 Summary of chi-square test of independence results between various students' demographic variables and perceptions of peer pressure and acquaintance rape

Variable	H_0	X^2	df	Sig.	Significance
Gender	There is no difference in perceptions of peer pressure and acquaintance rape between males and female students	6.561	4	.161	Not significant
Age	There is no difference in perceptions of peer pressure and acquaintance rape between different age ranges	25.470	12	.013	Significant
Level at college	There is no difference in perceptions of peer pressure and acquaintance	6.911	8	.546	Not significant

		X^2	df	Sig.	Significance
	rape by level at college				
Resident status	There is no difference in perceptions of peer pressure and acquaintance rape by resident status	3.829	4	.430	Not significant
Institution	There is no difference in perceptions of peer pressure and acquaintance rape by institution	8.458	8	.297	Not significant

There was significant difference in perceptions on peer pressure and acquaintance rape by students' age ranges, $X^2(12, N = 45) = 25.470$, p = .013. However, there was no difference in perceptions on peer pressure and acquaintance rape: between male and female students $X^2(4, N = 45) = 6.561$, p = .161; by students' level at college, $X^2(8, N = 45) = 6.911$, p = .546; between resident and non-resident students, $X^2(4, N = 45) = 3.829$, p = .430; and by institution, $X^2(8, N = 45) = 8.458$, p = .297.

Table 4.11 shows a summary of chi-square test of independence results between various staff .members' demographic variables and aggregate perceptions of peer pressure and acquaintance rape.

Table 4.11 Summary of chi-square test of independence results between various staff members' demographic variables and perceptions of peer pressure and acquaintance rape

Variable	H_0	X^2	df	Sig.	Significance
Gender	There is no difference in perceptions of peer pressure and acquaintance rape between males and female staff members	8.322	3	.040	Significant
Age	There is no difference in	8.229	6	.222	Not significant

	perceptions of peer pressure and acquaintance rape by age of staff members				
Experience	There is no difference in perceptions of peer pressure and acquaintance rape between staff members of different working experiences	14.150	15	.390	Not significant
Institution	There is no difference in perceptions of peer pressure and acquaintance rape by institution of staff member	6.300	6	.514	Not significant

There was significant difference in the perceptions of peer pressure and acquaintance rape between male and female staff members, $X^2(3, N = 18) = 8.322$, p $= .040$. On the other hand, there was no difference in the perceptions of peer pressure and acquaintance rape: between staff members of different age ranges, $X^2(6, N = 18) = 8.229$, p $= .222$; by staff members' work experience, $X^2(15, N = 18) = 14.150$, p $= .390$; and between staff members working at different institutions, $X^2(6, N = 18) = 6.300$, p $= .514$.

The subsequent section represents participants' responses to open-ended questionnaire items on the influence of peer pressure on students in higher education's perception of acquaintance rape.

4.5.1 Participants' responses on peer pressure and acquaintance rape

4.5.1.1 College administrators' responses

Peer pressure just like culture and gender was believed to have an effect on the perceptions of students in. Responses from college administrators from open-ended questionnaire items revealed that peer pressure has an effect on students in higher education's perceptions of acquaintance rape in Masvingo.

The following extracts confirm the above:

Peers fail to resist acquaintance rape due to peer pressure **(Principal 01).**

Victims fail to resist acquaintance rapists because they regard peers as acquaintances so to show that they accommodate them they do not resist them **(Vice Principal 03).** *Peers regard sexual activities as part of an interaction process* **(Principal 02).**

Copying and accepting actions and deeds of peers is part of traditional learning process **(Vice Principal 01).**

Peers cannot resist acquaintance rape because peer support is a powerful tool for peers' actions including acquaintance rape **(Principal 03).**

Perpetrators of acquaintance rape normally receive positive gratifications from their peers hence they regard acquaintance rapists as role models **(Vice Principal 03).**

4.5.1.2 Non-academic staff's responses

Like the administrators, non-academic staff's responses from open-ended questionnaire items also revealed that peer pressure affects higher education student's perceptions of acquaintance rape in Masvingo. The following extracts confirm the above:

Peers fail to resist acquaintance rapists due to peer pressure **(Hostel Warden 01).**

Peers fail to resist acquaintance rapists due to fear of rejection **(Assistant Hostel Warden 02).**

Peers fail to resist acquaintance rapists because they need to be accepted by the peer group **(Hostel Warden 03).**

Peers fail to resist acquaintance rapists because they would be under the influence of drugs and alcohol **(Assistant Hostel Warden 003)**

Peers regard acquaintance rape as a sexual activity which is socially accepted and justified **(Hostel Warden 03).**

Peers simply just find themselves in it **(Assistant Hostel Warden 001).**

Peers fail to resist acquaintance rape due to peer pressure **(Nursing Sister 01).**

Peers fail to resist acquaintance rapists due to fear of rejection **(Assistant Hostel Warden 02).**

Peers fear to be discriminated by their peers **(Nursing Sister 03).**

Peers fail to resist acquaintance rape because they view it as part of college life **(Disciplinary Chairperson 01).**

Peers don't want to be regarded as failures or too primitive **(Disciplinary Chairperson 02).**

Because they get financial and assistance in their academic studies from peers **(Disciplinary Chairperson 03).**

4.5.1.3 Students' responses

Like administrators and non-academic staff, students' responses from open-ended questionnaire items in this study also revealed that peer pressure has an influence on higher education students' perceptions of acquaintance rape in Masvingo.

The following extract confirms the above:

Peers fail to resist acquaintance rapists because peers want to remain part of the peer group as well as to be socially accepted **(Student 002).**

Because it seems to them as a normative behaviour amongst significant others, so they cannot resist it- **(Student 027).**

Because of peer pressure **(Student 003).**

Lack of knowledge on dating tactics **(Student 004).**

Peers commit acquaintance rape due to drug abuse **(Student 006).**

Peers will see you as having a weakness and it will be hard to remain as part of the peer group **(Student 013).**

Because they are afraid of being referred to as loose by members of the peer group **(Student 022).**

They are afraid of losing their peer group membership if they resist it **(Student 028).**

They are shy to report assailants and perpetrators of acquaintance rape **(Student 012).**

They are afraid of rejecting and regarding acquaintance rape as bad among peers **(Student 011).** *They are scared that they will be laughed at by their peers* **(Student 045).**

They fear to be regarded as naïve **(Student 03).**

They are interested in it **(Student 036).**

They didn't want to be laughed at by their peers **(Student 039).** *They fear to be isolated by peers* **(Student 017).**

They think it is part of peer group members' sexual benefits **(Student 021).** *To protect their relationships* **(Student 03).**

They avoid being labelled as social outcasts of the group **(Student 019).**

The subsequent section presents the findings of this study on the effects of policy, legislation or law on students in higher education's perceptions of acquaintance rape in Masvingo province.

4.6 Policy, Legislation or Law and Acquaintance Rape

The fourth sub-section question posed in section 1.4.4 of chapter 1 examined the extent to which policy, legislation or law affects the perceptions of students in higher education institutions' perception of acquaintance rape in Masvingo. Table 4.12 presents the responses by staff and students on peer pressure and perceptions of acquaintance rape in Masvingo.

Policy, legislation or law and students' perceptions of acquaintance rape (N=63)

Aspects	Responses				
	SA	A	N	D	SD
1. Students in higher education do not know the law of consent.	4(22.2%)	6(33.3%)	4(22.2%)	2(11.1%)	2(11.1%)
2. There are no policies, regulations or laws in institutions of higher learning guiding ' sexual behaviour.	3(16.7%)	6(33.3%)	1(5.6%)	3(16.7%)	5(27.8%)
3. College administrators do not consider acquaintance rape as a serious crime.	1(5.6%)	4(22.2%)	1(5.6%)	7(38.9%)	5(27.8%)
4. Interference between traditional and modern laws causes confusion to understand ance rape.	1(5.6%)	4(22.2%)	1(5.6%)	3(16.7%)	9(50%)
5. Administrators favour male perpetrators of acquaintance rape.	1(5.6%)	4(22.2%)	1(5.6%)	7(38.9%)	5(27.8%)
6. Law of sexual consent is also subjective in nature.	2(11.1%)	6(33.3%)	2(11.1%)	6(33.3%)	2(11.1%)
7. Acquaintance rape victims do not have faith with the justice system.	2(11.1%)	7(38.9%)	4(22.2%)	2(11.1%)	3(16.7%)
8. Forced sex by male acquaintances is tolerated among Africans.	5(27.8%)	5(27.8%)	1(5.6%)	3(16.7%)	3(16.7%)
9. Victims and perpetrators of acquaintance rape have limited knowledge on the city of the crime	1(5.6%)	7(38.9%)	3(16.7%)	3(16.7%)	3(16.7%)
10. Courts tend to try victims of acquaintance rape instead of perpetrators.	2(11.1%)	7(38.9%)	1(5.6%)	3(16.7%)	5(27.8)
Total	22(12.2%)	56(31.1%)	19(10.6%)	39(21.7%)	42(23.3%)
36. There are no policies, legislation or laws which protect rape victims.	0(0%)	1(2.2%)	0(0%)	18(40%)	26(57.8%)
37. College administrators perceive acquaintance rape as a petty crime.	8(18.2%)	12(27.3%)	3(6.8%	15(34.1%)	6(13.6%)
38. College administrators, security guards and even the police are not interested in with acquaintance rape cases	3(6.8%)	15(34.1%)	1(2.3%)	14(31.8%)	11(25%)
39. Police officers, college administrators tend to favour male perpetrators of ance rape.	3(6.8%)	12(27.3%)	3(6.8%)	14(31.8%)	12(27.3%)
40. Laws of the country give license to male rapists of acquaintance rape.	9(20.5%)	10(22.7%)	4(9.1%)	13(29.5%)	8(18.2%)

sex by males both strangers and acquaintances is tolerated within the context ...ips in Zimbabwe.	3(7.0%)	6(14.0%)	3(7.0%)	15(34.9%)	16(37.2%)	)
of acquaintance rape have limited knowledge on the authenticity of the	16(36.4%)	16(36.4%)	3(6.8%)	3(6.8%)	6(13.6%)	
of acquaintance rape are vulnerable to both societal and institutional blame.	7(16.3%)	9(20.9%)	2(4.7%)	15(34.9%)	10(23.3%)	)
...tance rape is difficult to understand.	8(17.8%)	14(31.1%)	4(8.9%)	10(22.2%)	9(20%)	)
	85(17, 5%)	**130(26,7%**	**44(9, 0%)**	**124(25, 9%)**	**104(21, 4%)**	**487(10**

Table 4.12 shows information at administrators and non-academic staff and participated students' level of contribution and findings on the perceptions of policy, law or legislation and acquaintance rape. There was high internal consistency with regards to responses on perceptions of policy, law or legislation and acquaintance rape as shown by the computed alpha values for both staff, (α = .755) and students (α = .634). As a result, the 10 question items for staff were aggregated into a single representative value. This was also done for the 9 question items for students.

Table 4.13 Summary of chi-square test of independence results between various students' demographic variables and perceptions of policy, law or legislation and acquaintance rape

Variable	H_0	X^2	Df	Sig.	Significance
Gender	There is no difference in perceptions of participants on policy, law and legislation and acquaintance rape between male and female students	17.597	3	< .001	Significant
Age	There is no difference in perceptions of participants on policy, law and legislation and acquaintance rape between different age ranges	17.192	9	.036	Significant
Level at college	There is no difference in perceptions of participants on policy, law and legislation and acquaintance rape by level at college	3.238	6	.778	Not significant
Resident status	There is no difference in perceptions of participants on policy, law and legislation and acquaintance rape by resident status	1.304	3	.728	Not significant
Institution	There is no difference in perceptions of participants on policy, law and legislation and acquaintance rape by institution	6.805	6	.339	Not significant

Source: Tafirei, 2023

Chi-square tests of independence were conducted to establish the patterns of responses of both staff and students' demographic variables with respect to the aggregate variables on policy, law or legislation and acquaintance rape. 0.05 was used as the level of significance. Table 4.13 shows a summary of chi square tests of independence results between various students' demographic variables and aggregate students' perceptions of policy, law or legislation and acquaintance rape.

There was significant difference in perceptions on policy, law or legislation and acquaintance rape: between male and female students $X^2(3, N = 45) = 17.597, p < .001$; by students' age ranges, $X^2(9, N = 45) = 17.192, p = .036$. However, there was no difference in perceptions on policy, law or legislation and acquaintance rape: by students' level at college, $X^2(6, N = 45) = 3.238, p = .778$; between resident and non-resident students, $X^2(3, N = 45) = 1.034, p = .728$; and by institution, $X^2(6, N = 45) = 6.805, p = .339$.

Table 4.14 Summary of chi-square test of independence results between various staff members' demographic variables and perceptions of policy, law or legislation and acquaintance rape

Variable	H_0	X^2	df	Sig.	Significance
Gender	There is no difference in perceptions of policy, legislation and acquaintance rape between male and female staff members	5.283	3	.152	Not significant
Age	There is no difference in perceptions of policy, legislation and acquaintance rape by age of staff members	9.771	6	.135	Not significant
Experience	There is no difference in perceptions of policy, legislation	16.133	15	.373	Not significant

	and acquaintance rape between staff members of different working experiences				
Institution	There is no difference in perceptions of policy, legislation and acquaintance rape by institution of staff member	7.467	6	.280	Not significant

Table 4.14 shows a summary of chi-square test of independence results between various staff members' demographic variables and aggregate perceptions of policy, law or legislation and acquaintance rape. There was no difference in the perceptions of policy, law or legislation and acquaintance rape: between male and female staff members, $X^2(3, N = 18) = 5.283$, p = .152; between staff members of different age ranges, $X^2 (6, N = 18) = 9.771$, p = .135; by staff members' work experience, $X^2(15, N = 18) = 16.133$, p = .373; and between staff members working at different institutions, $X^2(6, N = 1 8) = 7.467$, p = .280.

The following section represents the participants' responses to open-ended questionnaire items on the influence of policy, legislation or law on acquaintance rape in Masvingo.

4.6.1 Participants' responses on policy, legislation or law on acquaintance rape

4.6.1.1 College administrators' responses

College administrators in this study perceived policy, legislation or law as having an influence towards acquaintance rape.

The following excerpts confirm the above:

College administrators and the police have negative attitudes towards acquaintance rape because in institutions of higher education there are no policies, regulations or laws governing sexual relationships **(Principal 01).**

College and university administrators, security guards and police officers do not consider acquaintance rape to be a serious crime **(Vice Principal 03).**

The interference between traditional laws and modern laws makes it difficult for college administrators and campus police officers to deal with acquaintance rape cases **(Principal 02).**

Acquaintance rape victims have no faith in the justice system hence they see it as unnecessary to report their assailants **(Vice Principal 02).**

Forced sex by male acquaintances is tolerated among Africans hence acquaintance rape is not taken as a serious sexual offense **(Principal 03).**

Courts tend to try victims of acquaintance rape instead of perpetrators hence victims are afraid to report their assailants **(Vice-Principal 01).**

4.6.1.2 Non-academic staff

Like administrators, non-academic staff in this study also revealed that policy, legislation or law has effects on higher education students' perceptions of acquaintance rape in Masvingo.

The following extracts confirm the above:

College administrators and the police have negative attitudes towards acquaintance rape because acquaintance rape is a tricky issue to handle **(Hostel Warden 01).**

There are no policies, regulations or laws governing sexual relations in institutions of higher learning **(Hostel Warden 03).**

College and university administrators also lack knowledge on the existence of policies, regulations and laws governing sexual relationships **(Assistant Hostel Warden 002).**

College administrators do not know the application of sexual policies, regulations and laws due to cultural erosion **(Hostel Warden 02).**

Rape laws tend to favour acquaintance rape perpetrators **(Assistant Hostel Warden 001).**

Sexual crimes are not clearly defined according to African culture **(Assistant Hostel Warden 003).**

Law of consent does not apply in sexual relationships among Africans, so it is difficult to differentiate acquaintance rape from consented sex **(Nursing Sister 01).**

Institutions of higher education do not have policies, regulations or laws governing sexual relationships **(Nursing Sister 02).**

Perpetrators, victims of acquaintance rape, college and university administrators have no faith in the justice system **(Nursing Sister 03).**

It is because men have negative attitudes towards acquaintance rapists that's why acquaintance rape cases are not reported **(Disciplinary Chairperson 01).**

Most cases are not reported because there are no policies, regulations and laws governing acquaintance rape cases **(Disciplinary Chairpersons 02).**

4.6.1.3 Students' responses

Like non-academic staff, students in this study's responses from open-ended questionnaire items also revealed that policy, legislation or law affects students in higher education's perceptions of acquaintance rape in Masvingo.

The following extract confirms the above:

College administrators and the police have negative attitudes towards acquaintance rape **(Student 021).**

College administrators have negative attitudes towards acquaintance rape because norms contradict modern laws **(Student 017).**

There is interference between traditional and modern laws **(Student 039).**

Most college ladies are a prostitute, that's why they tend to ignore acquaintance rapists **(Student 036).**

College administrators have negative attitudes to protect their institutions' regulations **(Student 038).**

College administrators regard it as a petty crime **(Student 045).**

College administrators regard it as a misunderstanding between partners **(Student 011).**

Administrators see it as a thing which is non- existent among college students **(Student 012).**

Victims of acquaintance rape have limited knowledge on the crime **(Student 028).**

College administrators and police officers belong to the same culture, so they don't see any harm or sin in acquaintance rape **(Student 022).**

They see it as a way of disturbing students' sexual relationships **(Student 008).** *Lack of evidence may lead to negative attitudes* **(Student 007).**

College administrators blame acquaintance rape victims instead of acquaintance rape assailants **(Student 004).**

They regard it as a petty crime and assume that the victims have consented to sex **(Student 003).**

They want to protect the image of their institutions **(Student 004).**

They think that both the perpetrator and the victim are to blame **(Student 006).**

They view students as adults therefore they are said to be responsible for their behaviour **(Student 007).**

They promote victims' dignity **(Student 027).**

They think both perpetrators and victims are to blame **(Student 036).**

They see it as negligent behaviour on the part of the victim **(Student 019)**

The next section presents the findings.

4.7 Discussion of Findings

This book focused on the factors affecting perceptions of students in higher education's perceptions of acquaintance rape in Masvingo. In this section, the findings were discussed under four subheadings derived from sub-research questions 1.4 of Chapter 1 that guided this book. The subheadings are culture and acquaintance rape; gender and acquaintance rape; peer pressure and acquaintance rape; policy, legislation or law and acquaintance rape. The findings of this study were discussed in relation to both local and international literature.

The following sub-headings below discuss the views of college administrators, non-academic staff, and students on how culture affects students in higher education's perceptions of acquaintance rape in Masvingo.

4.7.1 The influence of culture on acquaintance rape

This discussion focused on the views of college administrators, non-academic staff and students on the factors affecting students in higher education's perceptions of acquaintance rape in Masvingo as indicated by the findings of this study. This section addressed the sub-research question posed in section 1.4.1 of Chapter 1 which reads: To what extent does culture affect students in higher education institutions' perceptions of acquaintance rape in Masvingo? Reference is made in the present book to international, regional and sub-Saharan African literature available on the factors affecting perceptions of higher education students' perceptions of acquaintance rape in Masvingo.

It emerged from this book that culture has an influence on the perceptions of students in higher education institutions' perceptions of acquaintance rape in Masvingo. For example, culturally, victims of acquaintance rape are blamed. College authorities, non-academic staff and students who participated in this book viewed society as having a tendency of victim blaming because of cultural reasons. The finding that victims, perpetrators and society at large have a culture of victim blaming in acquaintance rape cases concurs with the research by Mediterranean institute of Gender Studies (MIGS (2008:11) in Cyprus, Greece, Latvia, Lithuania and Malta which revealed that society blames victims of acquaintance rape instead of the assailants. The finding that society blames acquaintance rape victims is in line with Bandura's social learning theory which informed this book and which states that learning takes place within the social context. Victim blaming is the product of social learning. Social learning theory examines the process of socialisation through which sexual abuse, sexual harassment and acquaintance rape become inextricably linked and this explains males' treatment of females through cultural sexual scripts, values, norms, folkways, attitudes, gender roles and rape myths.

The study further revealed that students in institutions of higher education perceived acquaintance rape as a private issue and not an issue for public consumption. Members of society normally do not want to discuss their sexual experiences or encounters with other individuals. The above finding that students in institutions of higher education perceived acquaintance rape as a private issue and not an issue for public consumption concurs with Date Rape Cases among Young Women: Strategies for Support and Prevention's (2008:11) study that revealed that in Cyprus there is a perception that acquaintance rape is a private issue. The finding is also in line with social learning that acquaintance rape assailants learn raping tactics through socialisation, values, taboos, common thoughts and common practices in private places.

This book established that sexual issues, besides being private in nature, are generally treated as taboo and females are expected to be passive in romantic and sexual relationships and that men should not control their sexual desires is in line with Gravelin *et al.*'s (2019:16) study finding that men associate love with sexual aggression. Society perceives acquaintance rape and sexual relationships as taboo hence sexual acts and sexual intercourse are treated as private issues. The finding of this study that sexual issues are treated as taboo, and females are expected to be passive in sexual relationships are also in line with the social learning theory which guides this study because individuals develop perceptions of appropriate sexual behaviour by learning from society and social groups such as peers.

The finding of this book that aggression among boys during sexual activity is natural and normal and that girls and ladies are taught by the society to be sexually passive is a product of social learning. The finding of this book on sexual aggression among boys and passiveness of girls during sexual activity concurs with Johnson and Johnson's (2017:2) book in the United States, Dixie (2017:44) in America and Gravelin *et al.* (2019:13) in the United States which revealed that aggressive behaviour among boys and men is natural and normal and girls and ladies are taught by the society to be passive. College authorities and non-academic staff who participated in this book seemed to perceive love, dating and sex as associated with aggression hence students in institutions of higher education apply sexual aggression on their acquaintances. Johnson and Johnson's (2017:2) book finding on boys' aggression and girls' passiveness are also in line with Bandura's (1978:12) social learning theory which is a lens which guided the present book. Society's teachings on the normalisation of acquaintance rape have normalized the act. International literature from the United States (Harsey & Freyd, 2020:4; Dixie, 2017:41; Gravelin *et al.*, 2019:4; Johnson & Johnson, 2017:1), South Africa and Latin America (World Health Organization, 2017:4; Hungary, 2019:1) supported the notion that acquaintance rape and sexual aggression are products of social learning.

The other finding of this book that society does not blame acquaintance rape as a social vice but regards it as a normal dating practice concurs with the American Association of University Women: Police Documents and Reports' (2015:371) book in America which established that acquaintance rape is normalised due to both its high prevalence and cultural disposition towards sexuality and sexual relationships. College authorities, non-academic staff and students who participated in this book do not blame acquaintance rape because, according to African cultural dating practices, there is no sexual consent. It is the responsibility of the female partner to defend her territory. If she fails to defend her territory, then she is labelled a prostitute. Cultural norms also teach women to be submissive and passive and speaking against male advancement may also be looked down. .

The finding of this study that acquaintance rape is blurred to such an extent that a "no", according to African culture means a "yes" concurs with studies by Gravelin *et al.* (2019:1) in America and Right To Be Free From Rape (2018:12) in the United States which affirmed that acquaintance rape is complicated because consent in sexual relationships is not easy to define. An acquaintance rape victim's verbally saying "no" is subject to interpretation in a court of law, hence it is common for defence lawyers to inform the jury that "no" does not always mean "no" to lovers, and it can sometimes be interpreted as a "maybe", also interpreted as a token resistance. The above finding is in line with social learning theory which happened to be a pillar anchoring the present book. Robinson, Gibson Beverly and Schwartz (2004:44) propound that the socialisation process affects human interaction has contradictory perceptions of women. Societal practices and common thoughts have a bearing on students' perceptions of acquaintance rape because sexual consent, according to African culture, is also ambiguous in nature.

It emerged from this book that African culture tends to favour males hence it gives male perpetrators advantages over females, that is why most victims of acquaintance rape are females and most perpetrators are males. It originates from patriarchy which holds that males are natural leaders and females are followers; so, men lead in sexual activities as well. This finding that culture tends to favour males contradicts Zeira *et al.*'s (2002:152) book finding in their survey which they conducted using samples from Jewish and Arab public high schools which revealed that Jewish and Arab girls' sexuality as compared to that of boys is highly valued. In Jewish and Arab societies females are valued more than males. Jewish and Arab societies regard acquaintance rape as a social vice.

The finding that acquaintance rape is justifiable within cultural levels concurs with Johnson and Johnson's (2019:14) study in the United States which revealed that acquaintance rape is socially viewed as an extreme form of sanctioned male-female sexual interaction. This study's finding that acquaintance rape is justifiable within cultural levels is also in line with societal beliefs, language, societal values, common thoughts and common practices within the cultural context. The other finding of this study that college administrative staff, non-academic staff and students believe that acquaintance rape is influenced by acquaintance rape myth acceptance concurs with Mittal *et al.*'s (2017:1)'s findings in India that culturally, males as compared to females, hold lesser acquaintance rape myth acceptance but have more negative attitudes towards victims of acquaintance rape. Culturally, acquaintance rape in marriages is commonly perceived as the gateway to continuous and lifelong sexual access by a sexual partner. On the other hand, the finding of this study that college administrators, non-academic staff and students believe that acquaintance rape is influenced by acquaintance rape myth acceptance contradicts Vandiver and Duplo's (2012:1) study in South Western United States which established that the majority of participants in their study did not believe in rape myth acceptance, hence they did not have negative perceptions towards acquaintance rape. Participants in Vandiver and Duplo's (2012:1) study view acquaintance rape as a social evil.

The finding that acquaintance rape is not influenced by culture but by other variables such as tribe, residential area and level of education contradicts Odu and Olusegun's (2012:10) study in Nigeria (an African country) which revealed that acquaintance rape is a product of culture. Human beings' actions, thoughts, behaviour and perceptions of acquaintance rape are acquired through social learning. Both victims and perpetrators of acquaintance rape believe and practice standards, principles, perspectives as well as interpret acquaintance rape based on their cultural backgrounds and experiences.

The other finding of this study that victims and perpetrators of acquaintance rape practice a culture of silence by not divulging what would have happened concurs with Gravelin *et al.*'s (2019:15) study in the United States which revealed that perpetrators and assailants of acquaintance rape practice the norm of silencing victims, particularly in cultures where acquaintance myth are promoted and accepted. Victims of acquaintance rape keep quiet to preserve their dignity. Even members of the society also encourage victims of acquaintance rape to keep quiet in order not only to preserve their dignity but also not divulge that society is evil. Victims end up questioning themselves about their behaviour as well as wondering if their sexual encounters were rape or not. A culture of silence is observed by both offenders and perpetrators of acquaintance rape. This culture of silence is also a product of social learning theory among Africans, Asians and Europeans who happen to be most participants in the recorded studies in this study. Many perpetrators of acquaintance rape commit the crime as a function of living in a society that excuses or encourages sexual exploitation of women. Culturally, it is common knowledge and practice for individuals to believe that women are generally men's sexual objects.

Statistical evidence revealed that college administrators and non-academic staff are of the opinion that culture plays a role on students in higher education institutions' perceptions of acquaintance rape in Masvingo. Thus, college administrators and non-academic staff's perceptions differ with students' opinions which indicated that culture does not play a role.

The discrepancies in opinions from participants of this study could be emanating from the differences between the two research approaches adapted in the study. Results from the quantitative approach are objective while those from the qualitative approach are subjective and flexible giving participants' room for expressing different opinions.

The subsequent sub-section discusses the extent to which gender affects the perceptions of students in higher education institutions' perceptions of acquaintance rape in Masvingo as revealed by this book.

4.7.2 The influence of gender on acquaintance rape

This sub-section discusses the effects of gender on the perceptions of higher education students' perception of acquaintance rape in Masvingo as revealed by the findings of this study. In this discussion, reference is made to the available literature on the effects of gender on higher education students' perception of acquaintance rape in Masvingo. The sub-section addresses the sub-research question in section 1.4.2 in chapter 1 which reads: To what extent does gender influence students in higher education institutions' perceptions of acquaintance rape in Masvingo?

It was established from this study that gender has an effect on higher education students' perceptions of acquaintance rape. College administrators, non-academic staff and students' responses revealed that gender has a bearing on higher education students' perception of acquaintance rape. The above finding that gender has an effect on higher education students' perceptions of acquaintance rape in Masvingo concurs with Okeke's (2011:39) research in Nigeria, Dixie (2017:43) in the United States, Cotter and Savage (2019:30) in the United States, Walker et al (2019:5) in Australia, Gravelin *et al.* (2019:2) in the United States which revealed that gender differences emanate from gendered ideology of male dominance over females. Males unlike females perceive more situations as being sexually or potentially sexually accommodative hence they view acquaintance rape or sexual harassment as being normal and appropriate for courtship. Responses from all participants in this study also revealed that in Masvingo, acquaintance rape is socially accepted and justified especially by males who tend to look down upon females; hence, gender affects participants' perceptions towards acquaintance rape. The above finding is also in line with social learning theory since women victims of acquaintance rape are perceived as sexual objects whose main function in the society is to satisfy men's needs such that in certain situations, acquaintance rape or sexual coercion is seen as normal and acceptable by members of the society. In social set ups, because of gender differences, people have different perceptions towards acquaintance rape.

This study revealed that college administrators, non-academic staff and students in Masvingo perceived that when females limit their sexual inclinations, they would be able to avoid sexual abuse from their acquaintances because perpetrators of acquaintance rape would not have varied perceptions of victims' actions and expectations. If victims are positively inclined to their male acquaintances, those male acquaintances might misconstrue the inclination and interpret it as a sexual relationship which would have developed non-verbally. Acquaintance rape assailants would perceive the sexual encounter as a social technique of dating hence would also justify their sexual encounters. In most cultures, males commit acquaintance rape unaware of the fact that there is rape among acquaintances if there is no sexual consent. This study's finding of limiting females' sexual inclination is in line with social learning theory.

This study's finding that males dominate in social, political and economic spheres which is the reason why they dominate in sexual relationships concurs with Oshiname *et al.*'s (2013:137) study in Nigeria, Hester and Lilley's (2018:175) study in Canada and Okeke's (2011:39) study in Nigeria. The study found that males who revealed gender dominance in sexual matters were influenced by gender, perceptions and attitudes which promote females' differences to males in decisions on sexual matters and that accounts for why the males have negative attitudes towards acquaintance rape. The males' social, political and economic dominance enable them to perceive females as not having sexual consent hence they fall prey to acquaintance rape. Whatever actions or sexual encounters males perform on females, they would perceive it as having been done in good faith, which is the reason why they perceive acquaintance rape as part of males' sexual rights guaranteed by society. The finding of this study that the male gender dominates in social, political and economic spheres of life and is the reason why it dominates in sexual relationships is also in line with Bandura's social learning theory which guided this study, which states that individuals learn through active, direct and indirect learning as they interact and socialise with each other and this applies to how victims and perpetrators of acquaintance rape learn and perceive acquaintance rape tactics.

The finding of this study that ladies' first experiences are associated with acquaintance rape concurs with Ben-David and

Schneider's (2005:385) study in Israel which revealed that punishment given to a sexual partner or neighbour is less as compared to that of a stranger.

This study also established that acquaintance rape victims do not acknowledge rape by an acquaintance as rape and this concurs with the following studies: Oshinmae, *et al.* (2013:146) in Nigeria, Mittal *et al.* (2017:2) in India and Gravelin *et al.* (2019:6) in the United States. Most ladies, if not all, find it hard to consent to sex during their first sexual encounters hence they become victims of acquaintance rape. Since females cannot consent to sex on their first sexual encounter, they do not define their encounters as rape. They can define a sexual experience as rape if perpetrated by strangers. Female victims also do not perceive acquaintance rape experiences as rape. The finding of this study that victims of acquaintance rape do not acknowledge their experiences as rape is also in line with Bandura's social learning theory. Bandura's social learning theory which informed this study states that individuals' perceptions and attitudes are linked to their learning experiences in the environment and that the way individuals perceive variables determines their actions and perceptions of acquaintance rape. Males and females are given different orientations towards love and sexual relationships; hence they have different perceptions of acquaintance rape.

The finding that sex-role stereotyping influences perpetrators and victims of acquaintance rape to have wrong or negative perceptions about women victims of acquaintance rape concurs with Gravelin *et al.*'s (2019:6) study in America which revealed that females in their sex-role stereotyping groups feel that acquaintance rape victims would have given the perpetrator the room to do so. Sex-role stereotyping influences the females to have wrong perceptions towards women victims of acquaintance rape. From a gender perspective, females are seen as fuelling acquaintance rape hence society seems to have a negative perception of victims of acquaintance rape. Societies also perceive that victims of acquaintance rape would have led the man on and blame them after the acquaintance rape experience. The perception of having led the man on gives both the assailant and the victim the wrong impression about their intentions.

The finding that the male gender blames victims of acquaintance rape more than the female gender concurs with Xenos and Smith's (2001:1103) study in Australia which found that males were more blaming of acquaintance rape victims than females. It is from common societal knowledge and practice that gender wise, in sexual assaults and acquaintance rape, females are blamed. Even if the female victim reports acquaintance rape to significant others, she is blamed for initiating a rape. In most social institutions, males are likely to engage in acquaintance rape since they have negative attitudes towards women due to social learning. David and Lee's (1996:788) study in America also noted similar gender differences in perceptions of acquaintance rape that males in America, unlike females, are blamed targets of acquaintance rape and sexual harassment.

The other finding that males unlike females perceive more situations as sexually or potentially sexually accommodative concurs with Okeke (2011:39) study in Nigeria which established that males unlike females perceive acquaintance rape as being normal. College administrators, non-academic staff and students who participated in this study perceived acquaintance rape as being normal and did not see the evil in it since it is regarded as a common practice in human beings' dating and courtship practices. Males can indulge in acquaintance rape due to other factors beyond the scope of this study such as biological factors.

McCabe *et al.*'s (2009:252) study in America in support of the above finding, found that males think about sex between every 6 to 15 seconds on average. Sex is regarded as important to male gender and is perceived as a reflection of their masculinity by both genders in the society. If the male gender does not express any desire for sex, it becomes a societal concern hence acquaintance rape is perceived normal within the social context.

Gender differences emanate from social learning theory (Bandura, 1987) which acted as a research lenses in the present study. Individuals develop attitudes through interaction. Attitudes, just like perceptions, can be viewed as feelings of different variables which cannot be balanced with reasoning hence perceptions also cannot be balanced with reasoning. In social learning, there are also variables like social values, beliefs, languages, norms, folkways, common thoughts and common practices and these cannot be balanced with reasoning just like male gender's negative attitudes of acquaintance rape.

The finding that males are socially and culturally considered as bulls who can sleep around with women concurs with Johnson and Johnson's (2017:4) study in the United States which revealed that men believe that women are merely sexual objects for men's pleasure.

Participants in this study, from a gender perspective, seemed to view females as sex objects hence they view every woman as men's potential lover. Culturally, society perceives males to be sexually active and females to play subservient roles. If males fail to play leading roles in sexual relationships, it would be regarded as a social problem.

It emerged from this study that females' actions at times are suggestive of sex, so if the perpetrator misconstrue, this will lead to acquaintance rape without the perpetrator's knowledge. According to gender stereotypes and prejudices, failure to have sex with the victim in the full knowledge of the perpetrator shows his/her weaknesses. International literature by Sampson's study (2002:12) in the United States, Sleath and Bull (2017:1) in the United Kingdom, Date Rape Cases Among Young Women: Strategies for Support and Prevention (2008:12) in Canada, Australia, New Zealand, the Netherlands and Scandinavia also support the current study that when individuals, perpetrators and victims interact, they classify their experiences, encode or decode situations and as such can end up indulging in acquaintance rape. College authorities, non-academic staff and students from Masvingo who participated in this study viewed acquaintance rape as a product of misinterpreting their experiences, mis-encoding and miss-decoding of situations. Love, sex, forced sex and rape cannot be simply differentiated since they are common practices when it comes to expressing love, hence both victims and assailants of acquaintance rape would not differentiate love from acquaintance rape. All participants in this study seemed to perceive victims of acquaintance rape as real perpetrators of acquaintance rape.

The finding of this study that women should consent to sex contradicts international literature by Russo (2000:3) in the United States which states that young women are inclined to perceive sexual coercion in acquaintance sexual relationships as acceptable behaviour. Both male victims and male perpetrators perceive acquaintance rape as a product of perpetrators' misconception of love and dating tactics. The responses from college administrators, non-academic staff and students in this study that both male victims and male perpetrators perceive acquaintance rape as a product of perpetrators' misconception of situations concurs with Edwoldt et al.'s (2000:808) study which revealed the belief that a women's sexual consent is derived automatically from an intimate heterosexual relationship. International literature in the United States by Russo

(2000:3) also has supported the idea that young men would force sexual intercourse if they knew they would not be caught, and a substantial minority admitted to having committed sexual violence. According to the findings of this study, the perception that women should consent to sex is against traditional customary law as has been alluded to and supported by both local and international literature.

The finding that males are the main perpetrators and females are the main victims of acquaintance rape contradicts the international literature from Israel (Ziera *et al.*, 2002:161) which alluded that more boys than girls are victims of acquaintance rape. Reviewed international literature from Israel and other parts of the world revealed that boys unlike girls are now more vulnerable to acquaintance rape from both male and female acquaintance rapists. Female assailants of acquaintance rape, since they are not blamed for it, take it as an advantage to rape their acquaintances. Males are the main perpetrators of acquaintance rape and practice more sexual activities and their actions are justified by members of the society. In love affairs, females are the main victims of acquaintance rape. This contradiction in findings between this study and former studies could be due to gender differences, values, beliefs, common thoughts, common practices and age. On the other hand, the finding that most perpetrators of acquaintance rape are males, and most victims are females concurs with Tade and Udechukwu's (2020:3) study in Nigeria which found out that sexual violence and acquaintance rape among girls and ladies is quite rampant in Nigeria and some other parts of Africa. In Africa and the world over, girls and women are mostly abused by their acquaintances especially if they are young.

In Canada, Conroy and Cotter's (2017:3) study revealed that acquaintance rape is higher among 15-to-24year-old females (15%) and males (11%) than any other age-group. As age increases, the risk of victimisation decreases, with Canadians aged 65 years and older having a much lower risk of victimisation than those who are younger. Most males also drink and smoke drugs and even watch pornographic videos so they possess raping tactics and so females can be easily raped by their acquaintances quite unawares. That is the main reason why both perpetrators and victims perceive acquaintance rape as a normal dating practice.

Quantitatively, participants disagreed on the role of gender with regards to perceptions on acquaintance rape. College administrators and non-academic staff, on one hand thought that gender does not play a role while students on the other hand felt that gender plays a role. This difference in opinion could have attributed differences in age groups and life experiences.

The discrepancies in the quantitative and qualitative results might also be due to the fact that quantitative results were scientifically generated whereas qualitative results were subjectively generated.

The subsequent sub-section discusses the extent to which peer pressure affects the perceptions of students in higher education institutions on acquaintance rape as revealed by the findings of this study.

4.7.3 The influence of peer pressure on acquaintance rape

This discussion investigated the effects of peer pressure in part, on the perceptions of acquaintance rape in higher education students in Masvingo. In this sub-section the findings from this book were discussed under the sub-research question posed in section 1.4.3 of chapter 1 which reads: How does peer pressure influence acquaintance rape to students in higher education institutions?

It emerged from this book that students fail to resist acquaintance rape due to peer pressure. Some of the participants in the present book seemed to believe that peer pressure is a factor which influences acquaintance rape. The finding that peer pressure affects acquaintance rape from this book concurs with Do and Mark (2020:1) who conducted a research in the United States and found that peers might try to give up on the art of peer life but could not do so due to peer pressure and that is why victims and perpetrators of acquaintance rape accept and justify it. Do and Mark (2020:1) further established that both males and females want to be accepted by peer groups, so they accept acquaintance rape to be maintained in the peer group. The finding of this study that peer pressure affects acquaintance rape also concurs with the following studies: Armstrong (2006:483) in India, Lightfoot and Evans (2000:1160) in New Zealand and Dekeseredy (2007:295) in America which found out that male and female peers suffer from peer pressure and peer norms hence they influence how peers think, behave, interact with others and what they expect from others and what others may expect from them.

The finding of this study that male sexual abusers also happen to receive male peer support and adhere to the ideology of familial patriarchy concurs with De Leon's (2013:18) large body of quantitative and qualitative research which indicated that male peer support is a determinant of male perceptions towards acquaintance rape. In most acquaintance rape cases, males are triggered to commit the crime inadvertently due to peer pressure and other variables beyond the scope of this study. All participants in the present study revealed that college life is associated with adolescence period which is also full of storm and stress and peers themselves, especially in African countries, associate acquaintance rape with modern life. The fact that students in institutions of higher learning associate acquaintance rape with modern life causes confusion among acquaintances. Perpetrators of acquaintance rape seem not to know whether what they do to victims of acquaintance rape is good or bad. Victims themselves also do not know whether their acquaintances' sexual behaviour is right or wrong.

The finding of this study that in most cases in the occurrence of acquaintance rape, assailants would be under the influence of alcohol concurs with Hester and Lilley (2018:5) in England, Dixie (2017:35) in the United States, Sleath and Bull (2017:1) in the United Kingdom who found out that because of intoxication, victims of acquaintance rape could not be able to give an account of what would have transpired. If the victim happens to be a female who is intoxicated and would have received financial or academic assistance from the assailant, the victim will perceive the assailant as a nice guy. In such a scenario, both the perpetrator and the victim of acquaintance rape would perceive the act as normal and would also justify it as well. College authorities, non-academic staff and students who participated in this study perceive acquaintance rape as a product of peer pressure among adolescents. The other finding of this study revealed that assailants of acquaintance rape perceived that when an individual acquires raping tactics from acquaintances, he/she perceives acquaintance rape as normal peer group practice which is socially accepted and justified concurs with Thacker's (2017:91) study in the United States and Dekeseredy *et al.*'s (2007:295) study in Ohio in America who found out that both assailants and victims of acquaintance rape are more likely to accept peer group rape culture and engage in acquaintance rape when they happen to frequent and have close contact with significant others. The finding that both assailants and victims of acquaintance rape perceive acquaintance rape as a normal peer group practice which is socially acceptable and justified also concurs with De Leon's (2013:14) study in America that revealed that male peer assailants of acquaintance rape perceive their girlfriends as replacements for a hook-up, so they don't perceive acquaintance rape as a social vice. College authorities, non-academic staff and students who participated in this study perceive college ladies as campus prostitutes; hence there is nothing wrong for college men to have sex with prostitutes whom they know. In most social institutions where peers happen to be assailants of acquaintance rape, besides their peers, they are even supported by their neighbours and police officers for committing such a crime.

The finding of this study that higher education students view acquaintance rape as part of college life concurs with international literature by Johnson and Johnson (2017:1) in the United States, Sleath and Bull (2017:1) in the United Kingdom and Sampson (2002:12) in Canada, Australia, New Zealand, the Netherlands and Scandinavia and that of Olusegun in Nigeria who found that learners in institution of higher learning do not view acquaintance rape as a social vice because of the confusion between peer members' experiences, backgrounds, tribe and residential locations. College authorities, non-academic staff and students who participated in the study perceived that acquaintance rape is part of college rape culture, so it is institutionally accepted by most college students as part of college experiences. According to peer culture, sexual activities, just like acquaintance rape are regarded as part of the interaction process. Copying and accepting each other's behaviour through social learning are both traditional and modern methods which are applicable in tolerating acquaintance rape as a social norm due to peer pressure. It also emerged from all the participants of this study that peers cannot resist acquaintance rape due to peer pressure. Peer pressure is a powerful tool for peers' actions including acquaintance rape. The finding that acquaintance rape is tolerated and justified as a social norm by both perpetrators and victims of acquaintance rape is in line with social learning theory which is guiding this study.

The finding that assailants of acquaintance rape get positive gratifications from both assailants and victims of acquaintance rape concurs with Dixie (2017:44) and Kaplan *et al* (1987) studies study in the United States. Kaplan *et al* (1987:227), for instance, found that deviant peers, through interaction and socialisation with significant others, would get positive gratifications for the individual acquaintance rapist than the ordinary peer that would have learnt to value behaviour that would have been imposed by a group. Positive comments from peers which are part of a hidden curriculum on social life, dating and courtship act as a form of encouragement for both good and bad behaviour among peers. College authorities, non-academic staff and students who participated in this study seemed to believe that peers, especially male ones, praise their acquaintances for successfully managing to have sex with female peers whom they think are decent. The motivation in form of positive comments for acquaintance rapists' sexual achievement makes acquaintance rape to be labelled as a college game.

The other finding of this study that students in higher institutions perceive that women peers believe that in general women should be docile and submissive in all spheres of life concurs with Okeke's (2011:28) study in Nigeria which found that if the victim of acquaintance rape reports the assailant, she would have deviated from the social norm of being docile and submissive hence she would be rejected by the peer group. The rejection would be because of failing to observe the peer group norms hence vicarious reinforcement applies. The above finding that women should be docile and submissive contradicts literature from Odu and Olusegun's (2012:918) study which established that female students are natural targets of sexual coercion and every female student can be a. victim of acquaintance rape irrespective of age.

Quantitative results from this study's two groups of participants differ, while the elderly staff members are of the opinion that peer pressure does not play a role, the youthful students opinionated that it plays a role. The differences in opinions between members of staff and students could be due to differences in age groups, life experiences and socialisation patterns.

Results generated from the quantitative approach are consistent with those generated from the qualitative approach. The results from the two approaches coincide due to the participants' backgrounds, status, lifestyles and culture.

The following section discusses the extent to which policy, legislation or law affects students in higher education's perceptions of acquaintance rape in Masvingo as revealed by the findings of this study.

4.7.4 The influence of policy, legislation or law on acquaintance rape

The current sub-section discusses the effects of policy, legislation or law on students in higher education's perceptions of acquaintance rape in Masvingo as revealed by the findings of this study. The discussion is based on the available literature on the effects of policy, legislation or law on students in higher education institutions' perceptions of acquaintance rape in Masvingo. In this sub-section, the findings from this study were discussed under the sub-research question posed in section 1.4.4 of Chapter 1 which reads: How do policies, legislation or law influence perceptions of students in higher education institutions' perceptions of acquaintance rape in Masvingo.

It emerged from this study that courts tend to try victims of acquaintance rape instead of assailants of acquaintance rape. College administrators, non-academic staff and students who participated in this study seemed to have a perception that courts tend to favour assailants of acquaintance rape due to corruption. The above finding concurs with Sleath and Bull (2017:1) in the United Kingdom who revealed that victims of acquaintance rape were blamed more than victims of stranger rape. Human Rights Watch's research (2017:2) in India revealed that there are still persistent gaps in enforcing the laws, relevant policies, legislations and guidelines specifically for victims of acquaintance rape and sexual violence.

It also emerged from the study findings that acquaintance rape cases are not reported. All participants in this study revealed that most acquaintance rape cases are not reported due to psycho-social reasons among both perpetrators and assailants of acquaintance rape. Apart from the fact that acquaintance rape cases are not reported, they also differ from other rapes. The finding that acquaintance rape cases are not reported concurs with Salaz's (2005:13) study in America which established that most acquaintance rape cases are not reported to the police. This American study (Salaz, 2005:13) also shares similar views with European study by the Right To Be Free From Rape Report (2018:23), Tade and Udechukwu's (2020:3) in Nigeria which found out that most acquaintance rape cases are not reported to formal agencies of social control due to trust gaps, associated stigma against the victims, fear of re-victimisation, cultural barriers, religious sentiments and the powerlessness of the victims in pursuing justice. The finding of this study that acquaintance rape cases are not reported to the police also supports Koss's (2018:40) study which revealed that only 30% of women in the 1980s who had a man who climbed on top of them, held them down, and attempted unwanted sex acts, reported to the police. Forty-two percent of the victims of acquaintance rape told no one at all. Koss's (2018) survey also revealed that more than 45% of college women kept silent about sexual assaults by acquaintances and only 2.6% who experienced attempted or completed rape reported the incident to police.

It emerged from this study that there is no mandatory policy, legislation or law governing students' sexual relationships and acquaintance rape in institutions of higher education in Masvingo. College administrators, non-academic staff and students who participated in this study seemed to have a perception that, acquaintance rape is not taken as a serious crime in institutions of higher education because of lack of policy, legislation or law governing students' sexual behaviour in institutions of higher learning. All participants in this study believed that although there are other policies such as sexual harassment and sexual assault policies, they are too broad such that they do not well define acquaintance rape. The above finding concurs with Sampson (2002:15) in the United States, the United Kingdom, Cananda, Australia, New Zealand, the Netherlands and Scandinavia and that of the Mediterranean Institute of gender studies (2008:32) in Cyprus, Greece, Lativia, Malta and Lithuania which revealed that there are no policies, legislative acts or laws in institutions of higher learning which specifically differentiate acquaintance rape from other forms of sexual violence which govern students' sexual relationships. What it means is that institutions of higher education the world over do not have prescribed procedures to deal with acquaintance rape.

Institutions of higher education do not have either common approaches or any policy mechanisms to combat acquaintance rape hence college administrators, non-academic staff, victims and perpetrators of acquaintance rape perceive it (acquaintance rape) as just a hidden crime. Instead of dealing with acquaintance rape cases, college authorities simply ignore them as if they are non-existent. The major cause might be lack of technical knowhow. Some victims and assailants of acquaintance rape do not even know its existence. The finding that there is no policy, legislation or law in institutions of higher education in Masvingo specifically for acquaintance rape on the other hand contradicts international literature which states that there are policies, legislations or laws governing students' sexual behaviour in institutions of higher education in America such as the Campus Security Act of 1990, Title II of Public law (USA), Sexual Assault Policies (USA) (Date Rape Cases Among Young Women: Strategies for support and prevention, 2008:40).

This study revealed that there are no laws governing sexual relationships including acquaintance rape in Masvingo. Contrary to this scenario, the world over laws are there but do not cover acquaintance rape (Du Toit, 2012:465). Those laws cover stranger rape and other sexual assaults only hence acquaintance rapists get scot free. The absence of mandatory policy, legislation or law that govern sexual behaviour of students in higher education institutions in Masvingo is likely to negatively affect their perceptions of acquaintance rape. Victims of acquaintance rape are less likely to classify their sexual experiences as "rape" than those raped by a stranger. College administrators also blame victims of acquaintance rape instead of assailants because acquaintance rape is not only a hidden crime but also a controversial crime. College administrators are afraid of sending acquaintance rapists to courts because the justice system itself is corrupt. Campus police officers and college administrators are also afraid to disclose that acquaintance rape occurs more often at their institutions than at others. Even if the law is there, victims often refuse to testify.

Victims and assailants of acquaintance rape perceive policy, legislation or law as being there in theoretical terms but in practice, it is non-existent. This is in tandem with the findings of this study from participants. In America there are sketch laws governing the behaviour of acquaintance rapists. These sketch laws are not specifically for acquaintance rapists. In America the existing law guarding against sexual violence in institutions of higher learning was amended and renamed "The Jeanne Clery Disclose of Campus Security Policy and Campus Crime Statistics Act" in honour of a 19-year-old female college student, Jeanne Ann Clery who was raped and murdered in Lehigh dorm room in 1986 was also not specifically for acquaintance rapists. The Clery Act was amended several times, most recently in 2000, to require institutions of higher learning make information available to the campus community concerning possible presence of registered sex offenders on campus.

This study also established that college administrators and even campus police officers do not know how to deal with acquaintance rape cases due to the contradiction between modern laws and customary law hence students in institutions of higher education in Masvingo perceive it as part of living together and do not report the crime. Some of the participants in this study seemed to believe that both perpetrators and victims of acquaintance rape do not consider it as a crime since sexual crimes are not clearly defined according to African culture hence, they perceive it as a normal dating practice. The confusion as to whether a lady has consented to sex or not depends on the tone of the "no", if it is low tone it means a "yes". This law of consent is also ambiguous because it does not have an international definition. This law of consent is also subjective in nature due to cultural reasons hence college, university administrators or even security/police officers find it difficult to deal with acquaintance rape cases, as a result victims of acquaintance rape do not report these cases. Victims of acquaintance rape are reluctant to report acquaintance rapists because they do not recognise acquaintance rape as a crime.

The finding of this study that acquaintance rape cases lack evidence contradicts Skinneder et al. (2017:xi) study in the Asia-Pacific region which revealed that most acquaintance rape cases in Thailand and Vietnam, even if evidence is there, can be filtered out at every stage of the justice process. In other contexts, like those of Africa, it was revealed that acquaintance rape lacks evidence because culturally it is taboo to watch or witness sexual crimes but the world over, especially in European countries there is nothing wrong in giving evidence in courts pertaining to acquaintance rape. Even if evidence is there courts themselves are corrupt in nature and, the world over, they lack sanity. Location gaps between this book and international studies have also been put into consideration during the study. The book also established that female reporting cases in Thailand and Vietnam by acquaintances encountered significant societal, legal, institutional policies, legislation or law and practices act as barriers to justice.

The finding of this book that acquaintance rape cases lack evidence further corroborates the study by the World Health Organisation (2017:4) in a study by Palemo, Black and Peterman on masculinity where it was revealed that even if evidence is there, victims were also unaware of the law, or regarded the law as inappropriate. Acquaintance rape cases have reporting barriers which range from societal, legal, institutional policies, legislation or law and practices. Personnel in the justice system have positive attitudes towards sexual offences, victims of acquaintance rape and alleged perpetrators. When college administrators and non-academic staff attempt to try these acquaintance rape cases, they fail to get witnesses and as a result they would tend to favour acquaintance rape assailants rather than victims. Victims of acquaintance rape also have very limited knowledge on the nature of the authenticity of the crime.

Another finding of this study was that the policy, legislation or law were revealed as not protecting victims of acquaintance rape but acquaintance rapists hence victims of acquaintance rape do not have faith in the justice system. This concurs with Walker *et al.* (2019:6) study in England and Hester and Lilley's (2017:1) study in England who found that acquaintance rape victims have no faith in the justice system because society and its criminal justice system offer no real protection and both have the potential to victimise all women in general and victims of acquaintance rape in particular, forcing them to remain in abusive relationships and situations. Chireshe and Makura (2013:4) observed that policies and outcomes are influenced by the immediate context in which they are implemented. Viewed in this way, college administrators regard the justice system itself as weak and corrupt in nature such that even its outcomes are biased towards assailants of acquaintance rape. The finding of this study that acquaintance rape cases are difficult to investigate because judges and prosecutors think that women always lead men on, and cry rape concurs with Gravelin *et al.*'s (2019:10) study in America which revealed that women provoke acquaintance rapists by wearing revealing or provoking clothing. Policy, legislation or law itself is sketchy to such an extent that it also confuses college administrators in its implementation and, as a result, does not protect victims. Administrators in institutions of high education perceive victims of acquaintance rape as prostitutes if acquaintance rape occurs. The criminal justice system in any nation has an important symbolic role of shaping community perceptions of what is perceived as legitimate or illegitimate, legal or criminal behaviour. Society, administrators of higher education institutions, college security officers and students themselves perceive acquaintance rape as a product of negligence on the part of acquaintance rape victims hence they tend to blame victims of acquaintance rape. Victims of acquaintance rape also tend to blame themselves hence they keep quiet because they know that everyone would blame them.

Results from college administrators and non-academic staff and students on policy, legislation or law as factors that influence perceptions of students on acquaintance rape in institutions of higher education in Masvingo differ. While college administrators and non-academic staff felt that policies do not play a role, students thought they play a role. This discrepancy in opinion might be due to differences in common thoughts, common practices, norms and cultural values between the elderly and the youth.

4.8 Chapter Summary

This chapter has presented, analysed and discussed the findings in the context of the sub research questions in chapter 1, section 1.4. It emerged from this study that college administrators, non-academic staff and students raised factors such as culture, gender, peer pressure and policy, legislation or law as factors affecting students in higher education's perceptions of acquaintance rape in Masvingo.

The subsequent chapter presents the summary, conclusions and recommendations of the book.

Chapter 5

Towards the Elimination of Rape Culture in Higher Education

5.1 Introduction

The main aim of this book was to establish factors affecting perceptions of higher education students' perception of acquaintance rape in Masvingo. In this chapter, a review of the research problem presented in Chapter 1 is offered. A summary of the literature, research methodology and the findings of the empirical study on each sub-research question are also presented. This chapter also presents the conclusions of the study and recommendations for the improvement of the welfare and sexual health of students in higher education institutions' perceptions of acquaintance rape in Masvingo. A proposed model for reducing acquaintance rape is also suggested. Matters requiring further research and final comments are also included. A review of the research problem is presented first.

5.2 A Review of the Research Problem

The background of the book has established that acquaintance rape is quite rampant in high schools and institutions of higher education the world over (Chireshe & Chireshe, 2009; Dixie, 2017; National Victims Centre,1999; Santrock, 2005;Shumba et al., 2008; Shumba & Matina, 2002; Kottack, 2000; Koss *et al.*, 1988 ; Johnson & Johnson, 2019, Lyness, 2009; Dziech, 2003; Withowska & Menckel, 2005; Abuya *et al.*, 2014; Rosetti, 2001; Leach *et al.*, 2000; Human Rights Watch Report, 2001; Okeke, 2011; Banya, 2003; Mapfumo *et al.*, 2007). Chapter 1 revealed that internationally different researchers have established the effects of acquaintance rape (Dixie, 2017:35; Mittal *et al.*, 2017:1), perceptions of acquaintance rape (Suprakash *et al.*, 2017:001; Carlson *et al.*, 2012:82; Sleath& Bull, 2017:41; Dixie, 2017:41; Harsey & Freyd, 2020:12; Gravelin *et al.*, 2019:4; World Health Organisation, 2017:4; Dolan, 2019:1; Kahan, 2010:1; Ben-David Schneider, 2005:385; Oshiname *et al.*, 2013:1370), prevention of acquaintance rape (Finn, 1977:vii), and address of acquaintance rape issues to students in institutions of higher education (Colantonio-Yurko, Miller & Cheveallier, 2018:10).

As was highlighted in Chapter 1, to the knowledge of the researcher, there are no studies that have been carried out in Masvingo on the factors affecting students in higher education's perceptions of acquaintance rape in Masvingo. This book sought to investigate factors affecting higher education students' perceptions of acquaintance rape in Masvingo.

The following sub-section presents a summary of literature review.

5.3. Summary of Literature Review

This section presents the summary of literature findings on the factors affecting students in higher education's perceptions of acquaintance rape in Masvingo.

5.3.1 Culture and acquaintance rape

Reviewed literature in this book established that culture plays a fundamental role when it comes to interpreting acquaintance rape (Mittal *et al.*, 2017:1; Deming, 2017:11; Dixie, 2017:44; Flood & Pease, 2006: 27; Kamal *et al.*, 2010:108). Both local and international literature reviewed also established that acquaintance rape is under-recognised as a crime due to tacit cultural normalisation in dating relationships (Johnson & Johnson, 2017:3; Oshiname *et al.*, 2013:138; Dixie, 2017:41; Boswell & Spade 1996:134; Gravelin *et al.*, 2019:1). The reviewed local and international literature also established that culture, just like any other social variable, has a bearing on students' perceptions of acquaintance rape.

It was also revealed by this study that acquaintance rape, besides being a hidden crime (Flintort, 2010:2), is also controversial and ambiguous.

5.3.2 Gender and acquaintance rape

Reviewed literature findings established that globally both victims and performers of acquaintance rape perceive gender as a factor patriarchal in societies which enables men to possess social, political and economic powers hence they tend to dictate the pace in sexual relationships as well (Hester & Lilley, 2018:175). This gendered ideology of male dominance over females brings about different perceptions between both male and female perpetrators. Reviewed literature also established that males are the main perpetrators and females are the main victims of acquaintance rape, hence society does not acknowledge acquaintance rape as a crime but as a normal dating practice (Dixie, 2017:44; Gravelin *et al.*, 2019:13; Johnson & Johnson, 2017:2). It was also established that male gender blames victims of acquaintance rape more than female gender (Person *et al.*, 2018:7).

5.3.3 Peer pressure and acquaintance rape

Reviewed international, regional and Sub-Saharan Africa literature established that students fail to resist acquaintance rapists due to peer pressure (Do & Mark, 2020:1; Armstrong, 2006:483; Lightfoot & Evans, 2000: 1160; Dekeseredy, 2007:295). Peers might try to give up the art of peer life but cannot do so due to peer pressure and that is why victims and perpetrators of acquaintance rape accept and justify it (Dixie, 2017:45; Armstrong *et al.*, 2006: 483; Lightfoot & Evans, 2000:1160; Dekeseredy, 2007:295; Leone & Parrott, 2018:42). It was revealed in the reviewed literature that male sexual abusers happen to receive male peer support and adhere to the ideology of familial patriarchy (De Leon, 2013:18).

Reviewed literature also established that there is a lot of rape culture among peers at fraternity parties in colleges and Universities (Johnson & Johnson, 2017:2; Boswell & Spade, 2010:133; Peters & Besley, 2018:458; Dixie, 2017:41), so students in institutions of higher education perceive acquaintance rape as a social norm. Such a perception enables higher education peers to view acquaintance rape as part of college life (Johnson & Johnson, 2017:1; Sleath & Bull, 2017:1; Sampson, 2002:12). It was also established that performers of acquaintance rape get positive gratifications from both assailants and victims of acquaintance rape (Dixie, 2017:44).

5.3.4 Policy, legislation or law and Acquaintance rape

Reviewed literature revealed that institutions of higher learning in Masvingo lacked mandatory policy, legislation or law governing both sexual relationships and acquaintance rape among students (Sampson, 2002:15). This non- existence of mandatory policy, legislation or law that governs students' sexual relationships and acquaintance rape in institutions of higher education in Masvingo has a bearing on students' perceptions of acquaintance in institutions of higher education in Masvingo. Reviewed international, regional and sub-Saharan African literature also revealed that acquaintance rape cases are difficult to deal with because they lack evidence (Skinneder *et al.*, 2017: xi). It was established that courts tend to try victims of acquaintance rape instead of perpetrators (Sleath & Bull, 2017:1).

Findings from reviewed international literature revealed that acquaintance rape victims have no faith in the justice system. Both perpetrators and victims of acquaintance rape perceive it not as a crime but as part of college life. International literature also revealed that college administrators and even campus police officers do not know how to deal with acquaintance rape cases and as such individuals, perpetrators and victims have no faith in the justice system hence they view the vice as a minor crime (Odu & Olusegun, 2012:919).

The next sub-section presents a summary of research methodology.

5.4 Summary of Research Methodology

This book was informed by the positivist paradigm. The researcher employed the quantitative approach to investigate factors affecting the perceptions of higher education students' perceptions of acquaintance rape. Descriptive survey design was employed. A total sample of 63 participants comprising principals, vice principals, hostel wardens, assistant hostel wardens, nursing sisters, disciplinary chairpersons and students from Masvingo was randomly and purposely selected for this book. Descriptive statistics, inferential statistics and tables were used to analyse generated data.

The following sub-section presents a summary of the findings of this book.

5.5 Summary of the Findings

The present section summarises the research findings with special reference to sub-research questions and objectives in Chapter 1.

5.5.1 Sub-research question 1: To what extent does culture affect students in higher education institutions' perception of acquaintance rape in Masvingo?

It emerged from this study that culture affects students in higher education institutions' perceptions of acquaintance rape in Masvingo. The findings of this study indicated that most perpetrators and victims of acquaintance rape do not regard acquaintance rape as a social vice due to cultural reasons. All participants in this study, that is, college administrators, non-academic staff and students in institutions of higher learning accepted and justified acquaintance rape as a normal cultural practice due to cultural norms, values, beliefs, folkways, language, common thoughts and common practices. It further emerged from this study that culture prohibits the revealing of sexual activities hence acquaintance rape also becomes taboo according to African culture. It also emerged from this study that acquaintance rape according to African culture, especially the Karanga culture, is controversial and ambiguous.

This book also revealed that according to African culture, women and girls cannot openly consent to sex, so a "no" means "yes" depending on the tone of the "no". If it is a "low" tone, it means go ahead and if it is a "high" tone, it means a "no". This book also revealed that women have subordinate roles in society whilst males have major roles hence the reason why African culture tends to blame victims of acquaintance rape. African culture tends to favour males since it gives assailants of acquaintance rape advantages over their victims.

5.5.2 Sub-research question 2: To what extent does gender influence students in higher education institutions' perceptions of acquaintance rape in Masvingo?

This book revealed that gender has a bearing on students in higher education institutions' perceptions of acquaintance in Masvingo. The findings revealed that society is patriarchal in nature and as a result males tend to force females into sex, especially acquaintances due to gender and power dynamics. Acquaintance rape is socially perceived as a good and normal dating practice and this perception emanates from gender stereotypes. The book also revealed that men are socially regarded as bulls that are culturally licensed to sleep around with women of their choice at will while women play a subservient role. It also emerged from this study that females are males' sex objects so there is no problem if they force women, especially acquaintances to have sex with them.

This study also revealed that females cannot ask for sex from men so what they do is simply to show actions which are suggestive of sex, and in such situations if men fail to have sex with them, men are viewed as cowards. If these actions are displayed by acquaintances, they would be perceived as asking for sex. In institutions of higher learning, students interpret it as begging for sex hence they force their acquaintances to have sex with them and they believe that it cannot be socially interpreted as rape.

5.5.3 Sub-research question 3: How does peer pressure influence acquaintance rape to students in higher education institutions in Masvingo?

The book revealed that peer pressure was perceived as a major cause of acquaintance rape. Students in institutions of higher education in Masvingo were perceived as failing to resist acquaintance rape due to peer pressure and as such they tend to perceive acquaintance rape as part of college life. College mates are peers, so they accommodate acquaintance rapists by either not resisting or reporting them to college authorities. College life is associated with adolescent period and modern life. It also emerged from this study that acquaintance rape is tolerated and justified as a social norm by both perpetrators and victims of it due to socialisation by students from different social backgrounds. As students interact and socialise with each other, they tend to copy and imitate their peers through social learning hence acquaintance rape is regarded as part of social life and positively tolerated. This study also revealed that in institutions of higher learning there is a lot of rape culture among peers hence acquaintance rape is perceived by students as part of college life. Since acquaintance rape is a hidden crime, if it comes in the open, the assailant would be regarded as a sexual hero and would get positive gratifications from both assailants and victims of acquaintance rape.

This book also revealed that acquaintance rape in institutions of higher learning takes place during parties and college functions when most students would be under the influence of drugs and alcohol, thus both assailants and victims would not give a clear and full account of what would have happened. In such a scenario, other college students would also tend to associate those functions and college parties with hooking up and acquaintance rape. Reporting assailants to the police or college authorities after these college parties would result in the victims being rejected by the peer group.

5.5.4 Sub-research question 4: How does policy, legislation or law influence the perceptions of students in higher education institutions' perceptions of acquaintance rape in Masvingo?

This book revealed that students in institutions of higher education in Masvingo have limited mandatory policies, legislations or laws governing both sexual relationships and acquaintance rape among students. The non-existence or limited mandatory policies, legislations or laws that govern students' sexual relationships and acquaintance rape in institutions of higher education in Masvingo affects the perceptions of students in institutions of higher education in Masvingo. It further emerged that lack of such mandatory policies, legislations or laws governing students' sexual relationships and acquaintance rape meant that it was also unlikely that a legally binding framework existed for conducive interaction among college mates in Masvingo. It also emerged that fair implementation of policies, legislations or laws that govern students' sexual relationships and acquaintance rape is compromised due to lack of knowledge on sexual crime by policy implementers. Furthermore, it emerged from this study that college administrators and even campus police officers do not know how to deal with acquaintance rape cases due to conflict between traditional and modern laws.

This book also further revealed that acquaintance rape cases are difficult to try because they lack evidence. The findings of this study also revealed that acquaintance rape victims have no faith with the justice system because courts try victims of acquaintance rape instead of assailants of acquaintance rape hence it is viewed as there in theoretical form but not in practicality. Perpetrators and victims of acquaintance rape perceive acquaintance rape not as a crime but as part of college life. Policy, legislation or law do not play a fundamental role in acquaintance rape cases in institutions of higher learning hence it is perceived by both assailants and victims as a defence lawyer for perpetrators of acquaintance rape.

The following section presents the conclusions.

5.6 Conclusions

The essence of this book was to assess factors affecting students in higher education' perceptions of acquaintance rape in Masvingo. The findings indicated that culture affects students in higher education's perceptions of acquaintance rape in Masvingo. It can also be concluded that college administrators, non-academic staff and students in this book did not regard acquaintance rape as a crime due to culture that prohibits the revealing of sexual activities (Flint, 2010:2). Acquaintance rape is also a controversial and ambiguous crime (Sampson, 2002:15). It can also be concluded that culture encourages acquaintance rape by its mandatory silence as a way of protecting relationships. The book also concluded that African culture tends to favour males hence it blames victims of acquaintance rape, especially females.

It can also be concluded that since society is patriarchal in nature, males tend to force females into sex hence acquaintance rape is perceived as a normal African cultural practice. It can be further concluded that patriarchal society considers males to be bulls that can sleep around with women at will whilst females play a subservient role. The other conclusion to be drawn from the findings of this study is that acquaintance rape is also a product of perpetrators' misconception of situations. Participants in this study revealed that according to African cultural practice, women and girls are not allowed to consent to sex hence victims of acquaintance rape suffer silently.

Based on the findings of this book, it can also be concluded that most students in higher education in Masvingo are adolescents hence they become both perpetrators and victims of acquaintance rape due to peer pressure. Peers regard sexual activities as part of the interaction process since copying and accepting peers is done with acquaintances through social learning. In institutions of higher learning there is also rape culture hence victims of acquaintance rape do not report their assailants.

It can further be concluded that there are no specific mandatory policies, legislations or laws in institutions of higher education in Masvingo for acquaintance rape cases, so college administrators, non-academic staff and students themselves do not have guidelines when handling acquaintance rape cases. Administrators of institutions of higher education in Masvingo do not report assailants as a way of protecting the images of their institutions and as a result victims of acquaintance rape also keep quiet as a way of protecting their own images. This culture of silence enables acquaintance rape to be a hidden crime although it is quite rampant in institutions of higher education in Masvingo.

The subsequent section presents recommendations of the book.

5.7 Recommendations

Based on the findings of this study and body of knowledge from the literature review, the researcher would like to provide several recommendations as suggestions to improve the negative perceptions of acquaintance rape in students in higher education in Masvingo.

The researcher makes the following recommendations about policy, practice and further studies.

5.7.1 Policy

There is need to establish clear and mandatory policies, legislations or laws supported by an Act of parliament which govern students' behaviour and improve their perceptions of acquaintance rape in institutions of higher education.

College administrators, non-academic staff as custodians of policy implementation should be empowered by policies which mandate students' dating and courtship practices. Good implementation of policy can be achieved if college and university administrators get in-service training on administration.

The policy governing students' sexual behaviour should be clear and straightforward such that they would be not ambiguous and misleading to college administrators in their implementation and governing of students in institutions of higher learning. Sketch policies, formulated from Acts such as the Sexual Offences Act (Chapter 9.21) 2001 and Domestic Violence Act (Chapter 5.16) 2007 in some of the institutions of higher education are not specifically for acquaintance rape.

5.7.2 Practice

5.7.2.1 Training

All stakeholders should be adequately trained in handling sexual and acquaintance rape issues. As the quantitative research results suggests, college administrators and non-academic staff in higher education do not know how to handle acquaintance rape issues therefore they should be trained to reduce acquaintance rape. College administrators and non-academic staff should also be trained and equipped with the necessary skills to identify victims of acquaintance rape. If they identify acquaintance rape victims, they will refer them to appropriate specialised services. Stakeholders should be made aware of policies, legislation or laws governing students' sexual behaviour so that they would be able to manage it.

Involvement and training of all stakeholders should be conducted so that there is total implementation of policies, legislations or laws governing students in higher education. Improving and implementation of existing policies, legislations or laws governing students' sexual behaviour, although seemingly too general as evidenced by this study, should be implemented to improve the welfare of college students as well as curb acquaintance rape. Involvement and training of stakeholders in policies, legislations or laws governing students in higher education should be also done to reduce cultural barriers, gender inequality, peer pressure, reduction and blaming and stigmatisation of victims of acquaintance rape. As part of training, rape aggression defence training should be part of college students' training to fend off would be rapists.

5.7.2.2 Peer Education

Since the study revealed that peer pressure was a main factor in affecting students' perceptions towards acquaintance rape, it is prudent that peer education on the effects of acquaintance rape be considered as peers are more likely to influence other peers.

Peers with leadership roles should be employed in acquaintance rape prevention peer education programmes. The peer educators need to be trained on the causes and effects of acquaintance rape so that they will educate other peers from an informed position.

5.7.2.3 Higher Education Curriculum

This study revealed that acquaintance rape is quite rampant in institutions of higher education because the current curriculum does not include the effects of acquaintance rape and risk life skills across the board. As such, acquaintance rape aspects need to be included in the curriculum. Inclusion of acquaintance rape and risk life skills in the curriculum helps students to acquire survival skills to reduce and manage acquaintance rape. It is recommended that cultural practices related to acquaintance rape be part of the curriculum in higher and tertiary education so that students are educated about the bad aspect of culture that perpetuates acquaintance rape.

5.7.2.4 Awareness Campaigns

Since the study revealed that there is need to improve students' welfare in institutions of higher education, acquaintance rape awareness campaigns should be conducted as a measure to reduce it. These awareness campaigns should be in the form of cultural tools of art and drama such as street theatre, competitions, murals, fostering grassroots men's and women's groups and networks for victims and perpetrators of acquaintance rape who are committed to advocate for reducing acquaintance rape and gender equity. Awareness campaigns would also overcome public prejudice and misconceptions about victims of acquaintance rape.

These awareness campaigns should aim at including the following: college students' behaviour change programmes, acquaintance rape prevention programmes for college students, college administrators, campus security officers and other key campus personnel's acquaintance rape handling procedures. These awareness programmes and activities should include aspects that help young people to negotiate sexual situations in their relationships that reduce acquaintance rape. Parents, guardians and society should also be involved in awareness campaigns to prevent acquaintance rape so that every member of the society will be able to reduce acquaintance rape from a societal up to national level.

5.7.2.5 *Accommodation of students in halls of residence*

Each institution of higher education should have safe accommodation for resident students. The government on behalf of institutions of higher education should provide well secured accommodation for residence students. To improve the welfare of resident students, there should be installation of cameras, lights, locks in students' residential hall rooms. To tighten the security system, there should be campus police officers manning students' residential halls. Policies, legislation or laws governing students' sexual behaviour should be well written on charts stuck on corridors of residential halls. Institutions of higher education should provide single sex halls to reduce acquaintance rape among students.

5.7.3 *Further studies*

This study was confined to three institutions of higher education in Masvingo from the six institutions in the province, therefore, the findings can be generalised to students' perceptions of acquaintance rape in Masvingo. This study employed both open-ended and closed-ended questionnaire items and produced both quantitative and qualitative data. It is therefore recommended that studies be carried out to survey all institutions of higher learning at provincial level using other research tools in order to compare the findings of this study and future studies.

Whilst this study revealed students' perceptions of acquaintance rape as influenced by culture, gender, peer pressure, policy and legislation or law, future studies may need to include other variables such as media, dressing, alcohol or substance abuse.

This book recommends that future researchers investigate strategies that should be used to popularise the effects of acquaintance rape in the society. The following section discusses the proposed acquaintance rape reduction model.

5.8 Proposed Acquaintance Rape Reduction Model

A proposed model to reduce acquaintance rape in higher education institutions is discussed in this section. This model is grounded in the social learning theory and is envisaged to improve students' welfare as well as to reduce acquaintance rape in higher education institutions in Masvingo (and elsewhere in Zimbabwe and beyond) using the following components: passing clear mandatory policy, legislation or law governing students in higher education's sexual behaviour, in-service training of college and university administrators on acquaintance rape and students' welfare, mounting awareness campaigns on the welfare of students in institutions of higher education, peer education on health and risk life skills and monitoring and evaluation of residential higher education students' welfare and perceptions towards acquaintance rape. Social reformers propound that policy, legislation or law should be implemented to protect human beings against exploitation as well as operating under dangerous conditions.

If this book's proposed acquaintance rape reduction model is implemented ,women rights such as; the right to good sexual practices, moral education to bring social and humanitarian changes may be promoted (Rasivhetshele, De Bruyn, Sotshononda & Uys, 2017:19). If institutions of higher education implement policies, legislations or laws, they might be a balance or equity in terms of how human beings treat each other hence acquaintance rape might be reduced or managed.

5.8.1 A Proposed Model to reduce acquaintance rape in institutions of higher learning

Figure 5.1 A Proposed P. Tafirei 2022 Acquaintance Rape Reduction Model

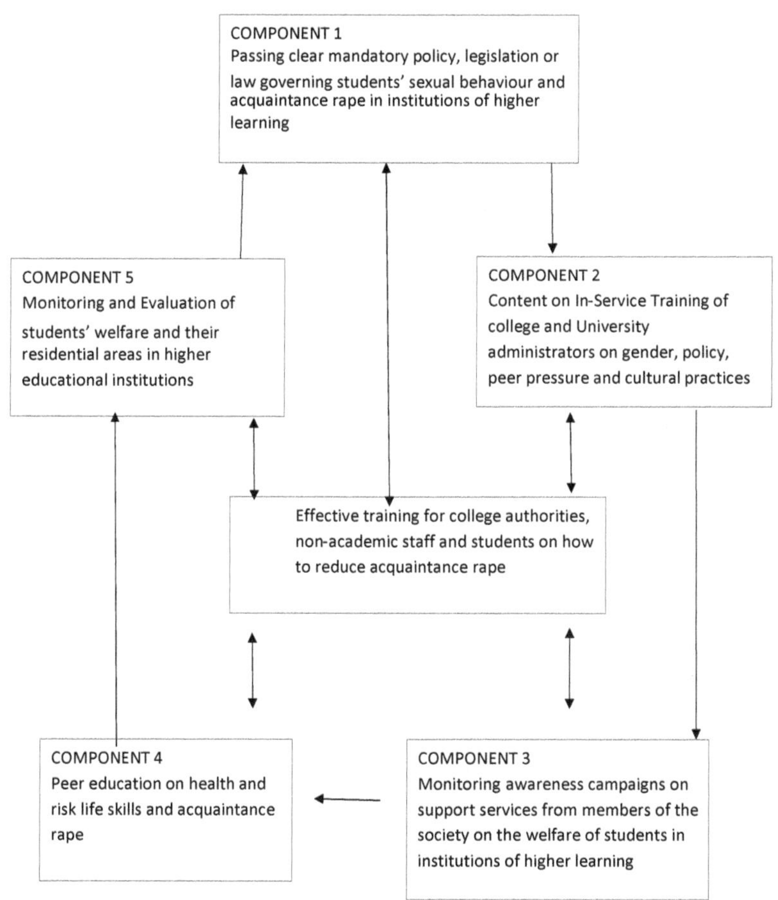

Component 1: Passing clear mandatory policy, legislation or law governing students' sexual behaviour

Students in higher education institutions should be empowered with skills to improve their welfare through the introduction of clear and concise mandatory policies, legislation or laws governing their sexual relationships as well as reduce the prevalence of acquaintance rape. These policies, legislations or laws should provide practical guidelines for preventing and dealing with acquaintance rape cases. The policies, legislations or laws need to clearly specify and clarify the roles, responsibilities and expectations of all key stakeholders in higher education institutions. These policies, legislations or laws governing students' welfare and sexual behaviour in higher education institutions should be supported by an Act of Parliament. The application of enacted policies or laws should be meant to protect students against exploitation and dangerous conditions especially acquaintance rape which is a hidden crime in institutions of higher education as suggested by Date Rape among Young Women (2018:11).

Component 2: Content on In-service training of college and university administrators on acquaintance rape and students' welfare

College administrators and non-academic staff should be offered in-service training courses to improve the welfare of students and reduce acquaintance rape in institutions of higher education. College administrators and non-academic staff should be trained to impart skills in students in higher education institutions to socialise and interact in a way governed by institutional policies, legislations or laws. The in-service training of college authorities may help to develop sound social skills, knowledge, attitudes and understanding of one another's culture, gender and individual rights in students hence this might also reduce acquaintance rape in institutions of higher education. Once students have gained awareness of the effects of acquaintance rape, they would be also able to help formulate their own institutional policies, legislations or laws to improve the welfare of ordinary students in institutions of higher education. Staff development in the implementation of institutional policies, legislations or laws may also help to improve management and administration of higher education students at the same time improving students' welfare. Through in-service training, college authorities might be also able to discourage blaming of victims of acquaintance rape.

Component 3: Monitoring awareness campaigns and support services from members of society on the welfare of students in institutions of higher education

Authorities in higher education institutions should also be equipped with knowledge and skills to inculcate in students' positive attitudes towards acquaintance rape through awareness campaigns mounted at both local and national levels. This is in tandem with the social learning theory which involves active participation through copying, imitating and observing expected behaviour which shun acquaintance rape from peers in institutions of higher education. These awareness campaigns inculcating positive perceptions in students and authorities in institutions of higher education might overcome public prejudice and misconceptions of victims of acquaintance rape. College administrators, non-academic staff and students might stop blaming victims of acquaintance rape and deal with the crime diligently since they might have been equipped with necessary skills.

Component 4: Peer education on health and risk life skills and acquaintance rape combating skills

Students in higher education should conduct peer education workshops and competitions at both local and national levels on reducing acquaintance rape in institutions of higher learning. Peer education workshops and competitions might help to reduce peer pressure and negative attitudes of acquaintance rape. When conducting peer education workshops and competitions, college administrators, non-academic staff and students might acquire skills to combat acquaintance rape through observational learning. The acquired knowledge on acquaintance rape might be used to effectively reduce exploitative or dangerous living conditions in institutions of higher learning. Students might be actively involved hence they may gradually acquire knowledge on how to reduce acquaintance rape as they interact and socialise with both assailants and victims of acquaintance rape.

Component 5: Monitoring and evaluation of students' welfare and their residential areas in higher educational institutions

Since acquaintance rape is a controversial and hidden crime in institutions of higher education, there is need for effective and timeous monitoring and evaluation of the safety of students' residential halls. Effective and timeous monitoring and evaluation of both students' residential halls and policies, legislations or laws might enable institutions to improve students' welfare and reduce incidences of acquaintance rape. Effective and timeous evaluation routines might also accumulate feedback that would serve as starting points for further implementation and formulation of policies, legislations or laws governing students' welfare in institutions of higher education.

The next section presents contribution of the book.

5.9 Contribution of the Book

To the best of the researcher's knowledge, the present book is the first of its kind to assess factors affecting students in Masvingo higher education's perception of acquaintance rape. Despite the limitations explained in Chapter 1, it is anticipated that this book has made a significant contribution by generating evidence on how culture, gender, peer pressure and policy, legislation or law affect students in higher education's perceptions of acquaintance rape.

The body of knowledge generated by this book on factors affecting students in higher education's perceptions of acquaintance rape is of paramount importance to the welfare of students in higher education institutions. The knowledge may go a long way in assisting and supporting stakeholders in higher education institutions in Masvingo such as principals, vice principals, hostel wardens, assistant hostel wardens, disciplinary chairpersons, nursing sisters, students, parents, policy makers and the society at large to develop ways of preventing and dealing with acquaintance rape. Further studies on the same problem could use this book as a starting point for references and consultations. The next section of this book presents the final comments.

5.10 Final Comments

This book assessed the factors affecting perceptions of students in higher education's perceptions of acquaintance rape in Masvingo. College administrators, non-academic staff and students provided valuable data to unearth the perceptions of acquaintance rape in students in higher education in Masvingo. This book entailed a body of both local and international related literature as well as an empirical study to gather data on the factors affecting students in higher education's perceptions of acquaintance rape. The data for this book was quantitatively analysed.

From this study, it was established that students in higher education's perceptions of acquaintance rape in Masvingo are affected by culture, gender, peer pressure and policy, legislation or law. Participants in this study revealed that most students and authorities in higher education blame victims of acquaintance rape instead of blaming assailants of acquaintance rape.

This study also revealed that administrators in higher education lack managerial skills and knowledge to deal with acquaintance rape cases, hence students in higher education also develop negative attitudes towards acquaintance rape. This book also revealed that there are limited and concise mandatory policies, legislations or laws to give managerial guidelines to college authorities as well as guide students' sexual behaviour in campuses of higher education

Despite this book's revelation that factors such as culture, gender, peer pressure and policy, legislation or law have a bearing on the perceptions of students in higher education of acquaintance rape, the Proposed Acquaintance Rape Reduction Model might help to improve the reduction of acquaintance rape if implemented by administrators in higher education institutions.

Abati, R. (2006). Domestic Violence in Nigeria: *Guardian. 16 April: 13.*

Abbey, A, Helmers, B. R., Jilani, Z, McDaniel, M. C. & Benbouriche, M. (2021).Assessment of men's Sexual Aggression Against Women: An Experimental Comparison of Three Versions of The Sexual Experiences Survey. *Psychology of Violence, 11(3), 253-263.*

Abuya, B. A, Onsomu, E, Moore, D. & Sangwe, J. (2004). A Phenomenological Study of Sexual Harassment and Violence Among Girls Attending High Schools in Urban Slums, Nairobi, Kenya: *International Journal of Psychology and Counselling,66 (5) 387-460.*

Action for Life: One Love: Protect: Respect: Connect: Loving Each Other (2010): Harare: Action.

Adeokun, O. A. (2004). Sexual Harassment in Nigeria Educational Setting: Preliminary Notes from Qualitative Lagos State University: Sexuality in African Magazine. *Adolescents. Sex Roles, 34 (11-12) 787-803.*

African Union Commission (2004). The Road to Gender Equality in Africa: An Overview. Addis Ababa. Ethiopia: OAU.

Akers, R. & Jennings, W.G. (2002). Social Learning Theory. In S. Cote (Ed) *Criminological Theories: Bridging the past to the future.* London, England. International and Professional Publisher.

Alder, F., Mueller, G.O. & Laufer, W.S. (2007). *Criminology and the Criminal Justice System:* Sixth Edition: Boston: McGraw Hill Higher Education.

Alsop, S. & Watts, M. (2003). Science Education and Affect. *International Journal of Science Education (25) 1043-1047.*

American Association of University Women: Police Documents and Reports (2015).

Anderson, K. B, Cooper, H. & Okamura, I. (1997). Individual Differences and Attitudes toward Rape: A Metaanalysis Review. *Pers.Soc. Psychol. Bull (23) 295-315.*

Anderson, V. N, Sampson-Taylor, D. & Hermann, D. J. (2004). Gender, Age and Rape Supportive Rules. Sex Roles: *A Journal of Research, 50 (1-2) 77-90.*

Archer, M.S. (2004). *Being human: The problem of agency.* Cambridge University Press. Cambridge.

Armand, K. & Pepitone, A. (1982). Judgment of Rape: A Study of Victim-Rapist Relationship and Victim Sexual History. *Personality and Social Psychology Bulletin (8) 134-139.*

Armstrong, A. (2000). *Rethinking Gender Violence: Beyond Inequalities:* Women in Southern Africa. Harare. SARDC.

Armstrong, A.K. (1989). *Culture and Choice: Lesson from Survivors of Gender Violence in Zimbabwe:* Institute of Southern Africa Studies: National University of Lesotho.

Armstrong, E, Hamilton, L & Sweeney, B. (2006). Sexual Assault on Campus: A Multilevel, Integrative Approach to Party Rape. *Social Problems,* 55 *(4) 483-499.*

Ashford, J.B. & Le Croy, C.W. (2010). *Human Behaviour in the Social Environment. A Multidimensional Perspective.* Fourth Edition. David Drive: Belmond.

Babbie, E. (2007). *The Practice of Social Research.* Belmont: Thomson Wadsworth.

Babbie, E.R. & Mouton, J. (2002). *The Practice of Social Research.* 9th Edition. Belmont Wadsworth.

Babbie, E.R. & Mouton, J. (2002). *The Practice of Social Research.* Cape Town: Oxford University Press.

Bandura, A. (1978). Social Learning Theory of Aggression. *Journal of Communication,* 28 *(3) 12-29.*

Bandura, A. (1986). *Social Foundation of Thoughts and Action: A Social Cognitive Theory:* Englewood Cliff, NJ: Prentice-Hall.

Beere, C.S, King, D.W, Beere, D.B. & King, LA. (1984).Sex-Roles. Egalitarian Scale: A Measure of Attitudes towards Equality between the Sexes. *Sex Roles (10) 563-576.*

Bell, S.T, Kuriloff, .J. & Lotters, I. (1994). Understanding Attributions of Blame in Stranger Rape and Date

Rape Situations: An Examination of Gender s' Race, Identification and Student's Social Perceptions of Rape Victims. *Journal of Applied Social Psychology (24)* 1719-1734.

Ben-David, S & Schneider, O (2005). Rape Perception, Gender Role Attitudes, and Victim Perpetrator Acquaintance. *Sex Roles (53)* 385-399.

Berkowitz, A.D. (1992). College Men as Perpetrators of Acquaintance Rape and Sexual Assault: A Review of Recent Research: *Journal of American College Health. (40) 175-180.*

Berkowitz, A.D. (2004). *Working with Men to Prevent Violence against Women: An Overview (Part one):* National Resources Centre on

Domestic Violence: VAW net Applied Research Forum, October.

Best, J.W. & Khan, J.V. (2014). *Research in Education.* 9th Edition. Boston: Alynn and Bacon.

Best, S.P & Khan, S.V. (2015) Research in Education. New Delhi: Prentice Hall of India Pvt Ltd.

Bogal-Allbritten, R. & Allbritten, W. (1992). *"An Examination of Institutional Responses to Rape and Acquaintance Rape on College Campuses" Family* Violence Bulletin: Fall.

Bohner, G, Siebler, F. & Schmelcher, J. (2006). *Social Norms and the Likelihood of Raping:* Perceived Rape Myth Acceptance of other Affect Men's Rape Prochivity: Personality and Social Psychology Bulleting. 32 *(93) 86-97.*

Boholm, A. (1998*).* Comparative Studies of Risk Perception: A Review of Twenty Years of Research. *Journal of Risk Research* 1 *(2) 135-163.*

Bongiorno, R, McKimmie, B. M & Masser, B. M. (2016*).* The Selective Use of Rape-Victim Stereotypes to Protect Culturally Similar Perpetrators. *Psychol. Women Q (40)* 398-413.

Bondestam, F & Lundqvist, M (2020). Sexual Harassment in Higher Education: A Systematic Review: *European Journal of Higher Education 10(4) 397-419.*

Boswell, A. A. & Spade, J. Z. (2010). Fraternities and Collegiate Rape Culture: Why are some Fraternities More Dangerous Places for Women? *Gender and Society*10 (2) 133-147.

Bridges, J. S. (1991). Perceptions of Date Rape and Stranger Rape: A Difference in Sex Role Expectations and Rape-Supportive Beliefs: *Sex Roles (24)* 291-30.

Brink, H. (2009). *Fundamentals of Research Methodology for Health Care Professionals.* Cape Town, Juta. Bryden, D. P. & Lengnick, S. (1997).Rape in the Criminal Justice System*: Journal of Criminal Law and Criminology (87) 1194-1384.*

Bryden, DP. & Mador, E. (2016).Patriarchy, Sexual Freedom, and Gender Equality as Causes of Rape. *Ohio State Journal of Criminal Law 13*(2) 299-345.

Bryman, A. (2004). *Social Research Methods.* London: Oxford University Press.

Buchwald, EP, Fletcher, P. & Roth, M. Ed (1993). *Transforming a Rape Culture:* Minneapolis. M.N: Milkweed Edition.

Burnett, A, Mattern, J. L, Herakova, L. L, Kahl J. R, D. H, Tobola, C & Bornsen, S.E. (2009).Communication/Muting Date Rape: A

Co-cultural Theoretical Analysis of Communication Factors Related to Rape Culture on a College Campus. *Journal of Applied Communication Research, 37 (4) 465-485.*

Burns, N. & Grove, S. K. (1991). *Social Cognitive Theory of Gender Development and Differentiation. Psychological Review*

Bussey, K. & Bandura, A. (1991).Social Cognitive Theory of Gender Development and Differentiation. *Psychological Review (106)* 676-713.

Cairney, K. F. (2012).Addressing Acquaintance Rape: The New Direction of the Rape Reform Movement. *St John's Law Review: Volume 69: Issue 1, Article 14.*

Campus Sexual Assault Statistics Don't Add up Centre for Public Accountability, Last Modified June 5, 2012,*http.//www.publicintegrity.org/2009/12/02/9045/campussexual-assault-statistics-don-t-add.*

Carlson, M, Kaminura, A, Trinh, H, Mo, W, Yamawaki, N, Bhattacharya, H, Nguyen, H, Makomenaw, Birkholz & Olson, L. (2015). *Perceptions of Violence against Women among College Students in Date Rape Cases among Young Women: Strategies for Support and Prevention (2008).* Nicosia University of Nicosia Press.

Chiresehe, R. & Chireshe, E. (2009). Sexual Harassment of Female Students in Three Selected High Schools in Masvingo Urban Zimbabwe. *Agenda (80) 88-96.*

Chireshe, R. & Makura, AH. (2013).Preparing Review of Related Literature, In SM Tichapondwa (Ed). Preparing Your Dissertation at a Distance: *A Research Guide:* Virtual University for Small States of the Commonwealth: Vancouver, CA *187-201.*

Chireshe, R. (2006). *An Assessment of the Effectiveness of Zimbabwean Secondary Schools.* DEd. Thesis in Psychology of Education, University of South Africa, Pretoria.

Chisaka, B.C (2013).*The Quantitative Paradigm in Action for Educational Practice* .Save the children ISBN: 978-079745531-3.

Christian, CG. (2005). *Ethics and Politics in Qualitative Research: The Sage Handbook of Qualitative Research.* London: Sage.

Christopher, FS. & Kisler, TS. (2004). *Sexual Aggression in Romantic Relations:* Mahwah: N.J: Erlbraum.

Churchill, SL. (2012). *Victim-Blaming: A New Term for an Old Trend.* Lesbian Gay Bisexual Transgender Queer Centre.

Clarkson, CMV, Keating, H.M. & Cunningham, S.R. (2007). *Criminal Law: Text and Materials:* Six Edition: London: Sweet & Maxwell.

Clemons, C. (2002). Wood-Plastic Composites in the United States: The Interfacing of two Industries: *Journal Forest Products. (53) 6.*

Cobb, NJ. (2001).*The Child Infants, Children and Adolescents:* Toronto: Mayfield Publishing Co.

Cohen, L, Manion, L. & Morrison, K. (2007). *Research Methods in Education.* 5th Edition. New York: McMillan. .

Coller, SA. & Resisk, PA. (1987). Women's Attributions of Responsibility for Date Rape. B The Influence of Empathy and Sex-Role Stereotyping. *Violence and Victims, 2 (2) 1987-2000*

Collins, H. (2010). *Creative Research: The Theory of Research for the Creative Industries.* London: AVA Publications.

Colntonio-Yurko, KC, Miller, H &Cheveallier, J. (2018)."But she didn't scream". Teaching about Sexual Assault in Young Adult Literature: *Journal of Language and Literacy Education (14) 2-10.*

Cook, T, Swain, J. & French, S. (2001). Towards an Affirmation Model of Disability. *Disability and Society 15 (4) 569-582.*

Cresswell, JM. & Plano Clark, VL. (2007). *Designing and Conducting Mixed Methods Research.* Thousand Oaks, C.A: Sage.

Cresswell, JM. (2009). *Research Design: Qualitative, Quantitative and Mixed Methods Approaches, 3rd Edition.* Thousand Oaks, C, .A. Sage.

Creswell, J.W, Ebersohn, I, Eloff, R, Ferreira, N, Ivankova, V, Janson, J.D, Neuwenhuis, J., Pieterson, J., Plano-Clark, V. L. & Van der Westhuizen, C. (2010) First Steps in Research. Pretoria: Van Schalk.

Creswell, JM. (2007). *Educational Research: Planning, Conducting and Evaluating Quantitative and Qualitative Research.* New Jersey: Merrill Prentice Hall.

Date Rape Cases among Young Women: Strategies for Support and Prevention (2008). Nicosia: University of Nicosia Press.

Davis, M & Sutton, CD. (2004). *Social Research: The Basics.* London: Sage Publications.

Davis, M, Rogers, P. & Whitelegg L. (2009). Effects of Victim Gender, Victim Sexual Orientation, Victim Response and Respondent Gender on Judgements of Blame in a Hypothetical Adolescent Rape. *Legal and Criminological Psychology (14) 133-338.*

Davis, T & Lee, C. (1996).Sexual Assault: Myth and Stereotypes among Australian Adolescents. *Sex Roles, 34 (11-12) 787-803.*

Deane, T. (2018) Sexual Violence and the Limits of Laws' Powers to Alter Behaviour: The Case of South Africa: Journal of International Women's Studies *(19) 84-103.*

De Leon, D. (2013). *Examination of Students' Personal Interactions and Rape*: Unpublished Msc in Psychology Thesis: Texas State University-San Marcoos.

De Vos, AS, Strydom, HV, Fouche, CB &Delport, CSL (2011). *Research at Grass Roots for the Social Sciences and Human Service Professions. Fourth Edition.* Pretoria: Van Schaik Publishers.

Dejoy, DM. (1992). An Examination of Gender Differences in Traffic Accidents Risk Perception. *Accident Analysis and Prevention 24 (3) 237-246.*

Dejudicibus, M & McCabe, MP. (2001). Blaming the Target of Sexual Harassment: Impact of Gender Role, Sexist Attitudes, and Work Role. *Sex Roles, 44 (7/8) 401-417.*

Dekeseredy, W, Schwartxz, M & Shahid, A. (2002). The Role of Profeminist Men in Dealing with Woman Abuse on the Canadian College Campus: *Violence against Women, 6 (9) 918-936.*

Delport, CSL. (2005). *Quantitative Data Collection Methods, in Research at Grassroots for the Social Sciences and Human Service Profession.* 3rd Edition. Edited by SA.

Deming, ME. (2017). Context Matters: Evaluating Social Judgement of Acquaintance Rape Myths (Doctoral Dissertation). *Retrieved from https://scholarcommons.sc.edu/etd/4068.*

Dencombe, M. (2010). *Ground Rule for Social Research Guidelines for Good Practice.* Second Edition: McGraw Hill.

Denzin, NK & Lincoln, YS. (2005). *Handbook of Qualitative Research.* Thousand Oaks, C.A: Sage.

Devos, H, Strydom, CD, Fouche & CSL Delport (2012). *Research at Grass Roots for the Social Sciences and Human Service Professions.* Pretoria Van Schaik 159.

Dixie, KOD. (2017). Defining Consent as a Factor in Sexual Assault Prevention. *McNair Scholars Research Journal. (10) 35-54.*

Do, MAF & Mark, VSMD (2019). Adolescent Sexual Assault and Statutory Rape. *Journal of Pediatric and Adolescent Gynecology: (11) 33-52.*

Dolan, EW. (2019).Perceptions of a Rape Perpetrator as a Successful Person Decreases the Likelihood of labelling it as Rape, Study Finds: *Social Psychology.*

Dube, D. & Tagntanazvo, OB. (2003). *Sociology for Health Sciences: Module BSNS 107:* Harare: Zimbabwe Open University.

Duff, KG. & Artwater, E. (2012). *Psychology for Living: Adjustment, Growth and Behaviour Today:* Eight Edition: New Delhi: Pearson.

Dumont, J, Miller, K. (2003). The Role of "Real Rape" and "Real Victim" Stereotypes in the Police Reporting Practices of Sexually Assaulted Women. *Violence against Women (9) 466-486.*

Dunnel, M, Pryor, J & Yates, P. (2009). *Becoming a Researcher: A Companion to the Research Process.* Berkshire Open University Press.

Du Toit, L. (2017) 'Sexual Violence, Religion and Women's Rights in Global Perspective', *Religious Studies and Theology* 36 *(2) 155-170.*

Dziech, BW. (2003). *Academic and work place sexual Harassment: a handbook of cultural, social science, Management and legal perspectives,* Prager: London.

Eboe-Osiji, C. (2012). *International Law: An Unsettled Tug of War?* Jstor. Brill.

Edwards, SR, Bradshaw, KA. & Hinsz (2014). Denying Rape but Endorsing Forceful Intercourse: Exploring Differences among Responders. *Violence and Gender 1(4) 188-193.*

Edwoldt, CA, Menson, CM &Robbing, J. (2000). Attributions about Rape in a Continuum of Dissolving Marital Relationship. *Journal of Interpersonal Violence (15) 1175 -1183.*

Ellis, L. (1989). *Theories of Rape: Inquiries into the Causes of Sexual Aggression.* New York. NY: Hemisphere Publishing Company.

Fanflick, PL. (2007). *Victims, Responses to Sexual Assault: Counterintuitive or Simply Adoptive?* Special Topics Series: Prospectors Research Institute.

Ferrao, MC, Goncalves, G, Giger, J & Parreira, T. (2016). Judge me, judge me not: The Role of Eye Size and Observer Gender on Acquaintance Rape. *AnPsicol. (32) 241-249.*

FindLaw.com. (2016). Texas Sexual Assault Laws. *Retrieved from http:// statelaws.findlaw. com/ texaslaw/ texas-sexual-assault.html.*

Fink, A. (2002). *The Survey Handbook.* 2nd Edition. Thousand Oaks, CA: Sage.

Finn, P. (1997). *Preventing Alcohol-Related Problems on Campus: Acquaintance Rape: A Guide for Program Coordinators:* Massachusetts: Higher Education Centre For Alcohol and Other Drug Prevention.

Finucare, M.L. Slovic, P, Mertz, C.K, Flynn, J & Satterfield, T.A. (2000). Gender, Race and Perceived Risk: The White Male's Effect. *Health Risk and Society (2) 157-172.*

Fisher, BS, Cullen, FT. & Turner, MG. (2000). *The Sexual Victimization of College Women:* Washington, D.C: National Institute of Justice.

Flintort, R. (2010). *Sexual Assault. In J Nicoletti, S Spencer-Thomas & C Bollinger (EDs), Violence Goes to College: The Authoritative Guide to Prevention and Intervention.* (2nd Ed).Springfield, IL: Charles C. Thomas.

Flood, M & Pease, B. (2009). Factors Influencing Attitudes to Violence against Women. *Trauma Violence & Abuse 10 (2) 125-142.*

Forward, F. (2020). *Date Acquaintance Rape and Gang/Group Rape.* New York. The Jesuit University of New York.

Frankel, RF. & Wallen, N.E. (2006). *How to Design and Evaluate Research in Education.* New York. NY: McGraw Hill.

Frese, B, Moya, M & Megias, J. (2004). Social Perceptions of Rape: How Rape Myths Acceptance Modulates the Influence of Situational Factors; *Journal of Interpersonal, Violence (19) 143-161.*

Glenn, N & Marquardt, E. (2001). Hooking up, Hanging Out, and Hoping for Mr Right in an Institute for America Values Report to the Independent Women's Forum. *Retrieved from http://fmmh.yedsb.ca/teachers/fmmhmcmanaman/pages/mfhook.pdf.*

Gravelin, CR. (2017). *Assessing the Impact of Media on Blaming the Victim of Acquaintance Rape.* Doctoral Dissertation, University of Kansa.

Gravelin, CR., Biernat, M & Bucher, CE. (2019). Blaming the Victim of Acquaintance Rape: Individual, Situational, and Sociocultural Factors. *Front Psychol: (10) 2022-2013.*

Guy, L. (2006). *Partners in Social Changes. Olympia. WA:* The Sexual Assault Prevention Resource Center, the Washington Coalition of Sexual Assault Programs.

Hackett, P.M.W. & Claire, K.S. (2012) Academic Challenge: Its Meaning for College Students and Faculty. *Journal on Centre for Teaching and Learning (4) 101-117*

Harmon, GA, Owens, G & Dewey, ME. (1995). Rapists Versus non-Rapists' Attitudes toward Women: A British Study. *International Journal of Offender Therapy and Comparative Criminology 39 (3) 269-275.*

Harsey, S & Frey, LL (2020). Deny, Attack, and Reverse Victim and Offender (DARVO): What is the Influence on Perceived Perpetrator and Victim Credibility? *Journal of Aggression, Maltreatment & Trauma (10) 1080-1092.*

Hester, M & Lilley, S.J (2017). Rape Investigation and Attrition in Acquaintance, Domestic Violence and Historical Rape Cases. *Journal of Investigative Psychology and Offender Profiling (14) 175-188.*

Hills, PS, Pleva, M, Selb, E & Cole, T. (2020). Understanding How University Students Use Perceptions of Consent, Wantedness, and Pleasure in Labeling Rape: *Archives of Sexual Behaviour. (10) 1050-2050*

Hird, M. & Jackson, S. (2001). Where 'angels) and "Wusses" fear to tread: Sexual Coercion in Adolescent Dating Relationships. *Journal of Sociology 37 (1) 27-43.*

Human Rights Watch. Everyone Blames Me. Barriers to Justice and Support Services for Sexual Assault Survivors in India (2017). *United States of America: http://www.hrw.org.*

Human Rights Watch (2017) Everyone Blames Me: Barriers to Justice and Support Services for Sexual Assault Survivors in India. Washington.

Humphries, D. (2009). *Women, Violence, and the Media: Reading in Feminist Criminology.* Boston, M.A.: Northeastern University Press.

Illinois Coalition against Sexual Assault. (1993). US Department of Justice: National Institute of Justice.

James Madison University: Office of Judicial Affairs (2011) Students Handbook. *Sexual 100-134.* .

Jewkes, R. (2012). *Rape Perpetration:* Pretoria: Sexual Violence Research Initiative.

Johnson, AM. & Hoover, SM. (2015). *The Potential of Sexual Consent Interventions on College Campuses: A Literature Review on the Barriers to Establishing Affirmative Sexual Consent.*

Johnson, NL. & Johnson, DM. (2017). An Empirical Exploration into the Measurement of Rape Culture. *Journal of Interpersonal Violence 00(0) 1-6.*

Jozkowski, KN & Peterson, ZD. (2013). College Students and Sexual Consent: Unique Insight. *Journal of Sex Research. 50 (6) 517-523.*

Kabaya, GT (2018*). Sexual Harassment in the workplace and the law.* Harare: Zimbabwe Women Lawyers Association.

Kahan, DM. (2010). Culture, Cognition, and Consent: Who Perceives What, and Why, in Acquaintance Rape Cases. *University of Pennsylvania Law Review (95) 729-813. Retrieved from http://www.jstor.org.ezproxy.emich.edu/*

Kalof, L & Cargill (1991). Fraternity and Sorority Membership and Gender Dominance Attitudes. *Sex Roles (25) 417-23.*

Kamal, A, Shaikh, I.A. & Shaikh, MA. (2010) Comparative Analysis of Attitudes and Perceptions about Rape among Male and

Female University Students: *J. Aub Med Coll Collabbottaba 22(2). Retrieved from http://www.popcenter.org/problems/pdfs/Acquintance Rape of College Students, pdf.*

Kaplan, HB, Johnson, R.S & Bailey, CA (1987). Deviant Peers and Deviant Behaviour: Further Elaboration of a Model. *Social Psychology Quarterly 30 (3) 277-284.*

Kathryn, M, Feltey, JJ & Ainslie, AG (2016) Sexual Coercion Attitudes Among Higher School Students: The Influence of Gender and Rape Education: *Youth & Society, 23(2) 229-259.* Sage Publication, Inc

Katz, J, Carino, A & Hilton, A. (2002). Perceived Verbal Conflict Behaviour Associated with Physical Aggression and Sexual Coercion in Dating Relationships: A Gender Sensitive Analysis. *Violence and Victims 17 (91) 93-109.*

Kim, B. (2010). Social Constructivism. Emerging Perspective on Learning, Teaching and Technology. Htt://projects.coe.uga.edu/eplyy/index. *Accessed on 20 December 2013.*

King, LA. & King, DW. (1990). Abbreviated Measure of Sex Role Egalitation Attitudes. *Sex Roles (23) 659-675.*

Kishwar, M. (1999). *Off the Beaten Track: Rethinking Gender Justice for Indian Women.* New Delhi: Oxford University Press.

Klar, HW. (2012). Fostering Distributed Instructional Leadership: A Socio-Cultural Perspective of Leadership Development in Urban High School. *Leadership and Policy in Schools (11) 365-390.*

Kombo DK. & Tromp, D.L.A. (2009). *Proposal and Thesis Writing: An Introduction. Nairobi:* Paulines Publications Africa, Makuyu.

Koss, MP & Dinero, TE. (2010). A Discriminate Analysis of Risk Factors among a National Sample of College Woman. *Journal of Counselling and Clinical Psychology (57) 133-147.*

Koss, MP, Dinero, TE. Siebel, CA. & Cox, SL. (1988). Stranger and Acquaintance Rape: Are there Differences in the Victim's Experience? *Psychology of Women Quarterly (12) 1-24.*

Koss, MP, Oros, C.J & Chery, J. (1980). *The "Unacknowledged" Rape Victims:* Ohio: Kent State University.

Kottack, CP. (2000). *Cultural Anthropology: 13th Edition:* New York: McGraw-Hill.

Labovitz, S & Hagedorn, R. (2007). *Introduction to Social Research.* Michigan: McGraw-Hill.

Lam, & Roman, (2009). Date Rape: Risk Factors and Prevention. National Center for Biotechnology, US.

Lambert, AS, & Raichel, K. (2000). The Role of Political Ideology in Mediating Judgements of Blame in Rape Victims and Their Assailants. A Test of the Just World, Personal Responsibility, and Legitimization Hypotheses. *Personality and Social Psychology Bulletin (26) 853-863.*

Lanza-Kaduce, L, Capecce, M & Alden, H. (2016). Liquor is Quicker: Gender and Social Learning among College Students. *Criminal Justice Policy Review 17 (920) 127-143.*

LaPlante, MN, McComick, N & Brannigan, GG. (2010). Living the Sexual Script: College Students' Views of Influence in Sexual Encounters: *Journal of Sex Research (16) 338-55.*

Lassiter, JE. (1983). Culture and Personality Aspects of Socioeconomic Development in Swaziland: An Analysis of Student Attitudes and Values. *Doctoral Dissertation: University of Oregon.*

Lead, F &Machakanya, P. (2000). *Preliminary Investigation of the Abuse of Girls in Zimbabwe Junior Secondary Schools, Educational Research No 39:* London: DFID.

Leedy, PD. & Ormrod, SE. (2005). *Practical Research: Planning and Design: 8th Edition.* Saddle River N.J: Prentice Hall.

Le-Wiesel, R. (2004). Male University Students' Attitudes toward Rape and Rapists: *Child and Adolescent Social Work Journal 21 (91) 199-210.*

Lichter, EC. & McCloskey, LA. (2004). The Effects of Childhood Exposure to Marital Violence on Adolescent Gender-Role Beliefs and Dating Violence: *Psychology of Women Quarterly. 344-357.*

Lightfoot, S & Evans, I (2000). "Risk Factors for a New Zealand Sample of Sexual Abusive Children and Adolescents". *Child Abuse and Neglect 24 (a) 1185-1198.*

Linton, R. (1945). *The Cultural Background of Personality.* New York. D. Appleton-Century Company, incorporated.

Lisak, D, Gardinier, L &Nicksa, S and Cote (2010). False Allegations of Sexual Assault: An Analysis of Ten Years of Reported Cases. *Violence against Women, 16 (2) 318-1334*

Lonsway, KA. & Fitzgerald, LF. (1994). Rape Myths in Review. Psychol. *Women Q (18) 133-164.*

Lyness, D. (2009). Date Rape. Teens Health from Remours. *Retrieved from https/www.Teenshealth.org.*

Machisa, M, Jina, R, Labuschagne, G, Vetten, L, Loots, L, Swemmer, S, Meyersfeld, B &Jewkes, R. (2017).

Rape Justice in South Africa: A Retrospective Study of The Investigation, Prosecution and Adjudication of Reported rape Cases From 2012, Pretoria, South Africa. Gender and Health Research Unit, South African Medical Research Council.

Malamuth, NM. (1986). Predictors of Naturalistic Sexual Aggression. *Journal of Personality and Social Psychology. 50 (5953-962)*

Manson, KO & LU, Y. (1988). Attitudes towards Women's Familial Roles: Changes in the United States 1997-1985. *Gender and Society (2) 39-57.*

Mapfumo, J, Shumba, J & Chireshe, R. (2007). Sexual relationships in Higher Education in Zimbabwe: Implications on HIV/AIDS. *South African Journal of Higher Education. 121 (5) 515-526.*

Martin, PY. (2016).The Rape Prone Culture of Academic Contexts: Fraternities and Athletics. *Gender & Society (30) 30-43*

Matlin, MW. (2008). *Psychology of Women:* Sixth Edition: Mexico: Wadsworth.

Mazrui, AA. &Mari, AM (1985). *Swahili State and Society: The Political Economy of an African Language.* Nairobi: East African Educational Publishers.

Mbigi, L. & Maree, J. (2006). *Ubuntu: The Spirit of African Transformation Management:* Ransburg Knowledge Resources.

McMahon, S. (2010). Rape Myth Beliefs and Bystander Attitudes among Incoming College Students. *Journal of American College Health, 59 (1) 3-11.*

McMillan, JH & Schumacher, S. (2007). *Research in Education Evidence Based Enquiry.* New York: Pearson.

McMillan, J.H. & Schumacher, S. (2010) Research in Education: Evidenced-based Enquiry. Seventh Edition. New Jersey: Pearson Education.

Mcnair, K, Fantasia, HC, Harris, AL (2018). Sexual Misconduct Polices at Institutes of Higher Education: An Integrative Review. *Journal of Forensic Nursing 14(4) 238-247.*

Mediterranean Institute of Gender Studies (2008). *Date Rape Cases Among Young Women: Strategies for Support and Prevention.* Capline: University of Nicosia Press.

Mertens, DM. (2009). *Research and Evaluation in Psychology.* 4TH Edition. New York. NY: Guilford. Michalski, J. (2004). Making Sociological Sense Out of Trends in Intimate Partner Violences. The Social Structure of Violence against Women. *Violence against Women. 10 (6) 652-657.*

Mihalic, SW. & Elliot, D. (1997). A Social Learning Theory of Model of Marital Violence. *Journal of Family Violence, 12 (1) 21-47*.

Miller, B & Marshal, JC. (1987). Coercive Sex on the University Campus. *Journal of College Student Personnel (28) 38-47*.

Ministry of Health and Child Welfare (2001).Harare: *Health Magazine Publications*.

Mittal, S, Singh, T & Verma, SK. (2017). Young Adults' Attitudes towards Rape and Rape Victims: Effects of Gender and Social Category. *Journal of Psychology and Clinical Psychiatry 7(4) 2-6*.

Mooney, LA, &Sacacht, C. (2007). *Understanding Social Problems:* Belmont, C.A. Wadsworth Publishing.

Morgan, DL. (2007). Paradigm Lost and Pragmatism Regained: Methodological Implications of Combining Qualitative and Quantitative Methods. *Journal of Mixed Methods Research 1 (1) 48-76*.

Mouton, J. (2012). *How to Succeed in Your Masters' & Doctoral Studies: A South African Guide and Resources Book*. Pietermaritzburg. Van Schaik Publishers.

Muchlehard, CH. (1988). Misinterpreted Dating Behaviour and the Risk of Date Rape. *Journal of Social and Clinical Psychology 6 (1) 20-37*.

Muchlenhard, CL, Friedman, DE. & Thomas, CM. (1995). Is Date Rape Justifiable? The Effects of Dating Activity, Who Initiated, Who Paid, and Men's Attitudes towards Women. *Psychology of Women Quarterly 9 (3) 297-410*.

Murnen, SK, Wright, C. & Klauzy, G. (2002). If "boys will be boys", then girls will be victims? A Mete-Analytic Review of the Research that relates Masculine Ideology to Sexual Aggression. *Sex Roles, 16 (1112) 359-375*.

Mwamwenda, TS. (2010). *Educational Psychology: An African Perspective*. 2nd Edition: Burbon: Butterworths.

Narayanan, VAM (2005) Sexual Exploitation and Abuse in Emergency Context. A Basic Module for Staff Orientation. Available *efweb.int/ sites/ reliefweb.int/ files/ resources/ E96CC52FD6B7AF85257 2490073C66 E-care-protection-apr2005.pdf*

National Adolescent Sexual and Reproductive Health Strategy (2010-2015). Harare: Ministry of Health and Child Welfare.

National Adolescent Sexual and Reproductive Health Strategy (2010). Harare: Ministry of Health and Child Welfare.

National Sample of College Women. *Journal of Counselling and Clinical Psychology (57) 138-147*.

National Victims Centre (1992). *Rape in America: A Report to the Nation*. Arlington, VA: National Victoria Centre.

Neuman, WL. (2006). *Social Research Methods*. 6th ed. Boston, MA: Pearson.

Nyul, B, Kende, A, Engeyel, M & Szabo, M. (2018). Perception of a Perpetrator as a Successful Person Predicts Decreased Moral Judgement of a Rape. *Frontiers in Psychology*.

O'sullivan, C. (1993). *Fraternities and The Rape Culture: In Transforming a Rape Culture:* Edited by E. Buchaward, PRF & Roth, M: Minneapolis: Mildweed Editions.

Odu, BK & Olusegun, GF. (2012). Determinant of Sexual Coercion among University Female Students in South-West Nigeria. *Journal of Emerging Trends in Educational Research and Policy Studies (JETERAPS) 3 (6) 915-920*.

Okeke, CMA. (2011). *Impact of Sexual Harassment on Women Undergraduates' Educational Experience in Anambra State of Nigeria*. Unpublished DEd Thesis: Seton Hall University.

Oltedal, S, Moen, B, Klempe, H & Rundumo, T. (2004). *Explaining Risk Perception: An Evaluation of Cultural Theory:* Trondheim: Rotunde Publikasjoner.

Onyejekwe, C. (2008). The Dominance of Rape. *Journal of International Women's Studies. 10 (1) 48-63*.

Oshiname, FO, Ogunwale, AO & Ajuwon, AS. (2013). Knowledge and Perceptions of Date

United Nations Human Rights Of The High Commissioner (2014).Sexual and Gender. Available at*; https//www.ohchr.org/Document/Issues/Women/WRGS//One Pagers/Sexual and gender-based Violence. pdfbased violence in the context of transitional justice*.

Rape among Female Undergraduates of a Nigeria University. *African Journal of Reproductive Health 17 (3) 137-148*.

Page, AD. (2008). Judging Women and Defining Crime: Police Officers' Attitudes towards Women and Rape. *Sociological Spectrum, 28 (4) 389-411*.

Paludi, MA. (2004). *Sexual Harassment of College Students: Cultural Similarities and Differences:* New York: McGraw Hill.

Parahoo, K. (2006). *Nursing Research Principles, Process and Issues*. Second Edition. London. Palgrave McMillan.

Person, S, Dhingra, K. & Grogan, S. (2018). Attributions of Victim Blame in Stranger and Acquaintance Rape: A Quantitative Study. *Journal of Clinical Nurses. (27) 1-10.*

Pedagogies and Hashtag Internet Activism. *Educational Philosophy and Theory 51(5) 458-464.*

Peters, MA. & Besley, T. (2019). Weinstein, Sexual Predation, and "Rape Culture" Public

Peterson, Z.D. & Muchlenhard, C.J. (2004) Was it Rape? The Function of Women's Rape Myth Acceptance and Definition of Sex in Labelling their Own Experience. Sex Roles *(51) 129-144.*

Polansky, MJ. & Waller, D.S. (2010). *Designing and Managing a Research Project. A Business Student's Guide.* Second Edition: London: SAGE publication.

Polaschek, DLL & Gannon, T. (2004). The Implicit Theories of Rapists: What Convicted Offenders Tells Us. *A Journal of Research and Treatment (16) 299-314.*

Polit, DF. & Beck, CT. (2004). *Nursing Research: Principles and Methods.* 7th Edition. Philadelphia: bippincott, William and Wilkins.

Polit, DF. & Hungler, BP. (2009). *Essentials of Nursing Research Methods, Appraisal and Utilizatio.* Philadelphia: Lippincott.

Pratt, B & Loizos, P. (2003). *Choosing Research Methods: Data Collection for Development Workers.* London: Oxfam.

Ramalibana, K. (2005). *An Investigation into the Effectiveness of Staff Development Policies and Programmes of the Unisa Library.* Pretoria UNISA.

Rape and Sexual Assault: A Renewed Call (2004).Washington: The White House Council on Women and Girls.

Rape Crisis England & Wales (2017). *Rape Crisis England & Wales Headline Statistics 2016-17.* Retrieved January 6, 2017 from https: // rapercrisis. Org. UK /statistics.php.

Reeves, H & Baden, S. (2000). *Bridge Development-Gender: Institute of Development Studies. University of Sussex.* Retrieved. 15th September 2011 from www.medinstgenderstudies.org.

Rhodes, J. (2019).*Examining Collegiate Students' Perceptions of Date Rape and Sexual Assault. Masters Theses &Specialist Projects. Paper 3144. Https: //digital commons.Wku. edu /theses/3144.*

Rickert, VI, Wiemann, CM & Vaughan, RD. (2005). Disclosure of Date Rape/Acquaintance Rape: Who report and when. *Journal of Pediatric and Adolescents and Adolescence Gynecology. (18) 17-24.*

Right to Be Free from Rape: Overview of Legislation and State of Play in Europe and International Human Rights Standards (2018).Amnesty International. *EUR 01/9452/2018*.

Robson, A, Gibson-Bervely and Schwartz (2004). "Sorority and Fraternity Membership and Religious Behaviours: Relation to Gender Attitudes". *Sex Roles (50) 871-877*.

Roe, KJ. (2004). *Public Policy Consultant National Alliance to End Sexual Violence Newsletter of the National Sexual Violence Resource Center.* Spring/Summer.

Romeo, FF. (2004).Acquaintance Rape on College and University Campuses: *College Student Journal (4) 290-310*.

Rossetti, S. (2001). *Children in School: A Safe Place- Botswana: United Nations Educational and Cultural Organisation:* Wellesly: U.S. Agent for International Development.

Salazar, L. (2005*).* Moving Beyond the Individual: Examining the Effects of Domestic Violence Policies on Social Norms. *American Journal Community Psychology 32 (3-4) 1-12*.

Salkind, NJ. (2004). *Social Learning Theory: An Introduction to Theories of Human Development:* Newbury Park: Sage Publications.

Sampson, R. (2002). *Acquaintance Rape of College Students: Problem Oriented Guide for Police Services: (17) 1-5 Retrieved from www. Cops.usdoj.gov.*

Sanday, PR. (1990). *Fraternity Gang, Rape: Sex, Brotherhood, and Privilege on Campus:* New York: New York University Press.

Santrock, JW. (2005). *Adolescence. 10th Edition:* Boston: McGraw Hill.

Schneider, L & Silverman, A. (2008). *Global Sociology: Introducing Five Contemporary Societies:* Boston: McGraw Hill.

Schoellkopf, J (2012). *Victim-Blaming: A New Term for an Old Trend.* University of Rhode Island, juliesschoellkopf@gmail.com

Schuller, RA, Mckimmie, BM, Masser, BM &Klippenstine, MC (2010).Judgements of Sexual Assault: The Impact of Complainant Emotional Demeanor, Gender, and Victim Stereotypes. *New Criminal Law Review 13 (4) 759-780*.

Sellers, C, Cochram, J & Branch, K. (2005).Social Learning Theory and Partner Violence: A Research Note: *Deviant Behaviour 26 (4) 379-395*.

Sexual Violence Facts and Statistics (1993). Illinois Coalition against Sexual Assault.

Shalhoub-Kevorkian, N. (1993). *Fear of Sexual Harassment: Palestinian Adolescent Girls in the Intifada Palestinian Women: Identity and Experience:* London: Zed Books.

Shastri, VK (2008). *Research Methodology in Education.* Delhi.
Anthorspress.

Shumba, A, Gwirai, I, Shumba, J, Maphosa, C, Chireshe, R,
Gudyanga, E & Makura, AH. (2008). Pupils Perceptions of
Sexual Abuse by Teachers in Zimbabwean Schools: Issues and
Challenges: *Journal of Psychology in Africa.* 18 *(2) 279-282.*

Shumbai, A & Matina, A. (2002). Sexual Harassment of College
Students by Lecturers in Zimbabwe: *Sex Education 2 (1) 44-58.*

Silverman, D. (2006). *Qualitative Research Theory, Methods and Practice.*
3rd Edition. London: Sage.

Siomonson, K. & Subich, I. (1999). Rape Perceptions as a Function
of Gender-Role Traditionalist and Victim Perpetrator
Association. *Sex Roles (40) 7-8.*

Skinnider, E, Montgomery, R & Garrett, S. (2017). *The Trial of Rape.
Understanding the Criminal Justice System Responses to Sexual Violence
in Thailand and Viet Nam. UN Multi-Country Study.*

Sleath, E & Bull, B. (2017).Police Perceptions of Rape Victims and
the Impact on Case Decision Making: A Systematic Review.
Journal of Interpersonal Violence (25) 969-988.

Smith, M (2014).*Encyclopaedia of Rape and sexual violence:* California:
ABC-CLIO.LLC.

Stalan, L & Finn, M. (2000).Gender Differences in Officers'
Perceptions and Decision About Domestic Violence Cases.
Women & Criminal Justice 11 *(3) 525-554.*

Stubbs, J. (2003). Sexual Assault, Criminal Justice, and Order. Paper
to Practice and Prevention: *Contemporary Issues in Adult Sexual
Assault in New South Wales.* Sydney: University of Technology.

Spratt, C, Walker, R. & Robinson, B. (2004) *Module A5: Mixed-
methods research.* Cambridge. Commonwealth of learning.

Suprakash, C, Ajay, KB, Murthy, PS. & Biswajit, J.
(2017).Psychological Aspects of Rape and Its Consequences.
*International Journal of Psychology and Behavioural Science 2 (3) 555-
586.*

Sovino, J. O. & Turkey, BE (eds) (2011*): Defining rape and sexual
assault, in rape investigation handbook.* San Diego: Elsevier Inc

Tafirei, P, Makaye, J and Mapetere, K (2017:3) Stakeholders'
Perceptions of Campus Acquaintance Rape: The Case Study of
Masvingo Polytechnic of Zimbabwe. *Research Journal (DRJ)
Journal of Economics and Finance (DRJ-JEF) 2(9) 01-09.*

Timire, C (2014: 77). Sexual Behaviour and Practices Among
adolescents Blood Donors in Harare and Masvingi Province,

Zimbabwe: Master of Public Health Thesis: School of Public Health and Psychosocial Studies: Auckland University of Technology.

Tangri, SS, Burt, MR. & Johnson, LB. (1982). Sexual Harassment at Work: Three Explanatory Models: *Journal of Social Issues (38) 33-54*.

Taylor, N. & Mouzos, J. (2006) Community Attitudes to Violence Against Women Survey: A Full Technical Report (Paper One). Aus), Australian Institute of Criminology. Canberra.

Taylor, B, Sinha, G & Ghoshal, T. (2009). *Research Methodology: A Guide for Researchers in Management and Social Sciences*. New Delhi. PHL Learning Private Limited.

Taylor, SE, Peplaus, LA. & Sears, DO. (1994). *Social Psychology*. Prentice Hall: Englewood Cliff.

Terell, SR. (2012). Mixed-methods research methodologies. *The Qualitative Report 17(1) 254-280*.

Thacker, LK. (2017). Rape Culture, Victim Blaming and the Role of Media in the Criminal Justice System. *Kentucky Journal of Undergraduate Scholarship: Volume 1: (8) 89-98*.

Thomas, C. (2020). The 21st Century Jury: Contempt, Bias and the Impact of Jury Service. Criminal Law Review *(11) 987-1011*.

Tlali, MS. (2017). *Introduction to Marketing. MNM 1503*. Pretoria. University of South Africa.

Turner, JH. & Stets, J.E. (2005). *The Sociology of Emotions*. New York. Cambridge.

University of Zimbabwe Calendar Book (2014) Harare: University of Zimbabwe Printing Press.

Urombo, R. (2000). *Ethics in Counselling. Module Bscc 1041 BPSY 405:* Harare: Zimbabwe Open University. Van Den Aadweg, EM & Van Den Aadweg, ED. (1988). *Educational Psychology*. Pretoria: E & E Enterprises.

Van der Bruggen, M & Grubb, AR. (2014). A Review of the Literature Relating to Rape Victim Blaming: An Analysis of the Impact of Observer and Victim Characteristics on Attribution of Blame in rape cases. *Aggression and Violent Behaviour 19 (5) 523-531*.

Vandiver, DM & Dupalo, JR. (2012). Factors that Affect College Students' Perceptions of Rape: What is the Role of Gender and Other Situational Factors? *International Journal of Offender Therapy and Comparative Criminology xx (x) 1-21*.

Walker, MH. (2018).Taking to Your Teens about Acquaintance
    Rape. Psych Central. Retrieved on August 18, 2020, from
    https:// psychocentral. Com/lib/talking-to-yourtens-about-
    acquaintance rape.

Walker, SJL, Hester, M, McPhee, D, Patsios, D, Williams, A, Bates,
    L & Rumney, P (2019). Rape, Inequality and the Criminal Justice
    Response in England: The Importance of Age and Gender.
    Criminology & Criminal Justice 00(0) 1-19.

Webb, C. (2003.) Research in Brief. An Analysis of Recent
    Publications in JCN: Sources, Methods and Topics. *Journal of
    Clinical Nursing (12) 931-1040.*

WestMarland, N. and Gangoli, G. (2011) International Approaches
    to Rape. Bristol. University Press. Policy Press.

Weiten, W & Lloyd, MA. (2002). *Psychology Applied to Modern Life:
    Adjustment in the 21st Century.* 7th Edition. Pacific Grove, C.A:
    Brooks/Cole.

Wiersma, W &Jurs, SG. (2009). *Research Methods in Education.* New
    York: Pearson.

Wiid, J. & Diggins, C. (2015). *Marketing Research.* 3rd Edition. Cape
    Town. Juta & Co.

Wilkinson, D & Birmingham, P. (2003). *Using Research Instruments: A
    Guide for Researchers.* London: Routledge Falmer.

Withowska, E & Menckel, E. (2005). Perceptions of Sexual
    Harassment in Swedish Schools Experiences and Social
    Environment Problems: *European Journal of Public Health. (15) 78-
    85.*

World Health Organisation. (2017).Violence against Women.
    November 29. New York: United Nations.

Xenos, S & Smith, D. (2001). Perceptions of Rape and Sexual
    Assault among Australian Adolescents and Young Adult. *Journal
    of Interpersonal Violence 16 (11) 1103-1119.*

Ziera, A, Astor, RA. & Benbenishty, R. (2002). Sexual Harassment
    in Jewish and Arab Public Schools in Israel: *Child Abuse &
    Neglect 26 (2002) 149-166.*

Zindi, F. (1994). Sexual Harassment in Zimbabwe's Institutions of
    Higher Education. *Zambezia: 21 (2) 177186.*

Zindi, F & Makotore, S. (2015). *Educational Psychology. Module PGDE
    303.* Harare: Zimbabwe Open University.